To,

Bertha Jack

Christmas, 1976.

*How to talk to birds*

Richard C. Davids

# How to talk to birds

### and other uncommon ways of
### enjoying nature the year round

ALFRED A. KNOPF
*New York* 1973

THIS IS A BORZOI BOOK
PUBLISHED BY ALFRED A. KNOPF, INC.

ISBN: 0-394-47279-9
Library of Congress Catalog Card Number: 73-171148

Manufactured in the United States of America

Published April 27, 1972
Reprinted Two Times
Fourth Printing, October 1973

*To my brother Robert*

# Contents

16 PAGES OF PHOTOGRAPHS FOLLOW PAGE 150

*How to talk to birds*

# 🌿 *Witch water rising*

LIFE, SAID CARLYLE, is a little gleam of time between two eternities. But ah, what a gleam for those who treasure little things!

This book is aimed at adding a little more gleam, luster, fun, excitement, or whatever you might call it, to the everyday—that vast chunk of our lives commandeered by commuter trains and kitchen sinks. It is dedicated to all those who live beyond the golf course, who care about something more than getting on top, or winning friends and influencing people, who want instead to be less of a stranger to the earth and the riddle of existence.

The day I watched a wasp struggling with a worm across the pebbles of my sandpile, stuffing it into a hole beside a tiny egg and then sealing the hole shut, remains one of the most exciting moments of my life. I deduced that the worm was a kind of living pantry for the larva that would hatch from the wasp egg. I was seven, I think, but I have never forgotten my elation when I discovered why the Indian paintbrushes always died when I tried to move them home. Their taproots—coiled like a screen-door spring around the root of some other plant—must mean they were parasites! And what about the housefly whose body was full of worms—were they parasites? or (a correct deduction) simply young that had hatched before the fly had found the right spot to lay her eggs? What was the fluttering outside the screened-in porch of my rooming house at college? Male cecropia moths avid for the female that had just emerged from the cocoon I was keeping there. Somehow the fragrance of that gravid female must have been borne on the wind to the Mississippi River bottom two miles or more away! These are discoveries that have made my life gleam with excitement, from early childhood on through the prosaic years of making a living.

When I moved east to that welter of people along the seaboard I felt sure I was leaving my outdoor world forever. But wonder of wonders—those were muskrat houses just outside of Manhattan, and, along the railroad track just north of the city, within easy shotgun range of the train, dozens of Canada geese on a creek bank. Mornings in spring when I walked to work through the heart of Philadelphia, migrant birds would call out to me from every bush—towhees, catbirds, brown thrashers, veeries and other thrushes, flickers, and white-throated sparrows, whose sweet, tremulous whistle has thrilled me from earliest childhood.

There is hardly a place or a time when the outdoors can't add a little gleam to life, sometimes in a grim situation. I was in my dentist's chair on the sixteenth floor of the Medical Tower Building in the center of Philadelphia, my mouth stuffed with cotton and a drain hanging from my lip. A block away on the top of that genteel institution, the Hotel Barclay, perched on the guardrail, was a bird clearly not a pigeon. It seemed more like a hawk, but what was a hawk doing on top of a skyscraper? A flock of pigeons wheeled below. Suddenly the bird plunged down the deep brick canyon after them. I all but tore loose the drain as I jumped up to look. With a mouth full of cotton plugs it was no time to explain to my startled dentist that I had just seen a peregrine falcon—now on the verge of extinction

—and that its power dives reach 90 and some say 150 miles an hour! As I was walking to the Colonnade for lunch the next day, again a peregrine, perhaps the same bird, perched atop the giant Rohm and Haas Building, facing into the wind like a gargoyle, then flew off before my companions could spot it. And so my friends, like most people, still don't realize that appreciating the out-doors doesn't need to be reserved for weekends in the country, but is a pleasure that can light up drab moments anywhere, anytime, the whole year round.

In nature, there is always something good to look forward to. Frost blackens the garden and flowers? That's no disaster, but a signal of nice things ahead. Maple leaves will soon take fire, and birches and aspen and tamarack turn to gold. Any day now may come the first tracking snow, as exciting as it is beautiful. It carries on its fresh front page the news of who's in town and what's doing. At the feeders outside the windows visitors will soon return, as happy as kids home for Christmas their first year at college.

Those who love nature are always on the brink of something pleasurable. Will this be the morning that the purple finches return? Or the horned larks or meadowlarks? The weeping willows talk of spring when it's nothing but a rumor. They whet our anticipation, like the best advance agents. Sometimes surprises come before we even await them. Bluebirds and redwings seem to come long before it's legal. The first morels, too, take us by surprise. And suddenly one night at dusk, the fireflies are out.

Now is the time to drive the country roads to look for does with their spotted fawns. And soon pin cherries will be ripe, and wild blackberries and blueberries. Let's gather a carful or two of family and friends and go berry-picking.

A seer once said that happiness consists of three

things: something to do, someone to love, and something to look forward to.

I can't help you much with the first two, but nature can give you something to look forward to—every month of the year. Those who know the outdoors already will understand what I am talking about. For all others, I hope this book will open up a world of pleasure independent of where you find yourself, what time of year it is, or how old or young you happen to be. It is a sample of the fun I have had with nature.

I would like everybody to come to know and enjoy nature as I do, but something beyond that: I would like them to participate in it, too. Feed birds. Grow moths. Collect snowflakes. Track. Call birds. Grow plants. Graft trees. Collect mushrooms. Traverse swamps. Become a disciple of nature—and an apostle, too.

I may as well confess that I am an incurable missionary for nature, and that with this book I aim to make a million—converts, that is, who love and understand nature and will therefore safeguard it.

There may be mistakes in this book, but they won't come from other books or encyclopedias, they will be my very own mistakes, the result of my own personal experiences. In fact, this is a book so intimate that it seems indecent for any but my closest friends to read. It is a revealing book, one that reveals at once why I have never made money.

There are other revealing views. In one chapter a friend whose brilliant work at Beltsville has pushed aside a part of the cloak that shrouds the mystery of plants gives his views on life and God and the laws that govern the universe, laws of survival which no congress can abridge nor president veto.

It would be easy to frighten a reader with dire predictions about how that scientist's bean plants (guinea pigs of the plant world) barely grow in his greenhouses out-

side Washington, D.C., and how last summer he had to
suspend his vital work for a whole month. The air was
so foul his beans died. I prefer to leave that to others,
and to make enjoyment of nature my silent ecological
plea.

Today the world is concerned with the mysteries of
space and time and infinity. Nobody was more absorbed
with the idea of interplanetary travel than I. But if
other orbs are as lifeless as the moon appears to be, I
think I'll have to cancel my flight. It was the prospect of
discovering new forms of life—new mosses, new plants,
new insects, and higher forms of animal life—that ig-
nited my enthusiasm to go spaceward. Without them, I
think I'll stay right here.

There are mysteries on earth as tantalizing as those in
outer space. How can a luna moth pupa lie frozen in its
cocoon all winter and emerge flooded with life on a
night in June? How can a snow flea—without warm
blood in his veins—survive and leap about when it's
twenty below zero? And how can a plant signal its pe-
tioles to stop pushing forth new growth and begin
flower production?

This book cannot supply all the answers, because to
date many are missing. But it hopes to sharpen the eyes
and ears of its readers a little, to share with them the
marvels I have found this side of space in the magic
world of little things.

In the Blue Ridge, when the sun beats hard against a
blacktop road in summer, or against a bank of moss or
the bark of a tree in midwinter, there are those who say
that the "witch water is rising." There are unfortunate
others who never see the tremulous wisps of heated air
that dance above the surface. It is the intent of this
book to help everyone see witch water rising, and to
arouse a sense of wonder, which is the seed of knowledge.

And now let the curtain go up. The play is about to begin.

But where? At what point do you begin a circle, a tale without beginning or end?

At spring? Perhaps. But in nature there is life and death, a beginning and an end, at every season. And pleasures, too. Pleasures now, and just ahead.

For want of another place to begin, let the curtain go up on spring.

# 1 🌿 *The fires of spring*

I NEVER KNEW the virtues of foul weather until I stayed for a week on a Caribbean island where the weather was perfect. Each day the sun came on warm and bright, and a mild breeze riffled the palm fronds. I couldn't believe such glorious weather, and on the third day I remarked about it to my host, a former advertising man from Manhattan now in the resort business.

"Yes, darn it," he replied, "the weather is always glorious. It gets so monotonous I'd leave tomorrow if I didn't have all this investment here. I'd give anything for a good old snow or even a sleet storm."

By the end of the week I began to agree with him.

To most of us change is as vital as family and friends —and nothing gives us more change than weather and seasons. It is the darkness and cold of winter that cause us to treasure as we do the great renewal of life that follows.

Spring is pure suspense. Nature itself seems to feel it. So eager is the skunk cabbage for spring that it thaws the snow and ice around it. In February or March, depending on where you live, some internal urging—time clock or temperature—starts converting the starches of its thick taproot into sugars that give off heat. The frozen earth begins to melt under the debris of last year's vegetation. You can actually feel the heat of the emerging leaves; the air around them is twenty degrees warmer than elsewhere. Each plant is in effect a small

starch-burning stove and a natural radiator. Once its
stalk emerges above the snow, it absorbs the sun's heat
and melts the snow farther and farther from it—the
same way a piece of charcoal does, or a rock thrown up
by a snowplow.

The snow itself helps warm the earth. It's amazing
stuff. Although it reflects most of the sun's energy, it absorbs some, too, and actually passes along that heat to
the ground, warming it during the day and blanketing
it against heat loss during the night. So the soil under
the snow of early spring can get quite warm—well
above freezing. Did you ever see a snowbank with water
running from beneath it? In early spring, snow melts
from the bottom up, not the top down.

Spring is change. No two days are alike—and no two
places, either.

Why not, like the skunk cabbage, hurry spring along?
Go to a sandy woods and find a sheltered hillside that
looks south to the sun. Even a road bank will do. The
world may already be coming alive. The fires of spring
burn early on the sandy slopes. The pipsissewa sprouts
in the carpet of needles under a patch of pine, bear-
berry starts to trail, and perhaps an arbutus begins to
open, its fragrance of apple blossoms calling out to a
motley assortment of crawling things oblivious to the
chill air. How can it bloom so early, while snow still
lies over some of the land?

The answer is in microclimates—a word that describes the temperature and humidity and oxygen-car-
bon dioxide ratio at the soil's surface, at an inch above,
at six inches, and so on. The mossy surface may be 35
degrees with 75 percent humidity. An inch above it
may be 40 degrees by reason of reflected heat with 50
percent humidity. A foot above that it may be freezing,
and six feet from the soil, where man breathes, the
wind may be sucking off the heat and moisture so that
the reading may be only 20 degrees with 15 percent

humidity. The only world that matters to the arbutus and its insect admirers is at soil level; to them, spring is already here. So to steal a march on spring, bask in the microclimate of the arbutus: drop to your knees, or better yet, lie on your side and let the sun beat down. It's cheaper than Florida, and not so crowded.

High above, soaring in the cold sunlight of earliest spring, is an eagle, independent of microclimates. He can change his climate at will, gliding from the high thin air to the warmth of a mudbank beside a lake where he finds a fish that is a casualty of the winter's shortage of oxygen. Alongside him the ice is black and honeycombed from the brightening sun. Rifts appear in the black surface, and a few days later a wind lashes the thin sheets onto shore.

Suddenly, across the melting snow comes a sudden whiff of spring, an attar compounded perhaps of the first green shoots of grass, of swelling buds and rising sap, a cool fragrance tingling with power. It lasts only a second or two, and rarely comes more than once a spring, but it is unmistakable. Several people may be outside talking and their conversation stops immediately. There it is—spring! Did you smell it? And for the next few minutes—as we do every spring—we try to guess what it is and where it comes from. And though we try again to get a second whiff, we cannot. Perhaps the nerve endings in the nostrils grow accustomed to the smell that fast. At any rate, spring comes with that first mysterious breeze.

The air seems thicker now, with more body than the thin-textured air of winter. The sap is rising—in moss and lichen, in weed and flower and tree and mouse and in man. For all his air-conditioned homes, his sophistication and knowledge, man is still captive to spring, and responds with atavistic fervor, each in his own way.

For my shy little aunt (lovingly known as "Auntie" in our community) spring meant raking the yard, combing the earth, nudging the dark soil awake. Every spring when we were growing up, even before the snow and ice were gone, we'd see her out in the yard cleaning up the debris. It was a ritual she loved. She didn't mind the sawdust beside the cellar windows, or the bones the dogs had chewed on. But the year after we had raised Leghorn chickens, she was in a tizzy. She couldn't overcome the white feathers. They blew out of her basket, caught in her hair, defied every effort at capture.

Then one morning they were gone, and we all wondered why. Our answer came as soon as we put out a handful more of the white feathers. Tree swallows came out of nowhere and pounced on them, carrying them off to the dead trees near the lake. Every year from then on, when Auntie would give the upstairs bedrooms their spring housecleaning, she would save the feathers that would find their way out of pillows and feather ticks during winter, and when she felt the neighbors might not be watching, would drop them out of an upstairs window, a few at a time. On a sunny day, birds sometimes caught them in mid-air, before they reached the ground.

I have tried to analyze why Auntie got so much more joy out of spring than most, and I think this is the answer. She participated in it. She wasn't content only to look. In her quiet, gentle way, she took part in it, feeding bread crumbs to the red-capped chipping sparrows at the back step. She had never been taught to write, so she asked us to keep records of the birds and wild flowers we saw when we moved each spring from town to the farm where we lived for the summer. She had us putting up nests for wrens—simply tomato cans with a hole punched into one side and nailed to the top of fence posts. Soon we had families of wrens in a dozen nests all the way to the pasture gate, making the walk up the lane something of a Disney movie.

Spring stays longer when you participate. If it is May

or June as you read this, get hold of some feathers, preferably white ones. Where do you find them? I wish I
could tell you. I have trouble even here in the country.
Few farmers keep small flocks, and big poultrymen
clean so meticulously that there's not a spare feather on
the place. You might borrow from an attic pillow, or
else buy a live hen. If you think you have trouble
finding feathers, consider the poor tree swallow, with no
other resources than a pair of swift wings. And yet in
my experience, a tree swallow will hardly nest without
a few white feathers to arch over her as she broods her
six white eggs.

Horsehair, for chipping sparrows, orioles, and kingbirds, is easier to supply. I am fortunate in having a
horsey nephew who trims a mane or tail for me and
brings in a handful of horsehair which I tie to the porch
railing outside the window, along with a handful of
sheep's wool. For weeks the birds pay no attention
either to horsehair or wool as they buzz past on their
way to and from the feeder. And then, in a few days, it
is largely gone. Early in the morning the orioles are at
it, tugging away big beakfuls of horsehair. Phoebes
make repeated trips for the wool, but the kingbird—
that practical, no-nonsense bird—takes a fistful in a single haul, barely clearing the tulips as he flies off. Orioles
go wild over foot-long strands of bright yellow twine, or
bits of colored string.

Much has been written about birdhouses. For years,
Congressmen used to send out—in franked envelopes—
bulletins on birdhouses every spring about the time of
purple martins and primary elections with the calm
assurance that every voter would realize the humanity,
even the greatness, of a man who loves birds. The boxes
in those brochures were marvels of beauty. How many
times I tried hollowing out pieces of elm to make the
inviting-looking woodpecker nest in the diagram. The
dimensions were there—to the eighth of an inch—but

no hint of how you hollow out a long, gourd-shaped cavity in a solid log. Gnaw it with a jackknife? I never got deeper than an inch. Burn it out? Ah, that might work. But the fire, even aided by kerosene, would go out after a charred inch or two. A red hot iron! But that too didn't go deep enough for a thimble, let alone the $8\frac{1}{2}$-by-$3\frac{1}{4}$-inch cavity which would delight the eyes of a lady hairy woodpecker. In my maturer years, I have tried band saws, handsaws, and brace and bit, without success. And still, the bird books I see keep repeating the classic old dimensions of the cavity, copying the errors of their predecessors, with even more beautiful, haunting diagrams.

If you must have a natural nesting cavity for woodpeckers, use the Davids system, the product of real creativity. You simply split a two-foot stick of hardwood in two, and then in four pieces with an axe, then chop off the points of the pie-shaped pieces and nail them back together again. The result is a fine, natural-looking birdhouse—for a year or so, until the pieces shrink and fall apart. Beautiful as they are for the first year or so, and closely as they resemble a bona fide hole in a tree, I've never had a single occupant of any kind. Woodpeckers invariably drill their own holes in an aspen nearby. Chickadees much prefer the tree-swallow nests, which are as about as natural-looking as platinum blondes. In fact, my chickadees often nest in a pottery nest I suspend from the limb of a spruce tree.

The kind of box seems much less important than its location. Your box should be in the open, never in the woods. Most people realize that purple martins like lots of open area around their box. But so do tree swallows and bluebirds. Wrens use boxes in the shade, but prefer not too much shrubbery around them. Even chickadees —forest birds—prefer to nest in the open, adjoining the woods. The crested flycatcher, that big raucous boss of the deep woods, likes to nest in my martin house out in the stark open. Right now a pair of them are searching my meadow and fields for snake skins. Except for certain warblers and owls, few birds nest in the deep woods, preferring the edges where open field and forest meet.

During the years we were growing up on the farm, there were flickers everywhere, boring nesting holes in the acres of fire-blackened pine snags that remained after my father's logging operations. We called them yellowhammers, and loved to hear them hammer their challenges to the world on the sides of the dry stumps. Over the years as we hauled and burned and dynamited out hundreds of tons of such stumps to make room for our fields, the flickers diminished. But we left one stump—fifty feet or more high—that we called the yellowhammer tree. The wood must have acted like the sounding board of a stringed instrument when the flickers drummed on it. How the beats rang out! From the day in midwinter when someone stole the yellowhammer tree for firewood, the farm has never seemed the same. My brother, who still lives there, was determined to have the flickers again. He found a grotesque hollow stump that he mounted at the edge of his two-hundred-acre field on a post no more than five feet high.

I laughed at him. Didn't he remember how high the yellowhammers used to nest? In the South, they're called "high holes." I installed four of my marvelously natural-looking birdhouses in trees twenty feet or more high, nailing them to the bark so that they seemed like the tree itself. I sprinkled sawdust and wood chips inside. (As far as birdhouses go, I'm the thorough type.) I waited. Flickers came in flocks during migration. Not one gave my splendid houses as much as a pleasant look. But one pair chose a dead aspen at the edge of the grove. And on the farm my brother's monstrous contraption was filled at once, and has been every year since!

One reason may be that my brother's birdhouse was on its own post—mine were nailed onto trees—and birds much prefer a free-standing box on a pole of its own.

Why that should be is easy to explain if you fall victim to anthropomorphism—ascribing human motives and reasoning to animals. Birds "know" that predators are less likely to be traveling up a slender stalk apart from the woods. With that specious reasoning, you might expect birds to like best of all posts surrounded by aluminum spouting (the kind used to vent electric dryers)—a good idea for protecting your tenants. But of course they don't know the difference.

Flickers and other hole-nesting birds generally choose dead trees or those with few or sparse limbs, and a post perhaps seems most akin to that. So put up your boxes on posts. Cedar ones are light, long-lasting, and easy to install. So, too, are two-by-two's, although they're inclined to be unsteady. If squirrels bother your nests, give the posts aluminum collars. Flying squirrels will still be able to glide to the roofs of nesting boxes from distant high trees, and sometimes they do make raids on tree swallow nests (although I have no firsthand evidence), but the tin collars will thwart most predators.

A third injunction about birdhouses: see that the lids are hinged. Not because that makes cleaning them easier (which it does) but so you can enjoy the birds more. In twenty years of my looking in on wrens and tree swallows and bluebirds, no harm has ever come to any of them, and we show the nests and young to all the goggle-eyed kids and unbelieving adults who come into the yard.

A family of bluebirds is pretty impersonal when all you see of them are the adults flying to and from the nest. But when you can look in on their home any time of the day, you find yourself following their home-building like an overanxious mother-in-law.

Mark on a calendar the day the bluebird lays its first egg. The second one may be two or even three days later. The third, fourth, fifth, and sixth follow in quick succession, generally one every day. What excitement the day the eggs hatch! The male sings again as if he had just arrived. You can look in many times a day without upsetting the parents. Some bluebirds pay no attention to humans, and in fact seem happy to be close. One pair nested in a pottery birdhouse within six feet of the kitchen door, and fed their young while we ate our meals on the patio beside them. On the day they left with their six young, the patio seemed dead and cheerless. It was as if friends, as if a blessing, as if happiness itself had left us.

Not all bluebirds are that friendly. Our current pair leave their nest the moment we drive into the yard, and return only furtively. There is little pleasure in them. The same pair must have nested here last year, too, because we hardly knew we had bluebirds.

Hinged lids (with hooks to keep the wind from opening them) permit you to look in on wrens as well. One brood last summer had ten eggs, and though one egg had rolled out of reach in a corner where it couldn't be covered, all the rest hatched. It was hard to believe that all those young could crowd into a cavity smaller than a teacup without smothering.

Like bluebirds, wrens differ greatly in temperament, and though all are noisy, quarrelsome, and furiously industrious, some seem undisturbed by human visitors; others dive-bomb them.

All of our chickadees without exception have been a pleasure, however. None of the parents seem worried over our visits, and the young in their black bibs and caps are a delight. This year, though, their nest was in a clay pot that doesn't permit even a glimpse inside. We never once saw the young. We would take down the clay pots if it weren't that they are so decorative and that the chickadees seem to prefer seeking refuge inside them during cold winter nights.

The real charmer of all birds that nest in boxes is the tree swallow. Gentle and beautiful, the female looks out of her nesting hole curious and unafraid as you approach. Sometimes she will fly. More often she snuggles back down on her eggs, completely covering the six snow-white pearls as she looks up at you without fear. When the young hatch, the parents aren't thrown into a panic as you approach, but continue to go inside, even though you might be holding a fledgling in your hand. Often the parents will feed the bird you're holding.

One day my cousin and I were holding a nestling apiece when she appeared to let her bird drop. I was about to chide her, when mine too slipped from my hand and almost hit the ground. But a crucial few inches above ground they both beat their wings like moths and lifted up over the grass and flew off on wavering but strong-beating wings, their parents twittering excitedly above them. We had watched the young make the maiden flight of their lives. It was a moment we won't forget—something like seeing a child take his first steps. The remaining four nestlings had left the nest by nightfall.

These are the pleasures of participating with nature. If you would participate in spring still further, keep your suet feeders well stocked. You will be amazed at the way catbirds, orioles, and even warblers can use a little help during the uncertain days of spring.

Sometimes that help is crucial. A sudden snow that persists a few days can starve many kinds of songbirds, because most of them don't turn back once the fire of spring ignites within them, nor do they fly long distances to feeding grounds, as ducks and geese do. Resident birds like chickadees and cardinals can lie low during a cold spell, conserving their energy or foraging for the foods they find during winter. But early migrants are stuck with the weather. There is no turning back.

Several years ago, most bluebirds east of the Mississippi were killed off during several weeks of cold and snow. Only lately are they beginning to reappear in their old haunts. If that storm had hit today, with the great increase in conservation-minded people, a great many might have lived on emergency rations of suet and hamburger. Robins, with their cosmopolitan tastes, fare better during late snowstorms, and feast on over-wintering crab apples, rose hips, and kitchen handouts.

Several years ago, snow began to fall in Minnesota during the first week of June in big, smothering flakes that came down all day. Flocks of rose-breasted grosbeaks, all male, began collecting along the shoulders of the highways, searching for weed seeds and grain scattered from trucks during the previous fall's harvest. As the snow continued without lessening during the second day, more of them gathered, sitting on the highway in a torpid state so that motorists plowed into them. Scarlet tanager males, too, sat in clusters along the roads. I saw a dozen on a side road that barely flew when my car inched up to them.

No one could account for their sleepy, lethargic condition. Was it cold that numbed them, or approaching starvation? And why did they all crowd to the highway? Most people said they were searching for gravel. But wasn't it rather the lingering warmth of the pavement, which kept the snow melting? Never before nor since have I seen such strange behavior. It was gratifying how almost everyone but outsiders was concerned and drove with care. The outsiders, speeding by on the highways, killed a great many. My brother and I picked up twelve flickers and two catbirds in a mile.

The big kill, though, was of swallows and martins—birds that survive almost solely on flying insects. I saw them skimming low over the lake in the snowstorm, searching for emerging insects. They crouched on window ledges and huddled in my nephew's machine shed for warmth. On about the fourth day, when the storm let up and the snow thawed, there were dead birds everywhere. My nephew counted sixty dead cliff swallows around his farm buildings. Barn swallows lay dead in his machine sheds. Surely the swallow population must be doomed, it seemed. But the condition, we learned, was highly local, and outside of two or three surrounding counties, there had been little snow and no lost birds. And—strange to believe—the doughty little tree swallow whose two white eggs had lain cold in the nesting box beside our kitchen turned up out of nowhere and laid four more, all of which hatched and prospered.

Strangely, too, tanagers, grosbeaks, and flickers that summer seemed as numerous as ever. Perhaps the dead birds had been en route to more northerly regions. Migration has a way of overcoming local or regional disasters, and though most birds probably return to the area where they were hatched, they radiate out from overpopulated areas, eventually filling in the vacant spaces.

Much as we have learned about bird migration in recent years, the questions are still more numerous than the answers. A friend of mine, Paul Fluck, has been helping to fill in a few clues to the mystery of migration with a giant banding program begun twenty years ago at the Nature Education Center at Washington Crossing in Pennsylvania. Small birds had been generally thought to be short-lived, since few were found with bands more than two or three years old. But Paul noticed that many birds wore out their bands fast, sometimes in a year. He began replacing worn bands with stouter ones, which he induced the Fish and Wildlife Service to produce. Now almost a thousand birds banded in former years return to the center annually: three grackles he banded eleven years ago are still com-

ing to the feeder wearing their fourth bands, and a
hairy woodpecker was thirteen years old when he died
of a dose of DDT intended for elm trees in the park.
Paul's most spectacular migrant is a red-eyed vireo that
returned from the jungles of South America—a five-
thousand-mile trip over the tropical forests of Central
America and back again—every year for six years.
"That one-ounce bundle of fluff and navigational
knowhow," Paul says, "has made trips totaling more
than twice around the world—without benefit of radar,
airports, or catered lunches!"

Males of most migrants generally come days and even
weeks before females. Just as many animals mark the
edges of their territories with urine, and humans put up
NO TRESPASSING signs, so birds sing in part to advise the
world of their property, moving from perch to perch on
its periphery. The net effect is to prevent overcrowding
of a species.

A pair of loons need an entire lake to themselves, or
at least one bay of a large lake. Song sparrows may need
an acre or so to a pair. Wrens—much as they would like
to keep every other couple out of singing distance—will
settle for much less.

Certain birds, like the robin, will defend their nesting areas with song and beak and wing, but will feed together in undefended territory. Chickadees are like this,
too, and so are barn swallows and cedar waxwings.

The first birds to arrive are thought to be the oldest
ones. These old-timers often come to precisely the same
spot as the year previous, and literally pro-claim their
territory by singing up a storm. For two years, a pair of
catbirds nested in a tangle of woodbine behind my pool,
and the male showered the yard with song. In a foolish
attack of orderliness, I pulled out the woodbine and re-
placed it with two gooseberries which I thought would
be a suitable nesting site. The next spring the male sang
above the gooseberries in a plum tree until his spouse

arrived and considered the skimpy bushes. For two weeks the male chased off all other comers while the bushes leafed out. They were still too sparse. Finally, the pair nested in young white pines near the lake. Again last spring a catbird and his spouse wasted a couple of weeks in indecision over the gooseberries before nesting again in the white pines. It seems altogether likely that at least the male is the same catbird of four years ago.

There is a passion to spring, a quickened heartbeat to life, an exhilaration of the senses. A pair of common terns do aerial acrobatics high above the water of Red Lake, one dropping a stick two feet long to the other below who catches it in mid-air, flies up and drops it to its mate and so on, continuing for fifteen minutes before they let it fall to the surface. On the feeder outside the window, orioles drink from the orange halves as if they were thirsting to death and devour saucer after saucer of jam I've put there.

Birds otherwise songless begin to sing. The quiet little brown creeper bursts forth in a cascade of liquid notes, soft yet clear, that once heard can never be forgotten. The blue-gray gnatcatcher, which all year squeaks like a mouse as it moves incessantly about, for a few short days pours forth a soft but exciting cadenza of trills and intricate warbles, hardly pausing for breath. (The one time I heard it, coming from a tiny songster sitting motionless just above my head, made me an hour late to a dinner party.) Some birds that catch sight of themselves in the window rush at their image, attack the glass with claw and beak and wing until they must be chased away. The sapsucker drums at the metal rain gauge, an irregular staccato unlike the steady riveter's beat of the flicker atop the television antenna. Is there any way to dampen their ardor, especially at four a.m.? None that I know of.

Several years ago an impassioned flicker started

pounding at the shingle walls of the house where my mother lived by herself. The noise didn't worry her— she was often up at four making bread for the various branches of her big family—but she was concerned about the holes the bird was making above her bedroom window. She tried shooing him away. He would be back at his boring before she was inside the house. In desperation she rigged up a scarecrow, which kept him away for the rest of the day. Just before day-break, she awoke to more hammering, and looking out, she was startled to see a big man peering in through the window at her. She crept out of bed and stole into the bathroom, then slowly peered out from behind the door. The man never moved, and in the gray light, she laughed to herself as she slowly realized that the man was her own scarecrow. In a few days, the flicker was so occupied with nest-building that he had no more time for useless drilling.

And so it is that the quickened pulse of spring slows into serene, workday summer.

But you can hold it back a moment longer. Drive to a nearby marsh and stop the car and listen to the rhyth-mic singing of the frogs. Have you ever heard two cho-ruses singing in a soft syncopated beat? Some say this is no conscious effort on their part, that once one section begins, the other replies in haphazard fashion. But it sometimes seems that they are surely conscious of beat. And if frogs do respond to other frogs by singing, isn't it possible that they time their answers to others they hear? Sometimes cricket frogs will respond if you simply take two pebbles and tap them together. You may awaken an entire pond of songsters in midday.

Listen for softer songs at the edge of the dark marsh. The little twittering sound may be a woodcock. The whooshing sound comes from the charming little Wil-son's snipe as he dives through the air in a marvelous display of aeronautics, his tail feathers spread like a tiny turkey as the wind whistles past, making the soft whinnying sound. You can see him with binoculars as he performs, sometimes in midday, but more often as dusk shrouds the marsh and moist meadows.

There are other sounds as darkness falls. Listen for the vesper song of the ovenbird—a wild, uncontrolled rhapsody of notes far unlike his plodding, studied "teach-er, teach-er, teach-er" song of daylight hours. Thoreau described the beauty of that evening song and puzzled over the identity of its singer. It came from the vicinity of the ovenbird, he wrote, but only in the evening and at night. Other birds have impassioned evening songs, among them the song sparrow and the red-eyed vireo. Speaking anthropomorphically, it seems as if birds with patterned phrases must need to burst out periodically in a cadenza totally unlike their stilted songs.

Night in the swamp, or a thicket, or even your own backyard is seldom quiet in spring. A veery might sing. Sometimes a robin sings in a muffled voice. And all night the marsh wrens sing, stitching up the remnants of day with their excited little sewing-machine sounds.

In the torrent of activity and ardor of spring, only the oaks are unmoved, heedless of the warming sun, their buds still winter-tight. Nothing will budge them until spring is most certainly here. Over the centuries, perhaps, overeager ones have been weeded out by late frosts.

I watch the oaks and am glad they are waiting, for as long as they stand leafless, the great floods of warblers won't appear, and I tell myself that spring is still ahead. When the warblers do come at last, I try to arrange for a few mornings off to glory in that storm of birds that suddenly sweeps through the oaks, searching every shiny leaf for the half-inch green worms that try to escape by suspending themselves from a silken thread.

There is only one way I know of prolonging the fragile, beautiful moments in life, and that is to participate in them, not stand on the sidelines or watch out the window as a spectator. Take part in the drama: feed the birds, put up nests and watch over the occupants, listen with your ears and your heart and slow down the rush of that fleeting, haunting mood known as spring.

# 2 ⚜ *How to talk to birds*

NEXT TIME YOU MEET a chicken egg that is all set to hatch, talk to it. Try humming a high-pitched, steady note. The embryo, which starts going peep-peep inside the shell a day or two before hatching, will suddenly go silent. You have given it an alarm signal, the same one the mother hen uses to signal "danger overhead."

When men searched for a sound to convey the same warning, they hit on a nearly identical one—the high-pitched, steady hum generated by air-raid sirens. Men use it for the same reasons that birds do: It carries well and is ventriloquial—doesn't disclose the whereabouts of the caller the way a fluctuating sound does.

Now if you had gone "cluck, cluck" to the egg, the embryo would have continued peeping. The mother hen's reassuring speech is wonderfully suited to its purpose. It is low-pitched and has only a short carrying range that doesn't attract predators, but coming at regular intervals, the sound is an easy one for a lost chick to home in on.

Ever since time began, it seems, mankind has been trying to understand the language of birds. Aristotle in 350 B.C. was studying bird calls and knew many of the voices of those that nested in Greece. Legend has it that Solomon owned a ring that permitted him to understand bird talk. According to another legend, a caliph of ancient Baghdad and his vizier took a magic powder so they could change themselves into storks and so understand stork talk. What the men heard was so funny that they laughed and laughed and ever after forgot the words that would turn themselves back into men. Poets, of course, have no trouble translating bird songs, and St. Francis thought that birds were forever praising God.

A few birds actually do communicate to people. Africa has a fantastic bird called the honey guide, a robin-sized, otherwise inconspicuous bird that lives on beeswax. When the honey guide locates a bee tree, it flies to the nearest camp of a tribe of people known as the Wanderobo and sets up a noisy chatter until the people start following. Flying ahead, twittering as it goes, it may take them as far as five miles to a bee tree. Then as the natives start hacking open the tree it sits quietly nearby, waiting for the wax that the humans leave. The honey guide has other bizarre relationships.

Like the cowbird, the honey guide lays its eggs in other nests. The scrawny, potbellied fledgling, just out of the shell, backs up to the other eggs and pushes them out. If he already finds rivals in the nest, he pecks them to death with a horny point of his bill that falls off a few days after hatching. Just as the honey guide depends on man—or in some cases a bear that answers his call—to open the tree, he depends on wax-digesting bacteria within his gut to convert the otherwise indigestible wax into simpler substances.

Certain Eskimos can call up just about every game bird in the Arctic. The dove-callers of the high Pyrenees in Spain, though, are the real experts. With no more than wild hoots that sound like someone out chasing hogs they lure the doves into catching nets. Nobody I know has figured out why the birds respond. And dove-callers—a tight union—aren't about to give out their secrets, passing them along only to their sons.

In 1960 on a hunting expedition I learned that the Cree Indians of James Bay have the same reluctance about letting anyone in on their goose-calling. The way that snow geese and blue geese come to the human voice is thrilling, and when the Cree guides were away brewing tea—which happens ten times a day, nearly always when the geese are moving—I lifted my voice in a trial falsetto. Almost at once a family of five blues started toward me, led by a splendid gander with a frosty white head. I was so surprised that I lost my voice. When I tried to continue, all that came out was a tense quack like a startled duck. My companion in the blind, Ralph Wennblom, was kneeling on the wet ground with me behind a scanty barricade of willow whips stuck around us. He urged me on. Eventually I was able to repeat that elusive quavering yodel.

This time a flock of fifty came across the distant spires of black spruce and began flapping toward us over the boggy grass. I hunched over, squawking at the ground to muffle the call. They came on, but too far left. So I did what the Crees do, shunted my voice to the right using the palm of my hand. As if the geese were hung on strings, they veered right and now came in just over the grass. Then I gave the same reassuring gurgle that the Crees do, a sound exactly like someone juggling too big a swallow of mouthwash. Amazingly, the birds answered.

I don't remember that Ralph fired a shot. I know I didn't. I was too flabbergasted at my amazing performance. That night after supper on a gravel bar beside the vast bay, Ralph recounted my triumph to our two tent mates, who refused to believe it. The night was black—not a star or glint of light in the whole world around us. We built a big fire of driftwood and sat on stumps around it as Ralph expanded on my vast new talent. In the distance, perhaps half a mile off over the water came the call of a lone goose, probably looking for its mate.

"Now's your chance," said Ralph. "Go ahead and prove it."

I knew it was hopeless, but I lifted my muzzle skyward and squawked, plaintively, seductively. And to my amazement the goose came flying toward us into that utter blackness, I don't know how, answering each of my hoarsening yaps with a dozen excited ones. Straight to us she came, and for just a second we saw her dark form over the fire. Then she turned and winged out over the bay. There was complete silence now. Even the Cree guides, who had been chattering in the adjoining tent, fell silent. My two unbelieving friends started up.

"Just a fluke," they said, "you'll never bring her in again."

And then—with all the convenience of a high school drama script—my goose started calling again somewhere offstage in the blackness. And once again I responded, with more pathos than skill. She came again blindly through the darkness, and when she swept darkly over the fire we could hear the soft whistle of her wings.

It was my finest hour, believe me. To someone who has never been able to whistle properly—a secret that as a child I guarded desperately—I had done something my whistling friends couldn't, although in fairness I must admit they hadn't given it the same effort.

Next morning, though, my hour was over. The Crees faced me in stony silence. I had invaded their precinct, had made them a trifle less indispensable. For the rest of the week they barely tolerated me. But it did seem to Ralph that they brewed a little less tea.

🦅

Whistle or not, there's an easy way now of talking to the birds—just about any birds—calling them in close enough so you can see the red of their irises. It's a sneaky thing to do, I suppose, but you use recordings made by Cornell University.

You set your player on the windowsill, or better yet, play the record on a transistorized machine next to a lake or meadow or thin woods. The best time is during spring migration. That's when you'll get the biggest assortment of warblers, finches, and sparrows. But any time during the nesting season will work on resident birds.

You can order bird records direct from Cornell University Records, 124 Roberts Place, Ithaca, N.Y. 14850. *An Evening in Sapsucker Woods* uses one side to teach the songs of twenty-five birds and a few frogs and toads, the other side to give you an evening concert of bird music undisturbed by other voices. *Music and Bird Songs* is another favorite of mine. Here the songs of wood thrush and winter wren are slowed down to quarter speed and less, permitting a study of the intricacy of their melodies. Albums keyed to Roger Tory Peterson's guides are available and offer a good way to learn bird songs. Excellent records are also available from the Federation of Ontario Naturalists, Edwards Gardens, Don Mills, Ontario. My favorites here are an album of finch songs, including sparrows and grosbeaks, and another of warblers. A masterpiece of nature sounds is their *A Day in Algonquin Park*.

A few years ago I demonstrated bird-calling to a few of my unbelieving friends in a cabin in the Poconos north of Philadelphia. Ralph was one of them. You might expect that after my performance at James Bay he would never again doubt me in any particular, but that isn't his nature. Nobody paid much attention while I plugged in a portable player and opened the nearest window. I had heard a scarlet tanager singing so I set the needle at that point on the record. It was no more than thirty seconds later that half a dozen males flew up and perched in the tree just outside. There was such a rush to the window that it seemed as if the cabin would tip. My friends gasped with delight. It seems that scarlet tanagers are vivid even a treetop away. (Being color-blind to red, I wouldn't know.) At arm's length, my friends found them overpowering. Tanagers are placid, slow-moving birds, and they stayed for a long while to peer inside. My friends called them up again and again to admire them, though not as many birds responded as at first.

When the player went on to the song of the rose-breasted grosbeak, a splendid male came up immediately and perched, giving everyone a good look. During the morning I had heard a bobwhite somewhere below the mountain, and I started playing his call, plus the "rallying" call that birds use to find one another and reassemble after the flock has been dispersed.

"Quail don't live in woods," said Ralph—just as a plump little bird came running up the path, pausing only long enough to assure us with a call that he was coming. He flew to a rock where he could look in the window, then systematically circled the house, whistling a fervent "bobwhite!" at every window. My friends were speechless.

Bird records are a great way of introducing people to birds. Children, and most adults too, couldn't care less about a distant bird, flitting through the branches, even though it might be a Cape May warbler. Binoculars aren't the answer, either, because it takes practice to use them fast enough to follow most birds, and few people will bother long enough to learn. But an oriole or flicker close enough to see the gleam of the feathers is electrifying. A few exposures like that and your friends won't consider your enthusiasm for birds quite so strange. Kids especially like those closeup looks. (It's that curiosity that prompts small boys with their first guns to pink away at songbirds; they're not blood-thirsty as much as interested.)

My equipment for bird-calling has undergone a long evolution. Before battery-powered record players existed, I built one with a turntable that I ordered from an English firm and fitted into a cardboard filing box that I got from a law office. An RCA inventor lent me a big loudspeaker he had been testing in his laboratory. I'll admit that the resulting contraption looked a little weird, but it worked.

I could hardly wait to try it. Driving outside of Washington, D.C., one day, I stopped along a narrow road that went through a patch of woods, set the player on the hood with the loudspeaker on the roof, and started up the warbler record. A hooded warbler—the first I'd ever seen in my life—dived at the speaker and lit momentarily on a branch across the road. He was a brilliant yellow—a color that looms brighter than fire to my color-blind eyes—with a tricky trimming of black. Just then a police car came racing around a curve in the narrow road and hauled up to a stop. A big young officer walked up, obviously startled.

"What're you doing here?" he shouted.

"Calling birds," I said, swallowing. Somehow any police officer automatically makes me feel guilty.

"I said what are you stopping here for?" he said, more quietly.

"Just to call birds," I said, and seeing a look of discomfort, almost fright come over him, I warmed to a discussion, and continued.

"A hooded warbler over there just came in and dive-bombed me," I began. "Want to see him?" But the young man only backed up, keeping his eyes on me, but occasionally glancing at my contraption on top of the car.

"Just see that you don't get run over," he said as he hurried into his car and drove off.

My next bird-calling rig was a conventional record player that I could plug into the cigarette lighter of my car—via an odd, boxlike gadget called a converter, which added its own sound of a jet on takeoff. Surprisingly, the birds didn't mind. On a trip up the Alaskan Highway, a fox sparrow came to the car and sang his heart out, continuing long after I turned off the machine. In northern Alaska the records were really unnecessary. Birds sing all night in the glorious Arctic summer, and generally it isn't hard to see them at fairly close range. They've got too much going on in the few short weeks of summer to be bothered by humans. If you're in Alaska in midsummer, stop along a brushy road and listen to the olive-backed or the gray-cheeked thrush as they sing at midnight in the vast frozen silence. You'll never forget it.

My current bird-caller is a compact little battery-operated tape recorder that I picked up in Hong Kong several years ago and that works beautifully. You can get the same kind in the United States now for not too much and tape the calls you want from the Cornell records.

Now for the fun. During April or May, tape the warblers that your bird book indicates are likely to be passing through, and stop at the edge of a patch of trees or brush and turn on the player. I've had redstarts all but light on me, and Blackburnians—the warblers with their throats on fire—give a pass or two and light in a tree nearby. Black-throated blues, those tame little dudes in fancy dress, come even closer; after a few looks they lose interest.

Migration time is full of surprises. Birds you may never have seen before because they nest farther north may stop to look you over. Most of them will be males, which makes identification easier. Not all migrating birds come to the call, though.

Nesting birds are surer to respond. After a male has staked out his territory, he'll come like a bullet to defend his boundaries. And when he comes, he'll be warbling mad. The angrier he gets—in true operatic tradition—the more furiously he sings.

When I play the flicker call during nesting season, a big male flashes across the orchard and lights on the television aerial where he hammers out an insult to the intruding voice, then flies down to a branch just above the record player, ready for battle. House wrens get so agitated near their nests that I don't often call them, though I confess I sort of enjoy breaking through their crusty arrogance. The record player almost broke up a pair of towhees in New Jersey. The female was enchanted with the stranger's voice and flew back repeatedly, each time followed by a furious mate who chased her home.

Bird-calling with records is much more than a diversion. Besides hooking adults and children into bird-watching, it's a way of broadening your own knowledge of uncommon species, of their habits and habitats. Birds you would rarely if ever see come to you and identify themselves. Only a hermit thrush will come to the hermit thrush song, a water thrush to the water thrush song.

That doesn't mean, though, that a curious fox might not come sneaking in to see what the commotion is all about, as one did for me in the Adirondacks. That's part of the fun of the outdoors—you can never predict anything for certain. When I played a dying rabbit's call to attract foxes, three deer came loping up to see what was happening.

Recorded calls bring the tranquillity of wild bird songs into the comfort of the home—something men for ages have longed to enjoy, caging wild birds in hopes they would sing.

When Romeyn Berry, newspaper columnist, first played the records, he said that all the animals except the goldfish responded instantly, working themselves into a state of morbid excitement. "The two beagles went into neurasthenic frenzy and had to be let out to chase something—chase anything. The canaries, who had been singing gloriously themselves, stopped instantly, huddled together, ruffed up their feathers, squatted on the perch, and suffered in silence. But it remained for Bingo, the cat, to be completely duped. At the first note of the hermit thrush she dived under the sofa to become a crouching lion, and when the robin gave forth she all but leaped upon the phonograph."

The man who pioneered bird-song recording is my friend Peter Paul Kellogg, a silver-haired scientist at Cornell University, who ironically doesn't need electronic devices to call up birds. Scarlet tanagers he can summon up with a throaty whistle. One time as he was swimming in Beebe Lake on the campus he heard tanagers singing on shore. He rolled onto his back and floated, whistling to them. Several came out to see what he was, flying low over him.

Paul felt the need of recording birdcalls for his ornithology classes, and in the process of building the equipment he needed, studied enough engineering to earn a degree. The first records were dismal, marred by a roar of extraneous sounds. No matter how careful he was, something would spoil a take: the rustle of leaves, even his own breath. And no matter if he was up at daybreak, there were cars rumbling past, or dogs barking, crickets humming, or roosters crowing. He set out after the water ouzel, which lives near the roar of rushing streams, and watched a bird that frequented a rock in the center of a torrent. He set a mike on the rock and to Paul's delight, the bird sat on the mike and started to sing. But the result was a flop—marred by the shuffle of the bird's feet!

Eventually he and a friend built a "parabolic reflector," a saucer-shaped ear, six feet across, that caught and focused distant songs onto a microphone. When it was completed, he turned on the juice to test it, said "Boo"—and broke the meter. The reflector worked too well. He learned to be more careful. One day when he was playing a mockingbird song in Florida he heard the excited tapping of a mockingbird at the window. Could the bird actually mistake the record for the real bird? He set the speaker outdoors and when the sound came on, the bird walked around it, looking for the rival, then hopped onto a perch and tried to outsing the intruder. It dawned on Paul that here was a way to get perfect recordings. He hurried to a spruce-tamarack bog with a winter wren's song and a microphone. A wren that had been singing high up in a spruce flew down at once and sang for half an hour within two feet of the microphone, providing a brilliant study that is now part of a long-playing record. A song sparrow heard his own voice preceded by a human voice saying, "Song sparrow." After just one hearing the bird instantly associated the man's voice with what he thought was an intruder's voice and, the second time they were played, flew in to the man's voice before he heard his own. Paul chuckled. It would seem to an outsider that the bird recognized his name.

Still Paul didn't have the call of the horned owl— that throaty hoot pitched at middle C (262 cycles a second) in the case of the female and somewhat higher for males. It wouldn't be hard to call one in, Paul thought. All he need do is play the recorded drumming of a ruffed grouse—favorite food of the old predator. The first night, not one owl came, although Paul knew a pair was nesting nearby. The next night, none came. Nor the next. Slowly Paul came to realize in his study of birds' hearing that the horned owl can't hear the low drumming of a grouse's wings. Though the owl feeds on grouse, the frequency of the beat is too low for his ears.

Good as a bird's hearing is, it can't compare to man's. Starlings are the only birds who can hear notes as high as we can. Their range is from 700 to 15,000 cycles a second, while man's goes from 20 to 16,000. A man can hear tones five octaves below a starling's lower limit. Paul tells me that a pigeon's range is from 200 to 7,500 cycles. No bird sings that a man with good ears can't hear, although as men age they often lose the ability to pick up the wiry trill of the grasshopper sparrow or the thin buzz of Blackburnian, Cape May, and blackpoll warblers. My brother and my nephew can't believe that a grasshopper sparrow is singing beside them, though they can hear a grouse drumbeat only a fraction as loud.

Scientists know very little really about birds' songs. They believe that all singing serves some purpose, but just what they're not sure. Many birds sing most ardently before any females arrive, staking out territory in advance, then subside after they have found mates. Besides advertising territory and attracting mates, birds like siskins and goldfinches and grosbeaks call to keep the flock together. So do geese. Other birds call at or near the nest to alert the mate.

Birds understand each other's language to an extent. A series of interrupted squawks that say "Look, a cat!" or "Snake!" have interspecies meaning. A crow or a bluejay's alarm call generally halts all singing for a few seconds at least. And I've seen deer stop eating and flip their tails in alarm at those calls.

Most bird sounds, though, have meanings only for a particular species. In fact, all that keeps two races of Traill's flycatchers from interbreeding are their accents. Centuries ago the races were separated—perhaps by a sheet of ice—and those below the Mason-Dixon line began to call "fitz-bew" while the Yankee birds sang "fee-bee-o." And though the birds—identical in appearance—have recently mingled, their dialects seem to keep them segregated.

Not so, perhaps, the eastern meadowlark with its wheezy, lusterless song—and the western version with its golden, full-throated song. As the two races are beginning to mingle, they are interbreeding. I can tell how far west of the Ohio I am by the song a meadow-lark sings. The farther west you go, the richer the melody.

Some birds may have big vocabularies. Aretas Saunders, who spent his life studying bird songs, set down in written syllables 884 variations of the song sparrow, though he would not guess how many moods, emotions, or "words" they encompassed. Most bird songs are probably not given with any intent to communicate, but simply reflect the bird's mood at that moment. Yet the result is the same. When danger is past, a male ovenbird is said to sing an "all's well" to his mate, who sits in a covered nest with a view out one side. Parent birds—wrens, for distance—use a special baby talk to their young that causes the orange-rimmed mouths to split wide to be fed.

No one has worked out a dictionary of the sounds of any species of animal or bird. Here is something for the careful observer to tackle. Even a bird with such a limited repertoire as a chickadee keeps surprising me with its variety of calls. I haven't the slightest notion of when each kind is given.

The more sociable the bird, the greater his vocabulary. Birds that live alone except during mating have only a few calls. The bobwhite, on the other hand, has many, some of which when translated might say: "Come back," "I'm lost," "Help, I'm caught," "Food," "Danger but lie still," "Danger, scatter," and the rallying call which is so effective for the bird-caller. The most common call, "bobwhite," is made by the lonesome male and means, "I need a wife."

Some songs, however, seem completely without function. The "whisper song" of birds in the fall is as mystifying as it is beautiful. Once heard, you won't forget it. A robin, for example, will sing with his bill closed, a song that you might never notice unless you are very near. Recordings may help reveal whether it is a young bird practicing softly, or an old one humming to himself as he remembers the raptures of spring.

Cornell used a recording to teach a mynah bird to talk. A friend of mine was doing publicity work for the Burpee Seed Company and hit upon an idea that he felt sure would be the hit of the big spring garden show at Convention Hall in Philadelphia. He would get a young mynah bird that hadn't yet learned a word and train it to repeat Burpee commercials all week long. Cornell's Laboratory of Ornithology agreed to train it, and David Burpee himself—a man of no unwarranted modesty—was glad to voice the commercial: "This is David Burpee. Burpee seeds *really* grow."

The young bird was placed in solitary at Ithaca and a tape recorder played the words over and over again at feeding time.

A month later in a Burpee office, my friend was startled to hear the voice of David Burpee coming from behind the door. It couldn't be. Mr. Burpee didn't stand in corners behind doors. And yet the voice was positively his—in pitch, volume, timbre, inflection. Even as my friend turned and saw the bird, he could scarcely believe it.

What a crowd-puller he had! Live commercials via bird! Should he alert the press? No, rather let them make the discovery.

And so on opening morning there was no fanfare. And at the start, at least, no commercials either. The young bird sat in a cage above the burgeoning marigolds like that brooding raven of Poe's. Only this bird said nothing as he hunched there, head withdrawn among ruffled feathers. Nor did he have anything to say all afternoon as the crowds, unaware, swarmed below him. Nor did he utter anything save an occasional wolf whistle all week long.

Was it fear of crowds or strange surroundings or what? I prefer to think he just didn't like to be brainwashed.

Scientists are putting the recordings to many uses. Professor Oliver Hewitt of Cornell used the willow ptarmigan call to take a census of that bird in Newfoundland. "It was amazing the way birds came to the sound truck," he said. "I suspect that all the males for a quarter of a mile on each side came flying in over the tundra."

Scientists elsewhere are learning to talk to birds. A man and wife research team, Hubert and Mable Frings, now of Hawaii, have begun to decode the vocabulary of crows, gulls, and, in the case of starlings, with practical results. They have caught the crow's slow, drawn-out love call, its food call, its "Look, boys, an owl!" call, and with a microphone hidden in a favorite roost have listened in on an amazing variety of whispered sounds that may or may not have meaning.

"Do crows speak an international language?" a researcher in France, Dr. René-Guy Busnel, asked the Fringes. He borrowed their recordings. At the alarm call of the American birds, French crows circled over to investigate and then flew off. How about Yankee crows —would they understand the French? The Fringes tried Dr. Busnel's calls at a summer research station at Bar Harbor, Maine. Not a bird paid the least mind. Nor would birds in Pennsylvania, either, during winter. But in spring they flew away in alarm. Perhaps the Bar Harbor birds would respond in spring? Not at all. They were as impassive as ever. After prolonged experimentation, the Fringes have this explanation: that Pennsylvania crows, which move somewhat south in winter, may associate with fish crows and learn their somewhat different language—something the nonmigratory Maine birds don't, and that birds wintering in Pennsylvania are from farther north and haven't learned

fish-crow talk. The Fringses believe, as do most ornithologists, that the basic language of birds is inborn, but
is influenced by experience. On the island at Bar Harbor,
where crows seldom feed with gulls, neither responds to
the other's food calls. But just across the bay on
Schoodic Point, where tourists feed them both and
where they fraternize, both come pell-mell to the other
birds' mess call.

Like crows, gulls have a repertoire of discordant
squawks that sound alarms, beg for food, and have
other functions not yet decoded by naturalists. On their
breeding grounds around the nest they too have low,
whispered, mewing songs. Albatrosses have even a more
varied language of squawks and growls, some of them
sounding amazingly like conversation. As they settle on
their nests on Midway Island, they whisper. People there
say they are talking to their eggs.

Gull talk has been translated in part at Bar Harbor
by the Fringses. It is an amazing sight to watch gulls lift
off the rocks as the sound of the recorded food call
reaches them. Farther and farther down the bay you see
successive birds take to the air. You have the strange
sensation of seeing the sound travel. Later, when the
cloud of screaming gulls above you hears the recorded
cry of alarm, they all go silent, then spiral higher and
higher and are off.

Frings has cleared several towns of hordes of starlings
by driving through the streets at dusk in a sound truck
and broadcasting a tape recording of the starling dis-
tress cry. A few squawks and the birds head for the hills.
They come back. He gives them another "treatment."
After three or four nights, they're gone for the season.
It's cheaper, Frings believes, than firecrackers or guns or
some other measures that starling-ridden cities adopt.
All it costs is the occasional hire of a sound truck and
the price of a tape.

Bird-chasing records are being used in the cherry orchards that belong to the Cherry Heering family in Holland, and in U.S. corn and rice fields, where blackbirds, defying guards with shotguns on all-day watches, firecrackers hooked in sequence to fire at ten-minute intervals, and gas-powered cannons, often devastate a crop. To the successful bird-scarer, the stakes are high: birds do a million dollars' damage a year to eastern sweet corn, a million and a half to rice fields in Arkansas. Crop losses to birds are a worldwide worry. I have seen women and children patrolling rice fields all day in Thailand, India, and Taiwan.

The success of bird records has suggested similar uses. A Connecticut engineer has patented a device to electrocute male mosquitoes, luring them to a screen with the recorded siren song of the female. He has hopes the idea will work against flies, gnats, beetles, crickets, katydids, and tsetse flies.

Duck and goose records were too effective. A Maryland inventor had just put into production his *Call of the Wild* goose recordings when conservationists, alarmed at the prospects of mass slaughter, had the calls quickly outlawed all over the United States. One of his friends, testing the call for him, had geese flying in a cloud around him, and though normally a law-abiding, kindly soul, he kept on shooting and calling, even knowing he would in all likelihood be taken in by the law, which he was. "Something snapped inside of me," he told game wardens. Having watched the performance, they found they could hardly blame him.

Scores of people now are recording bird songs. Mexican bird songs, gathered over some twenty years by Irby Davis, a lab technician in a Texas hospital, are available in a magnificent album that includes what many people believe is the world's best songster: the slate-colored solitaire of the cloud forests of Mexico, which—believe it or not—whistles almost the complete melody of "Here we go round the mulberry bush." An

Emory University philosophy professor, Charles Hart-
shorne, in search of the world's finest singer, has made
recordings of the Japanese nightingale, our American
thrushes, and others. Other enthusiastic followers of bird
recording are a Syracuse industrialist who sponsored an
East African expedition with Professor Kellogg; a retired Texas oilman; a naval officer in the South Pacific;
and the vice-president of a bank in Hawaii, now retired
and studying bird songs in New Zealand.

Why not learn to recognize birds by their calls? At
first, you might think that's a gigantic job. But look,
you already know more of them than you might think:
the crow, robin, bluejay, phoebe, meadowlark, cardinal,
chickadee, quail, mockingbird, and probably others.
With these as an anchor you can devise your own system
of remembering like these! Scarlet tanager: it sings like
a robin in a hurry with a sore throat—a surprisingly
good description, and once you learn that song, you'll
be amazed at how many tanagers you can find in a summer. Rose-breasted grosbeak: like a richer, faster,
longer robin song. Soon you'll be hearing its song above
a crowd of bird notes like the voice of a favorite friend.
Yellow warbler: "Sweet-sweet-sweet, I'm so sweet."
Silly, yes, but a good aid. The yellowthroat sings "witchity, witchity, witchity." The chestnut-sided warbler
ends a somewhat similar song with a phrase that sounds
like "Pleased to meet you."

As I walk in the woods, I know the song of every bird
that sings. Many another person does, too. I only wish I
could tell you how pleasant that is. Maybe it's like the
added pleasure that a baseball fan gets who knows all
the players. Or like a symphony-goer who knows every
instrument and its score. Certainly, the music grows
sweeter every spring you hear it.

No need to uncase your binoculars to know that in
the willow thicket a yellowthroat is singing with a
veery and a whitethroat in the taller trees behind it. And

now a wood thrush begins its evening song, which recordings have verified consists of magnificent chords of
three distinct and simultaneous notes, the lowest one
sustained and the two upper notes alternated and vi-
brated like unending echoes. What a pity that the deaf
cannot hear him, and that others, who could, haven't
learned to listen.

☙

By now if you don't already have a ring like King Solomon's, at least you've made a down payment on one. By
the way, what would you call yourself now that you're
talking to birds by squeak, squawk, quack, or recording? Bird-caller? Bird-hearer? Bird-listener? An avis-
dropper? We need a name for the sport and for its
participants, and one that's a lot better than that of
bird-watching. If someone had devised even a halfway
decent alternative, I think the sport would have grown
far faster. I don't have anything much to propose. But if
you hanker to get in on the fun, just tell your friends
you're going bird-finding, or bird-studying, or just birding. Or take a child along, and say you're going for his
sake.

It's June now. The birds are nesting and offer much
longer looks than during spring migration.

The bird books are confusing? Don't let this deter
you. They're not easy to use; they were put together by
experts who sometimes forget that most people don't
know a flycatcher from a turnstone.

Try once again with the next chapter. It's my field
guide to field guides. Only don't work at it. Let the
learning be fun, as it should be. All I ask by way of
preparation is that you know three birds: crow, robin,
and sparrow. Fair enough?

# 3 ❦ How to identify birds the easier way

AT THE ASWAN DAM in Egypt a few years ago I was watching as Russian engineers were assisting Egyptians in assembling giant girders and trusses. An unfamiliar bird flew by and alighted on a far-off block of granite, and I pulled out my binoculars. Just as I had focused them, I felt a hand on my shoulder. It was my host, a charming Egyptian I had come to value as a friend. He looked at me reproachfully.

"Why do you not tell me what you wish to see?" he said. "We are not hiding anything from you."

I told him I had just seen a yellow wagtail, a bird.

There was pain in his eyes. Was this American he had learned to trust nothing more than a spy?

I pulled out my bird guide and showed him the picture. I could see he was unconvinced, and though we were together several days more, our relations were never again as cordial.

There is no explaining the lure of bird-watching to anyone. Nor will bird guides convince or convert anyone. The will to learn must come from inside.

The first thing to notice about a bird is its size. Bigger than a crow? That narrows the field considerably: a hawk, eagle, owl, vulture, or one of the water birds. The size of a robin or bigger? Still not too big a range. The important thing is to size up the bird by size, first of all, rather than worry about minor details such as length of tail.

The next category is easy. Where was it—on the ground, low in a tree or high, or soaring in the sky? Ground-feeding birds are sparrows, mainly, along with thrushes, blackbirds, finches, and a few others. Soaring birds are mainly hawks and vultures. Birds feeding high in the trees are probably warblers or vireos. Those feeding or sitting lower in the trees are probably sparrows or woodpeckers or thrushes.

But don't bother worrying about memorizing all this. I mention it only to emphasize the importance of noting size and location of the bird—and not the length of its tail.

Now the third thing to note is the bird's behavior. Did it dart out after a fly or gnat and then return to the same perch? If so, that narrows the choice to flycatchers or kinglets.

If you know these three things—size, location, and behavior—you have in all likelihood zeroed in on the family to which your bird belongs, and you'll know what part of the bird book to search in. You probably already have an extra mark of identification to go on—color, shape of head, presence of stripes or spots—that will match up with the picture in the book.

One more word to the beginner: small black birds are not "baby crows," small brown birds are not "baby brown thrashers." Except for ducks and grouse and a few other precocial birds whose young leave the nest immediately after hatching, all young birds stay in the nest until they are full size. They may differ from the adults in color and behavior, and generally do, but they will nearly always be as big as the adults. Sometimes they may even be bigger, living on their baby fat until they can forage for themselves.

One more injunction before you set out. Don't expect to see a forest bird in the open, nor a marsh bird far from wet ground. If you think you do, in all probability you are mistaken. If you see and hear what you feel sure is a chipping sparrow in the deep woods, you are mistaken. It is probably a worm-eating warbler. Neither one strays out of its habitat, even during migration. You are no more likely to see a meadowlark in the woods than a Vanderbilt on the Lower East Side of New York City.

Now then for your first bird walk, Davids style, across the open fields. No need for binoculars. Most birds we'll distinguish by size, location, and behavior. If it's early spring, you may see horned larks on the gravel shoulder of a side road: plump birds with a tail edged in white apparent as they fly. Probably before you see them, you'll hear their song—a soft tinkling of notes that has no point of origin—whether from the sky or ground is hard to tell. They nest in some places in February directly on the ground. During winter many horned larks feast on young lettuce plants in the Salt River Valley of Arizona, going down a row methodically pulling up each young plant. But for most of the rest of America, the horned lark is a welcome reassurance that spring, though a long way off, will one day come.

Other small early arrivals to the prairie or open country are the longspurs, sparrowlike birds smaller than horned larks. Look for them among the debris of cornfields, where they walk or run—never hop—and crouch out of the wind in sheltered spots.

Snow buntings may still be around, and they're easy to distinguish. Their other name, snowflake, describes them well. When snow buntings appear in great sweeping flocks, we look for a storm out of the north. Their restless energy as they drift like gusts of snow across the prairies is exhilarating. On their nesting ground in Alaska they are dressed in stark black-and-white feathers, and are all business. I have seen them among the oil drums at Point Barrow, Alaska, at the northernmost point of land in the United States. They seemed more like house sparrows, perching on the tops of buildings and playing hide and seek with me as I tried unsuccessfully to find their nests. I like them far better on wintry or early spring meadows and fields, ethereal in their white plumage and seemingly as carefree as the wind that blows them.

The big bird of the spring fields is the meadowlark, with a black V on his yellow breast. He's a bird that could stand dieting, flies heavily for a short way to alight on a fence post or telephone pole, or else plop down onto the ground. From Minnesota and westward, his song is a rich, throaty warble; east of that it is weak and insipid.

A bird on long legs the size of a robin that runs fast ahead of you would probably be a killdeer, a member of the plover family; flocks of birds that size would be either golden or black-bellied plovers.

A flock of black birds in tight formation would either be starlings, on their first visits to the country for building supplies and food, or red-winged blackbirds and grackles, though these are more likely to appear in marshy areas.

There you have it. You have learned most of the early birds of fields and prairies by family—the biggest step in becoming an expert. Now when you return home, listen to a record of their songs to fix them even more firmly in mind.

Soaring overhead may be any of four big hawks: red-tailed, red-shouldered, rough-legged, or Swainson's. Don't worry if you have trouble differentiating them at the start. That comes only with practice.

Later in the spring you can expect to find bobolinks, in behavior much like meadowlarks, but mostly black and singing up a storm as they fly over the fields. A little bird singing from the telephone wire and looking for all the world like a vest-pocket meadowlark will be the dickcissel. In the Midwest, you'll generally find him hanging around an alfalfa field.

Still without your binoculars you can learn to tell sparrows by the way they fly out of the grass to tall weeds or shrubs, or drop back to the ground. During spring when they are singing you can learn to differentiate them by song alone. A bird sitting on a telephone wire beside an alfalfa field singing a dreamy "tsick–tsee–tsay" can only be a Savannah sparrow.

One woodpecker and one alone frequents the eastern fields and that is the redheaded. You will probably see it on a telephone pole. In California, it would be the acorn woodpecker.

Now for a second trip in spring through a weedy pasture or abandoned field. By now you can recognize members of the sparrow family by the way they fly up from the ground when you approach. A big sparrow with a black stickpin on his heavily streaked chest is a song sparrow. His song is one you ought to learn. It may vary greatly by bird, but all have the same general rhythm, normally beginning with three accented notes. Remember this ditty and you'll quickly learn to recognize him: "Hip, hip, hooray, boys, spring is here."

A song something akin, but in a minor key, is sung by the vesper sparrow most often toward dusk. As he flies off, the vesper sparrow shows a tail with white feathers at each edge.

The field sparrow is easy to tell by his song, which is for all the world like a coin dropped on a table and coming to rest. Thoreau says that the field sparrow "jingles her small change, pure silver, on the counter of the pastures."

A winter sparrow that flies up to a tree rather than dropping to the ground or low shrubbery in the usual sparrow manner is aptly named tree sparrow. Look for a small black stickpin on a clear breast.

In a small bush, singing his heart out, may be a tiny tailored-looking sparrow. Tilting his head far back, he opens his bill wide to pour forth what certainly must be some of birddom's least entrancing melodies—nothing more than a few long bars of "bzzzzz, bzzzz, bzzzzz." He is the clay-colored sparrow.

There are other sparrows that you will encounter during spring migration, but they are easy to distinguish once you know they are sparrows. The glorious Harris sparrow is a tame bird that passes through the Mississippi Valley, pausing for two or three weeks some springs, passing on nonstop during other years. An account of the discovery of its nesting grounds in the far north is one of the gems of nature writing that everyone ought to read. You can find it in John Kieran's *Anthology of Great Nature Writing*. Harris sparrows and the big reddish fox sparrows are likely to appear suddenly around your house and at your feeder, giving easy, close looks at them, and favoring you with their splendid melodies, then quickly disappearing. Another that may come directly to your feeder is the splendid white-crowned sparrow, which nests far north. Still another is the white-throated sparrow, which nests across the northern states. Its song is one you ought to learn, because once you learn it, you will hear it coming from shrubbery everywhere from Central Park in Manhattan during spring migration all the way to a muskeg swamp in remote parts of Canada and Alaska.

There are other, less common sparrows that you will learn to know, but for now, it is important only that you can recognize a sparrow. I have left until last that enterprising little immigrant called the English or house sparrow, partly because he isn't a sparrow but a weaver finch, and partly because you probably already have made his acquaintance on some not too fastidious street.

On a trip through light woods or shrubby pastures, look for a family of birds easy to identify as flycatchers. They sit on a perch, generally a high dead branch, and from time to time dart out after a fly, sometimes with a clicking sound from their bills, then return to the same perch. The kinglets do this, too, but they are tiny, smaller than a wren, and restless, whereas the flycatchers seem relaxed and sit motionless between forays. Learning to know all the flycatchers is a hard job except during nesting season, when their songs quickly identify them. Early in the spring comes the phoebe, calling all day and day after day its querulous "phoebe," and eventually nesting on a ledge below your eaves or on a bridge truss. The least flycatcher calls "che-beck" from a more wooded area. The alder flycatcher sings "wee-bee-o." The olive-sided sings "Quick, three beers!" The pewee sings a soft, slow "pee-a-wee," ending on a rising note. The kingbird, another flycatcher, is easy to distinguish by the quick beat of its wings and its pugnacity. If you see a crow being chased by a bird that is not a blackbird, in all probability it will be a kingbird. There are other flycatchers, depending on where you live. The important thing for now is that you recognize the flycatchers as a family.

The thrush family has two famous members, the bluebird and the robin. Unfortunately, neither quite typifies thrush behavior. Most thrushes are shy, denizens of the deep woods, and consequently hard to see. But they share one habit that helps: they like to sit on a sizable limb within a foot or two of the main tree trunk where they sing or else observe you, completely motionless, until the moment they see that you see them. The thrushes are gifted singers, and the nearer you approach them, the more beautiful the song becomes.

My favorite of all thrush songs is the veery's. As children, we said it must be singing in a rainwater barrel the way the rich notes seemed to swirl about. The song of the olive-backed thrush seems to rise in spirals like a bird gaining altitude. I have seldom heard the gray-cheeked thrush, except in northern Alaska, where it sings all night long.

The most celebrated singer is the hermit thrush, whose song has inspired both musicians and poets. For several years I despaired of ever seeing a hermit thrush, until one evening I simply homed in on its song. I paused for a moment under a jackpine. Presently the bird began singing directly above me. Its song is remarkable in that each phrase is followed by another an octave or more different in pitch. There is a first opening note like someone sounding a pitch pipe, then eight or so notes slurring upwards; a pause, then another opening note somewhat higher than the previous one, followed by another phrase ascending upward. When the song has ascended almost above human hearing, the bird returns abruptly to its lowest register.

There are other bird families you will come to know: tanagers, towhees, sandpipers, with their spindly legs and sleek bodies, stockier plovers that often feed alongside them, gulls, ducks, mergansers, and others. Most of these are obviously members of a family.

Less obvious and much more difficult are those small greenish-yellow birds called vireos. A Latin word, vireo means "I am green," and this is a good distinguishing mark. Vireos are tough, adaptable birds, smaller than sparrows. They sing without interruption all day long, but are seldom seen, because their world is the treetops, where they forage for small worms somewhat the way warblers do, except that they are slower-moving and don't flutter. The best way to learn the family is by their songs, which link most of them together.

Learn to know the red-eyed vireo's song first. You will hear it almost everywhere in continental America except the Southwest, high above in dense foliage, an interrupted warble of three or four notes interspersed with a couple of seconds of silence, going on all day long with monotonous regularity. How the bird can snap up a worm and swallow it between phrases is more than I can figure out.

If it should descend to a low branch and sit there quietly for several minutes, keep watch on it. This may be where it will build its beautiful cup-shaped nest, and if so you have a pleasant experience ahead watching the brooding bird, and the young being fed.

One spring I wondered what was wrong with a pair of red-eyed vireos. While I was weeding a perennial border no more than ten feet away, they sat motionless side by side on the branch of a young apple tree no more than three feet above ground. The little tree was exposed and a hundred feet from the woods. Everything about their behavior was strange. Normally they are treetop birds. They are forever on the move. And I have seldom seen more than one at a time. After a few minutes they left, and I went to see what kind of worm they might have been feeding on. I could find nothing. In a few minutes they were both back and again sat motionless, almost torpid. I concluded that they were sick from insecticides, they seemed that listless and dispirited. All day they continued perching there off and on while I worked around the yard. Next morning they were still there, but their pensive mood was gone. They were weaving the first few strands of grass and birch bark around that branch. By nightfall there was the shell of a beautiful cup-shaped nest anchored like a hammock to a small fork in the branch. What a treat it was to watch them build, unmindful of me, and later to watch them brood and rear a brood of five fiery-throated young. The following spring in Pennsylvania I saw another pair sit for the better part of a day in quiet contemplation of their nesting site before they began to build.

Once you have learned the red-eye's song, listen for variations: a deeper-pitched voice, slightly husky but musical, with a longer interval between phrases, is the yellow-throated vireo; a higher-pitched voice and sweeter, with a slight rising and falling inflection, will be the solitary or blue-headed vireo; another song higher-pitched and less frequent than the red-eye's is that of the Philadelphia vireo. The warbling vireo, that frequents the elms of small towns, has a long jumble of warbled notes, with what I think of as a Scandinavian accent: it ends each sentence with a questioning upward inflection. The white-eyed vireo has a song all its own, easy to identify if you remember this line: *Chick a per weeo chick.* There are less common vireos with limited range that you will discover, but for now, consider yourself a friend of the vireo clan.

Now for the biggest, most difficult, and most interesting family, the warblers, which, by the way, do not warble. Some squeak, others buzz, a few have fine, fully developed songs, but none of them warble. They are as unlike one another as members of a human family. But most of them are small, smaller than a sparrow, or about like a wren. And nearly all are restless, quick-moving, on the go—there they are, no, there they were. On most occasions, about all you'll see is a flash of yellow. Even so you can identify many of them without binoculars. Here is a maverick warbler, yellowish, feeding on the ground in a pasture, wagging his tail continually. It can only be the palm warbler. This tail-wagging is an important behavior tic to note. Only a few birds do it. One is another ground warbler that feeds in wet woods and around swamp margins: the water thrush, whose songs pour out like the water-filled whistles we knew as children. Its tail wags continually, the way a spotted sandpiper's does. Another warbler clings to trees like a woodpecker, circling them in a search for food. This is the black-and-white warbler.

A few other warblers you will probably see and identify without binoculars. The black-throated blue may pause for a moment in a low branch in the deep woods and sing his hoarse little song, "zoo, zoo, zee" ending with a rising inflection. His suit is trimly tailored in black, white and blue. Another that may favor you with a good look is the black-throated green, with a longer buzzing song but with the same upward inflection, "see-see-see-Susie."

About now is the time for binoculars. I like a light-weight pair with a center focus, either 7 x 35 or 7 x 50. The seven means a magnification of seven times. The second number refers to the width of the front lens in millimeters; the larger it is, the more light is admitted.

Just about any binoculars on the market will do, providing they are inexpensive. Almost all are good, but they're not all cheap, and it's the cheap ones I favor. A cheap pair is one you can carry in your glove compartment, always on hand when you need them. If they're lost or stolen, you don't need to grieve so long. And you don't worry if children use them—and they ought to, because learning to focus, find a bird in thick shrubbery, and follow it quickly is something that takes plenty of practice.

I lost my only expensive pair somewhere on the northern end of the Alaskan Highway when I left them on the car top after watching a cow moose with twin calves. If they had been my usual pair at $19.95, I wouldn't have backtracked fifty miles to search for them. I have had at least two pair stolen at filling stations. I own a pair that zoom from 7 power to 15 at the twist of a lever—and are forever at the wrong setting when I need them quickly, besides being twice as heavy as my cheap ones. I have made gifts of at least twenty pair to relatives and friends. I feel, therefore, as though I must qualify as some kind of expert in the matter of what binoculars to buy. I repeat: buy lightweight, inexpensive ones, and see that each member of your family has a pair. But don't assume that binoculars will make bird enthusiasts out of them. For my twenty or so gift pairs, I didn't win a single convert.

Now then, for your final tour, your graduation from

the Davids bird-watching course. Watch when the oak leaves are just beginning to sprout. Rise at daybreak on some Saturday morning. (If I sound like a teacher, you're right; for two years when I was eighteen and nineteen, I held sway in a one-room country school with thirty-five pupils from age five to eighteen.) On your walk at daybreak, listen for small lisping sounds. These are the signals that mean a cluster of warblers is moving in. Watch those parts of the oaks that are touched with sunshine. A slight flutter of wings? Make a quick mental note: second tree back, third limb up. It's gone? Watch again with your naked eye. Don't use the glasses until you've spotted something. Try again. Still no luck? Keep trying.

From the moment you get your first good look at a Cape May warbler, forever after you will be a bird-watcher, and there's no more help for you. You'll be out every May morning looking for others of this brilliantly colored clan. To your friends, you'll be somewhat ridiculous, but no matter. You will find yourself smiling indulgently at their jokes, smug in your newfound pleasure—which, like certain other of mankind's pleasures, cannot be described but only experienced.

Since I am color-blind, you might think I would have difficulty in distinguishing warblers, but to me the birds in real life are much more colorful than those in books. The yellows are yellower, the blues are bluer, the chestnut of Cape May and chestnut-sided more vivid. It is no exaggeration to call warblers the butterflies of the bird world.

Each new warbler you discover for the first time will photograph itself on your consciousness for all time. You will remember precisely the place, the time, and the way it tilted and postured. At any time you can pull that photograph to mind and enjoy it. More than that, it will aid you in repeating the pleasure, because you

will find the same warbler in almost precisely the same
location or kind of location the following year.

I was driving along a country road in the Catskills,
windows down to hear any new bird songs, when I
caught an unfamiliar jumble of notes from an opening
in the woods. I stopped to investigate. Each time I
moved, the sound came from a new corner of the opening which lumberjacks call a slashing: a place where
young trees or the tops of tall trees have been dropped
and left helter-skelter. I fought my way over limbs, then
stopped to look for any movement. The song was always
just out of reach. It was a quick, accented song which I
decided to jot down in my mental notebook as "rackety,
rackety, sweet Bemidji" (Bemidji is our northern Minnesota metropolis, home of Paul Bunyan). For half an
hour I pulled myself over logs and limbs while the sunlight filtered down through surrounding trees. Suddenly, only partly concealed behind a branch, there was
a brilliant yellow throat with a "necklace of black
streaks" just as Roger Tory Peterson had promised me.
It was a Canada warbler, and I couldn't help but gasp
at its beauty. Each time I call that first one to mind I
can almost smell the May morning and the verdure of
yellow bellworts and sarsaparilla, the warm feel of the
sun on my balding head, and the ringing call of that
sprite, which disappeared then reappeared just as I
wondered if I had really seen it. My only disappointment came that evening at a nearby inn. There was no
one there to whom I could burst out my news, that
I had just seen a Canada warbler that day. The waiter,
for one, seemed a little startled, when I told him, but
whether from the news or the customer I couldn't quite
tell.

My first Cape May was in a ten-foot spruce in a
friend's yard in Toms River, New Jersey, where it
stayed most of the day, so tame I had no need for

binoculars. And other Cape Mays, too, have been in small spruces, feeding with a deliberateness surprising in a warbler. Each time I see one I can hardly believe it is real, or that such brilliance and beauty pass overhead every spring without even a mention in the newspaper, a mention on television or radio. I feel a compulsion to tell my family and friends about each one I see. Their interest, I can see, is casual.

"Why Cape May? It must be a long way from home," they say in Minnesota, forgetting it was the same response they made last year. Once again I explain that the little warbler was first identified and described from a specimen at Cape May, New Jersey, but that its more usual range is to the west and north.

This apathy of non-bird people is the only disappointment in bird-watching. Perhaps it would explain a mystery that for upwards of fifty years has haunted that august body of all-male bird-watchers, the Delaware Valley Ornithology Club, of which I am a member.

Nobody knows quite what happened when one member left a meeting and never returned—to the club, to his office or to his family either. Since he was a member of a prominent Philadelphia family, his disappearance naturally made a big stir. For years the search went on until eventually he was presumed dead. Six years after his disappearance, a fellow club member, Witmer Stone, began noticing articles on ornithology written by someone in a remote part of western Florida. The subject was egg collecting—the specialty of the former member. When an article came for publication in the *Auk,* of which Witmer was editor, the handwriting was unmistakable. Witmer alerted the wife and family, who went to investigate. The missing man returned home without a fuss.

Some of the older heads at my club say it was a case of amnesia; others aren't so sure. In any case—whether by accident or design—it proves a point: a man can forget his name, his wife and family, his place of residence and business, but not his birds.

I wish I could say that once a human has taken to bird-watching in earnest he is transmuted into finer stuff. Sadly, that seems not to be true. Few of my birding friends seem to care a rap about converting others, even their children, to the cause, which is hard for me to understand, because ever since childhood I have wanted others to share the excitement.

Each April in company with fellow members of my club, I make a pilgrimage to the Pocomoke Swamp on the border between Maryland and Delaware. The leaves are just coming out, and there are early migrants in profusion, including several rare ones. The commonest bird in the swamp is the resplendent prothonotary warbler, pure gold in the dappled sunlight filtering through sweet-gum leaves.

A few years ago two of my friends asked to accompany me because they felt they were missing out on something that could enrich their lives. I was delighted to get them up at dawn with me. Edgar and Ingri Parin d'Aulaire are co-authors and co-illustrators of about two dozen of America's most illustrious books for children, including biographies of Washington, Lincoln, and Franklin, plus excellent volumes on Greek and Norse mythology. They are enthusiastic people, eager for new experiences. Neither Edgar nor Ingri ever caught sight of the prothonotary. They hadn't learned how to look, and they most certainly couldn't follow with binoculars, though Edgar tried valiantly while Ingri finally napped in the car. The rare Swainson's warbler was lost on them as well as the worm-eating, yellow-throated, Louisiana water thrush, red-bellied woodpecker, and a score of others. They did see a pair of ospreys at their nest, which delighted them so much they stopped to make sketches. Later they saw a convention of vultures around a dead horse, which they sketched with great delight. Bird-watching is not a pleasure you pick up as you would bowling or even golf. Perhaps my ornithology club friends show more wisdom than indifference when they make no attempt to inoculate others.

Now for a few words of advice as you go out into the world of bird-watching. That bible of bird-watching, the Roger Tory Peterson guide, has a worthy successor: *Birds of North America,* a kind of Revised Standard Version, put out by Golden Press in both paper and case bindings. Its principal advantage, beyond offering birds of both eastern and western America, is that it provides maps with each species which quickly outline range.

My library includes more than a hundred bird books, including guides to birding in South America, Europe, Africa, India, Nepal, and Puerto Rico, and all of them are valuable in foreign travel. But my favorite volumes are paperback reprints by Dover Publications of books known as the Bent Series. Each one covers a family of birds, and contains the best observations of scores of naturalists. If you buy one, you will eventually buy them all. Because as sure as you find a hummingbird's nest you will feel compelled to find out all about hummingbird nests, how they're built, where, how high, and whether or not they're used in succeeding years. Right now on August 25, I see a pair either gathering spiders from the corners of the window outside or else gathering webs to reinforce their nest. Could hummingbirds possibly nest as late as this? Their shadows on the floor at my feet remind me that I must consult the Bent book. The answer: one observer saw fresh eggs as late as August 7, which he thinks may have been a third brood. I look again more closely at the birds. The male is watching from the telephone wire six feet away, and the female is indeed gathering wisps of webs and twisting them around her bill. There is no attempt to catch spiders. She is nest-building even though the first frost here will come in a few weeks. Saunders, an authority quoted by Bent, says he has never seen a hummingbird gathering or working with spider silk, although it is an important nesting ingredient. My rubythroat has afforded me a special privilege. (My friend Wheeler McMillen, as astute a bird-observer as he is a commentator on U.S. agriculture, saw an occupied nest at Cape May in early September.)

A book I frequently consult is Headstrom's *Bird Nests*. So ingenious is his sorting system that I find little trouble identifying any nests even though long vacant.

There are certain aids you may want to buy for birding, such as the Audubon squeaker, in which metal rubbing against wood makes a variety of sounds that often bring a curious bird out of the bushes. You can sometimes lure a bird out of shrubbery in the same way by kissing the back of your hand, or by simulating the sound of a barn owl. Often a reticent bird will come out of hiding when it sees a person leave, and you and a companion can take turns at being a "go-awayster," while the other remains hidden. But all these are makeshifts compared with the really important ingredient of bird-watching.

Optimism is the key to seeing wildlife of all kinds as well as birds, and perhaps this book should have opened with the subject. The person who sets out knowing he will see wildlife is the one who does. He keeps searching the corners of the fields for deer, knowing he will find them, and does. The person who searches a flock of gulls for an Iceland gull eventually finds one. The person who turns his binoculars on a flock of myrtle warblers for the hundredth time is the one who finds a magnolia warbler.

Such a person is the leaven of any group, whether of duck-hunters, deer-hunters, bird-watchers or fishermen. My cousin Tobias Sunderland was such a human being. We might already have waited hours in the dark of an ice-fishing house for a fish that never came, but no matter.

"Just you wait a minute," he would whisper. "As soon as I light my pipe, a great big one is coming in." The way he said it, you somehow felt it would happen. Your whole outlook brightened. And if no fish came, Tobias would take off one decoy and substitute another.

"Now then, just watch that big one come in."

A day without a fish could still be a pleasure with Tobias; you never felt skunked. To an optimist, and to all those lucky enough to associate with him, a day without ducks or deer or birds is never a catastrophe. Like the skunk cabbage, which thaws its way through the frozen earth and heats up the air around its emerging leaves, so does the optimist like Tobias create his own sunny atmosphere and live in his own friendly environment. The vicissitudes of life don't bother such a person unduly.

A final injunction. In your walk through life as a graduate of the Davids bird-watching school, I hope you will do more than watch. I hope you observe. What do migrating killdeer feed on when they stop each spring on the arid lawns of the Bahamas? Paul Fluck was curious. He could see no insects, no seeds, no worms. The only inhabitants were hundreds of six-inch curly-tailed lizards that lived in holes in the sand and beneath the concrete sidewalks. Obviously the birds weren't feeding on them because they continued as numerous as ever. Except that something was happening to them—they were losing their tails! A lizard caught by the tail can shuck it and grow a new one. This apparently was what they were doing when grasped by the plovers. Paul's discovery will not reshape the world but will delight all of us who love the world of little things.

# 4 🦋 You too can grow moths in your closet

It is mid-summer now, deep July, and the days are growing hot. But once again nature has something exciting in store for you, in the cool evenings of summer. It's a sport you may never have heard about, perhaps even more an experience than a sport. Or call it an adventure into philosophy, a quest for the secret of eternal youth.

🦋

On the island of Rhodes is a small ravine that tourist guides call the Vale of Butterflies, where billions of butterflies gather in late summer, clinging to tree trunks, leaves, and rocks so that hardly an inch of space is uncovered. When someone whistles, they rise in a cloud that defies all efforts to photograph them, then quickly settle again. Where they eventually go, or for that matter, where they come from, is a mystery.

When I asked the guide whether they weren't really night-flying moths, he agreed.

"But we think not many people would come if we call them moths," he said.

Perhaps when I suggest that you grow moths in your closet or basement or spare bedroom or garage, I should rather say that you should grow worms there, but that would be incorrect. What I have in mind is your growing the caterpillars or larvae of moths—not the kind that destroy clothes, but the kind that spin silk. You'll have an experience you won't forget. To the timid soul who must keep an eye out for his neighbors and office associates, let me suggest two ways to escape ridicule: either raise them to entertain and educate your children, your neighbor's children or grandchildren, or else buy yourself half a dozen test tubes and assume the role of amateur scientist. One way you'll be lauded as a humanitarian and great family man, the other as an intellectual.

The simple truth is that big silk-spinning moths are among the most beautiful creations of nature. Perhaps you have seen them already, fluttering at night about the lights of a drive-in, their wings battered and torn, all but devoid of the haunting beauty of newly emerged ones.

The biggest kinds are cecropia, polyphemus, and luna, and these can be found almost everywhere in America. Perhaps if they were as common as monarch butterflies, or if they flew by day when you could get a good look at them, they would be less alluring. But they are creatures of darkness and moist June nights and cool woods, and always something of a rarity.

The thought of such beauty moving all about us while we slept captivated my sister and five brothers and me when we were children. It was Gene Stratton Porter's Girl of the Limberlost who brought moths into our lives. When she hunted the glamorous pale-green luna moth, so did we. No matter that five of the six brothers were color-blind and couldn't tell whether the pale green of the luna's wing was gray or brown or pink. The exquisite form with long curving tails was beauty enough. Tawny polyphemus with its giant owl eyes of blue on each hind wing looked ominous and otherworldly. Cecropias were so big they seemed like night birds at the window. We saw only two or three of each all summer. Generally they came about midnight when we would be playing a game of old maid or fantan or whist. All hands would be thrown in and we'd rush outside with quart jars and kettles, all giving instructions to everyone else, cautioning not to hurt the wings. We knew they were males by their heavily feathered antennae, so that collecting them wouldn't diminish the population.

But try as we might to preserve them, something always got to them and ruined them. One time it would be mice, which left nothing but the shattered wings. More often one of us would forget where they were kept in the cramped cubicle of the machine shed on the farm. The paper box that stored them would get sat on or thrown out or otherwise roughed up. So they never lasted. Once I stored them in the township safe that we kept in the granary, for which only my oldest brother and I knew the combination. The first time I reopened it, the treasured moths were mere husks; a parasite had eaten out the bodies. All this heightened the transient, ephemeral aura of the big moths. One brother and I went out into the woods after them, baiting trees with syrup and honey, and leaving lighted lanterns attached to trees. We didn't know—and might not have believed it had we been told—that the big moths not only never eat but don't have functional mouths to eat with.

It was the year after I left college and was working for a magazine that—while driving along a country road in Iowa just after the leaves had fallen—I caught sight of the big streamlined cecropia cocoons I had been looking for all my life. There were fifteen of them, all of them big and heavy and without a hole in them. The bluejays hadn't yet found them, and none of them had been parasitized by wasps. When I shook one of them, I could hear the pupa squirming gently in its sleep. I took them all home to the rooming house where I was living.

All winter they lay outside on a screened-in porch which was cold and moist, approximating the outdoors. Actually I had forgotten about them, until a warm night in June when I came home and heard a beating of wings against the window screen. Dozens of big cecropia males were trying to get inside at the females that had emerged on the porch and—so heavy with eggs they couldn't fly—were crawling up the screen. Others inside were just emerging, wet and crumpled. They climbed up the screen and paused as fluids pumped through the wings, causing them to unfurl and lengthen. It was like a dream. I had dozens of perfect males to choose from. This time I knew where I would keep my specimens. I had been walking to work past a furniture store that had a big, extravagant-looking table with a removable glass lid—a perfect display case for my newly mounted specimens. I walked downtown and bought it. It was the first piece of furniture I had ever owned, and though it crowded my rented room, it proved a safe repository for my cecropias.

Meanwhile the fertilized eggs I had gathered began hatching, and out of them came small larvae that raced around the side of the cheesecloth-covered glass bowl where I kept them. In a day they started eating, feeding on spirea leaves that I took from a neighbor's yard under cover of darkness. The larvae grew fast, but now and then one would look limp and watersoaked and die. By the end of summer I had half a dozen left out of an original hundred. Then apparently the neighbor must have noticed that something was eroding away his spirea hedge and unbeknownst to me he sprayed it with insecticide. In the morning my caterpillars were dead.

Since then I have become reasonably experienced in the art of moth-farming—which knowledge I find hard to inject into cocktail party conversations or with adults in general. Children—whose conversation has not yet ripened into the fruitful channels of making money and saving it, of oil furnaces vs. electric heat, of new cars—are eager to listen to my exposition.

My nephew raised thirty cecropias one summer, and

all of them spun sturdy cocoons, which he kept on a screened back porch. It was the same porch where a trio of flying squirrels lived in a large cage. For a few nights the squirrels were loose and when discovered, they had eaten out the pupa of every single cocoon.

Flying squirrels like the adult moths, too. I find the wings of luna moths in the grass below our all-night yardlight. I console myself that they were the wings of male moths. The females are so heavy with eggs that they can barely fly, even after they have been delivered of most of their load.

Nuthatches like the big adult moths, too. One morning I spied a perfect luna in the elm by our yardlight just as a nuthatch did. He pecked and held it while it fluttered just beyond my reach. And when I flailed my arms and shouted at the bird, he only glared at me, head down in nuthatch style. I have never before nor after seen a small bird glare, but this one did. I boosted a small boy up to scare him off, and even then the bird didn't budge until he was almost touched. The luna fluttered off to a pine tree, the nuthatch and I after it. Once again I lost the race, and again the bird, normally timid, stood his ground. I could almost hear him growl as he gave it up. By then the moth was so tattered that I let the bird repossess it.

Either that nuthatch was extra hungry, extra aggressive, or else the flavor of fresh moth is overpowering. Not possessed of quite enough curiosity to taste one, I wouldn't know.

To begin moth production you order the eggs or cocoons from one of several suppliers. (I order mine from Duke Downey of Sheridan, Wyoming 82801 or from The Butterfly Company, 2903 Long Beach Road, Oceanside, Long Island, N.Y. 11572.) Cocoons are only 75 cents or so, and a dozen eggs about the same. Eggs are air-mailed, since they hatch in twelve to twenty-one days, depending on the temperature. It's a good idea to divide up a large brood to avoid a total loss from "cage rot." The best place to keep larvae is a box enclosed with window screening on at least one side. Lacking that, you can use a pail or tub covered with screening or cheesecloth. Don't use a jar—they need much more air than that. Whatever you start with, you are sure to modify it as you go, because the larvae not only grow fast, needing more room, but they have a way of escaping. I know one eight-year-old boy who puts them out to pasture on the appropriate tree, enclosing each one in green mosquito netting, and is successful enough to have supplied a nature center with cocoons.

Luna larvae feed on a variety of plants, including walnut, hickory, sweet gum, and oak, especially the tender terminal leaves. Polyphemus feed on oak, elm, birch, and many others. Cecropia like maple, willow, cherry, and many others.

Some growers feed by scattering fresh leaves on the bottom of the container every day. I have had less disease when I let the larvae feed on an entire small branch stuck in a tin can or quart jar of water to keep it fresh. To prevent larvae from drowning, I cover the mouth of the jar or can with one of those imitation household sponges, through which I poke the stem of the branch. Every two or three days I install fresh branches in a second container and let the older ones dry up. No need to try transferring larvae onto the fresh leaves. They find them fast. Don't upset the larvae needlessly, especially when they are quiescent before and during skin-shedding. Stress probably activates intestinal bacteria which may kill them off like a plague. (Avoid disturbing the emerging moth, too, until the wings harden.)

For lack of anywhere else to keep them, I used the living room of my apartment one year. They have no smell, but as they grow bigger, they do make a noise. The first time I noticed it I was reading. I paused to listen closely. The sound was coming from the cecropia corner, and it was positively the sound of the worms chewing. In a few weeks the sound became a contented purr.

Watching them eat was something that interested even the most prosaic of my friends (the methodical kind who keep a continuous record of their car's gas consumption). The larva clasps the edge of a leaf between two knobs that serve as feet, then, beginning at the top of the leaf as high as he can reach, takes a long rounded bite down the edge in a sweeping arc. He is methodical about it and cleans up one leaf before going to the next. Every movement is graceful, flowing. As he travels from one leaf to the next, a pulse beat of energy ripples along his body, activating each set of claspers as it goes. A creature with something like sixteen appendages has to be methodical. Only when eight or more are firmly attached does he release the final pincers at the very rear and grasp a new hold.

Covering the body at hatching time are bristles growing out of protuberances along the body. As the larva grows, the bristles—vivid orange, blue, and red—make the larva look as if it were decked out in neon lights.

The bristles keep most birds away. But a wasp parasitizes them, injecting into the body a single egg which in some mysterious way divides into a dozen larvae that feed within the moth larva without killing it, eventually surfacing and pupating in a sac attached outside of the skin. (You often find the tomato hornworm larva—immature stage of the sphinx or hummingbird moth—traveling about in apparent good health with a crowd of white pupal cases attached to it.)

Although practically defenseless, cecropia larvae are adept at camouflage, freezing at the approach of danger and often assuming a stance that makes them resemble twigs.

Every few days, larvae stop eating, their skins turn

dark and wet-looking, they shed the skins, promptly devour them and return to eating leaves and growing. The first molt comes about the fourth day after hatching, the second molt on the ninth day, the third molt on the seventeenth day, and the final molt on the twenty-third day. Then about ten days later, towards the end of summer when they are almost the size of a hot dog, there comes a day when they stop eating completely. They will never again eat in their lives, though they will go on living for another year.

And this is what fascinates scientists: what is it that keeps the larva from becoming an adult? Is it a "youth" hormone that the worm keeps secreting which prevents it from reaching maturity and the downhill slide into senescence? Or is it a "maturity" hormone that the larva suddenly begins to produce which puts an end to childhood, and if so, what sets that hormone into production? Perhaps in the big silk-spinners is the answer to prolonging youth, or of postponing the onset of old age. Scores of top scientists in the United States and abroad are searching for answers. A synthetic food has even been developed, with antibiotics added to control the intestinal diseases that used to wipe out laboratory larvae. So far scientists have discovered two complex hormones that the larva secretes which forestall maturity, and a prize-winning chemist has even produced them synthetically from simpler compounds. Treated larvae never grow old, but keep on growing into giants which never pupate. It is the hope that these "Peter Pan" hormones, by preventing insects from reaching maturity, may some day replace toxic insecticides like DDT. With luck, we might some day have hormones, harmless to man and animals, that would keep harmful insects from ever maturing and reproducing. But such possible uses aren't alone what excites the basic scientist.

In a way, his wonder is like that of a child. No worry

over whether a discovery will make money. Wonder is reason enough and more. No embarrassment either. Why shouldn't a person study a larva?

To me the sense of wonder—of which Rachel Carson wrote so movingly—is a beautiful thing, almost tangible. You can see it in the eyes of children, glowing, luminous, lit from the soul inside. You can hear it in the questions: Why? Why? Why? Wonder feeds on wonder, too. One answer prompts another, perhaps a deeper question. It is a tragedy that society disdains a sense of wonder in adults. Life is so much richer for it.

My most prosaic friends get as excited as children when they watch the larva spinning itself into its silken shroud. Their questions come just as fast. They want to know more, more, more. Perhaps the sense of wonder that is a gift of God to humankind isn't lost somewhere during childhood but simply suppressed. It seems that way to me as we watch the larvae spinning.

The larva of luna moths prefers to spin on the ground, and it's important to provide earth for a caged larva. Polyphemus spins either on the ground or on twigs. But cecropia chooses a sizable branch, preferably one in which he can camouflage himself with leaves. He pulls a leaf toward him, secreting a dab of wet silk on the leaf, and attempts to attach it to an adjoining leaf or stem. Often his shroud lines let loose and he must anchor them again and again. But in an hour or two he has a few leaves hooked around him, and his serious spinning begins. At first it is hard to see that he is doing anything but moving his head back and forth. Only in good light can you see the first few filaments. Next time you look—perhaps in an hour or two—you'll see a cobweb film encircling the larva. All the while he will be spinning, moving his head back and forth endlessly. Only when he is bumped or moved does he stop.

How much silk would you guess he extrudes? Fifty feet or 500? The commercial silkworm of the Orient, a close relative, spins 2,500 to 4,000 feet according to most U.S. scientists. Others say 2½ miles of silk, of which 300 to 1,000 yards are commercially usable. At a silk factory in Korea I was assured that a single cocoon contains 3 to 5 miles of thread, and sometimes as much as 8, in a single unbroken thread. Take your pick of facts—United States or Oriental. Either length is phenomenal, especially when you consider that the tensile strength of silk is almost equivalent to that of iron wire, yet will absorb dyes of the intensity that made it famous. Even at the lower figure, the larva secretes half a mile of silk in four days, working with hardly a pause day or night, at the rate of 25 feet an hour, drawing from a reservoir of jellylike material which he extrudes from a hole in the lower lip and which soon hardens after exposure to air.

My cecropia cocoons are much bigger, but their silk is thicker. Is it possible that they could spin half a mile of thread? I find it hard to believe. And yet, the larva moves his head half an inch each second or so, and doesn't appear to pause except when jarred. At that rate, according to my computations—which my banker says are not always dependable—my larva would be able to spin almost 2 miles of thread in the three or four days it appears to continue spinning.

At any rate, he continues to spin for some time after the silken capsule takes form, his head moving in shorter and shorter arcs as his cell grows smaller. His actions are unhurried but purposeful as he closes himself off forever from the world he knew as a larva. Finally there is quiet, and a secretion from inside darkens the cocoon to a deep tan that approximates the color of dead leaves. So ends the life of the larva.

Friends who take home a larva for their children generally report that the whole family falls under its spell: the big colorful pet is easy to please, content and possessed of a kind of quiet charm. What excitement among all the members of the family when the larva starts to spin; there is regret, too, when the larva disappears. The moth that will emerge next spring (or later the same summer in the case of the luna's second brood) will have none of the easygoing contentment of the larva. From the time the pupal case breaks and the big wet creature starts unfolding its wrinkled wings, it is a frenetic creature, bent only on surviving against flying squirrels and birds so that it may reproduce before it dies. So tenacious of life is it that it withstands mammoth doses of insecticide, ether, and pinning. Even beheading will not quiet the big, powerful wings. The way to still it for mounting is to crush the heaviest part of the body, the thorax, by pinching between the fingers.

There is something beyond mystery in the life cycle of the silk-spinners: the long preparation of the larva, its continuous eating, the secret signal from somewhere inside that directs it suddenly to stop eating and begin spinning, and finally the long sleep, to awaken a wholly different, more beautiful being. It is a kind of death without being death, a rebirth, a resurrection. It is easy for me to believe in life after death as I watch the big silk-spinner emerge, spread its velvet wings, and fly off.

# 5   *How to welcome wildlife freeloaders*

SOMETHING ELSE is stirring in the summer dark outside your window. A hungry raccoon mother is foraging for food, her ravenous youngsters bobbing behind her. You might see them if you have a yardlight you can flip on occasionally, preferably an infrared light which doesn't disturb them. If you don't already have wildlife in your backyard during summer, there are ways to start them coming.

You attract wildlife in summer exactly the way you attract summer guests—with plenty of food and free lodging. Friendship is fine, too, but board and room—especially board—is the drawing card for most animals, whether they eat with silverware or bare paws.

Just ask any seal trainer and he'll tell you that it's food that does the training. Or if you don't know any seal trainers, ask your nearest lion tamer. Or failing that, just ask me, and I'll say that it's food that befriends and tames and tranquilizes me.

Apply that profound insight into animal behavior and you will have some great moments in attracting wildlife, and a rewarding interest that will last the rest of your life.

Even in the middle of Dayton, Ohio, animals started coming to feed at the hilltop house of Fred G. Stroop, a big, burly, no-nonsense lover of mankind and animals who managed farms for prosperous Ohioans. Fred had noticed that raccoons were eating dog biscuits that his big boxers had missed, so he put out feed especially for coons in the parking area outside his study. They came after dark, but he could make periodic checks of their numbers by turning on the floodlight. Presently a big female brought her family of five roly-poly youngsters. Each was as fastidious as its mother in eating habits. Fred wondered how they would handle a raw egg. Wouldn't they lose that Emily Post poise that was sometimes a bit annoying? They didn't. Holding the egg carefully in their front feet, they bit a hole in it and lapped out the contents daintily. Fred watched from a window, chewing gumdrops, his favorite candy. Aha, he thought, how about gumdrops? And this was the food that broke down that disturbing gentility. They chewed on them, shifted them to the back of the mouth, tilted their heads to one side and then the other, finally pawed at their mouths to dislodge the sticky morsels. But they kept on eating gumdrops, and have for the ensuing ten years.

The eggs brought a surprise visitor—a sleek gray fox that seemed more shadow than substance. A little later came another and then a red fox. All three would glide into the encircling shrubbery the moment the floodlight went on, but quickly return. The red fox tried his best to carry away two eggs at a time.

The day an opossum came at dusk to feed on eggs Fred saw trouble ahead, because a possum is practically defenseless against meat-eaters. Fred and his wife Dorothy watched from a dark window as the moon lit up the yard. The red fox came first, sniffed the air and gazed for a moment at the opossum, then fell to the dog biscuits. It was the same with three gray foxes that came next. Food was the tranquilizer, and if it didn't exactly make them friends, at least it prevented a massacre.

Fred is gone now, but Dorothy continues to feed, and

friends come to watch the nightly show of animals that begin at dusk to feed on lettuce, celery, apples, cabbage trimmings, and marshmallows in addition to the eggs, dog biscuits, and gumdrops. The opossums are first to arrive, and half a dozen may waddle in. They generally leave just as the fox appear. The coons come later, and though they sometimes quarrel with the fox, swelling themselves up to twice normal size, there is no fighting. Dorothy feeds dog biscuits enough for all, and in several places.

All of this might seem to be a disruption of nature for the sake of man's amusement, but it is something far more. Fred's army of influential farm-owning friends have learned the habits and food preferences of wildlife, the need for preserving hedgerows rather than cutting the brush along fences and farm boundaries. Farm owners who might otherwise demand clean-cut fields without borders, know without being told that wildlife feel uneasy without nearby thickets to escape to. If wildlife is so fond of apples, why not plant some on waste ground and in fence corners? Landowners who had been content with the profits from their fertile Miami Valley farms began counting something besides money—a feeling of partnership with wildlife. Stroop Agricultural Co. farms aren't generally manicured or picture-book neat, but they abound in quail and pheasants and cottontails. One might have a pond surrounded by marsh with a family of Canada geese and another of mallards. One farm that used to grow record-breaking corn crops now is largely lake, and brings bigger profits than it ever did. Some two hundred sportsmen buy family memberships in a club with the privilege of trout fishing. The spring-fed lake is stocked with rainbows, and members pay a fee per pound of fish. Members can bring guests and use the beautiful guesthouse for parties. Members enjoy putting up nesting boxes for wood ducks and platforms for geese. Others check periodically on the dog-proof fence. Fred set up a fee-fishing bass and bluegill lake for another friend, that warmly human, shy man, the late Walter Locke, editor of the *Dayton Daily News.*

Effective as Fred's conservation work has been, he was no expert. He loved to tell the story of the bird's nest he found one spring. It was a last-year's nest, on the ground in a shallow depression, big enough for a grouse, perfectly round, and made mainly of small spruce twigs. It was so perfect that Fred went home for a shovel and an apple box so he could bring it back intact. He was mystified by its symmetry and beauty, and so was the executive director of the National Audubon Society from New York City, who visited the Stroops not long after. They took it to the Aullwood Nature Center, outside Dayton, where the young director, Paul Knoop, studied it, probing into the soft rim. Running through the heart of the circle was a wire and bits of thread. It was a discarded Christmas wreath.

Fred forever studied the wildlife on his place. One noon while he was eating, Fred noticed a turtle munching lettuce at the edge of his lot. It was a big turtle, a foot across, and as Fred watched, it paused in its slow-motion eating, then turned and inched across the parking lot to a shallow pan of water where it drank deeply, lifting its head with each slow-motion swallow. Then it returned to its lettuce. Every noon it returned to feed, and eventually there were two at the feeder. Fred hadn't paid much attention to turtles up to then, but now he couldn't help but observe them closely. He liked especially to watch them eating corn on the cob, which they did by plucking a kernel at a time along an entire row, finishing a row in something like an hour, then proceeding methodically to the next. One foot generally held the ear of corn in place, and sometimes the turtle rotated the ear for easier eating. Fred found himself admiring the dignity and the resourcefulness of the turtle, as anyone does who watches the performance. And though Fred didn't talk much with friends at Rotary about his turtles, they became his cronies—easygoing, relaxing, and always there at mealtime.

Some of my friends at *Reader's Digest* have nightly visits by raccoons during fall. No matter how secure the garbage lids are, the coons unlatch them, thumbing through the contents and scattering the remains across the grass. Safety catches, springs, ropes, raised platforms —nothing stops them. Only once—after an infant grandson with disposable diapers had spent the day at one house—were the coons deterred, but repeating such a technique seemed both impractical and an affront to the dignity of these Einsteins of the animal world. I suggested that Chappaqua residents put out Ralston-Purina dog biscuits as food more suitable than garbage, but whether or not my advice has been taken I am not sure. I suspect that many residents would miss their nightly battle of wits.

I can't tell you how to discourage unwelcome guests, but I can offer an antidote against the ravages of one of them—and this advice is certainly worth the price of this book. When a skunk strikes, you can obliterate his scent with vinegar. If our cat could talk, I'm sure he would offer a testimonial. He suffered a direct hit across his face that left him writhing and leaping and howling with pain or humiliation, we couldn't tell which. When we could catch him, we doused him with vinegar, rubbing it into his fur. Almost at once the smell subsided. Another application the next morning and he was almost fit to return to the house.

Most visitors to your backyard won't announce themselves with such vehemence. Unless you have a patch of sand or soft earth somewhere you won't know the traffic of the previous night. Some of my friends with small children have hauled in a load of sand that serves as a play area during the day and a recorder of visitors at night. Cats and dogs move across it, but often there are tracks of opossum and skunk and coon. Now and then a young muskrat, dragging his tail amidships, crosses the sand patch in search of new living quarters. Smoothing the sand with a rake provides a fresh page to record the next night's callers.

When I was a child the sand outside our pasture gate was alive with tracks. I used to wonder if animals got the same pleasure out of the feel of it as my bare toes did. Ruffed grouse came to lie and dust themselves, as well as many smaller birds whose tracks I couldn't recognize. Flickers dusted themselves and dabbed stray ants on their wings. Almost every morning we could see the tracks of deer, and often the dainty hoof marks of a fawn, no wider than my index finger. The thrill of tracks for me was as great as seeing the animals themselves. Tracks are absorbing to children, especially when you tell them that every animal keeps making tracks, and if you only follow them long enough, you will find the track-maker. The child himself has been making tracks—good ones and bad ones—since the day he started to walk and will until he dies. A book printed years ago, *Animal Tracks and Hunter Signs* by Ernest Thompson Seton, is back in print and is one any child or adult can use.

To induce deer to come to your property you might consider putting out a salt lick, either a block of salt or a pile of it. You aren't serving them especially. They can get it elsewhere. Perhaps you might tell yourself that you're saving them from salt licks where the motive is more sinister than pure enjoyment. A few rows of rutabagas will lure deer up close for you to enjoy them, but don't expect them to overlook any carrots or lettuce you might want for your own use.

Besides feeding animals, try feeding birds in summer. They don't need it, but it's fun, and there's no harm done. Put out bread crumbs and you'll have friendly little chipping sparrows all summer, and they'll nest nearby. In Minnesota we have their cousins, the clay-colored sparrows, feeding with them and nesting in our five-foot pine trees, buzzing their earnest little insect song all summer.

Until you can see grackles feeding at arm's length on your window ledge feeder you have no idea of their beauty, the sheen of their purple-black feathers, the glowing eye that is incandescent, lit from within. Up close, the catbird, too, is a thing of beauty. But until you see the redwing flying straight at you making a landing on your feeder, you won't know the glowing brilliance of him—even to my color-blind eyes. His scarlet epaulets as he comes in shine like a plane's landing lights. This is the same gaudy view he offers a female when he postures before her. After he alights, black feathers quickly cover most of the scarlet and he is more subdued.

This summer on the feeder, not three feet from me, a male evening grosbeak gave a peck at a male cowbird. Instead of flying off, the cowbird waddled closer, bent down his head so as to expose the nape of his neck to the grosbeak and stood stiff as a statue. The grosbeak gave another light peck. The cowbird edged even closer, his neck still arched, and froze, only a couple of inches from the bigger bird. Like a dog that rolls over on his back, exposing his vulnerable underside to a bigger dog, the cowbird was offering the base of his brain to a bird which could have killed him with a single jab. The grosbeak gave another light tap, and then flew, whereupon the cowbird went back to feeding. Anthropomorphists would say that the cowbird was putting himself at the mercy of the grosbeak. Certainly this kind of behavior, noted by Lorenz in *King Solomon's Ring,* is mysterious.

Summer feeding brings a startling assortment of

birds. Robins come for a handout of jam. Bluejays and siskins continue feeding, as do an occasional crossbill and goldfinch. Woodpeckers continue at the suet, and may be joined by their summer cousin, the redheaded woodpecker, who likes an occasional meal of peanut butter, and will spend an afternoon carrying away whole corn to hide in a secret cache. Purple finches hardly leave the feeder when you go out to refill. One built its nest in the tuft of needles at the end of a red pine branch not more than twenty feet from the feeder. Rose-breasted grosbeaks—gentle, trusting birds—come occasionally. The male, with his American Beauty throat, is as exciting as his song is beautiful. The female, though plainer, is to me the quintessence of feminine charm, moving with an easy fluid grace quite unlike the quick, nervous movements of most birds. (How I wish that the beautiful blue grosbeaks came this far north! I'd certainly try coaxing them to a feeder. I have seen them eating grain in a pigpen in rural Delaware, and each time I can hardly believe they are real.)

By all means have a hummingbird feeder or two. The big ones aren't as good-looking as the small, but you won't need to refill them as often, and they aren't so likely to drip and call in all the ants from blocks around. Put up your feeder early, by the time the crocuses are in bloom, and you'll probably get takers. Four or five feed regularly at the big red feeder of my neighbors, Ruth and Albert Kragnes, and one nested on the limb of a red pine only a few rods away. The following year apparently the same bird returned, and made her nest on the same limb within a foot of the previous year's nest. A stepladder was all it took to enable the Kragnes grandchildren to look in on the two tiny eggs and later on the growing birds.

Orioles come to hummingbird feeders, fluttering awkwardly as they dip into the sap. And hummingbirds come to the oriole jam pot, battling wasps for the jam, leaving only when bumblebees and black hornets chase them off.

Country and suburban dwellers who have installed automatic mercury vapor lights to light up their property and deter thieves are feeding birds and animals, whether or not they know it. Night-flying insects come in swarms to the all-night lights, and these in turn attract flying squirrels. You will seldom see these charming little animals; more likely you will hear them thump as they alight on the roof.

For several years I kept a pair of flying squirrels that I had live-trapped from a friend's attic where their dusk to dawn scampering had proved annoying. There are few pets more appealing, especially to night people. Emerging from their daytime nests, they yawn, stretch, lap a little water, and then are set for a night on the town, racing up draperies to glide across the room to a table with a bowl of nuts. Their big expressive eyes win friends, especially among those who don't worry unduly about holes in upholstery. My pair of charmers produced a couple of young every spring, some of which I gave to nature centers, and others I freed.

If there are cats around your place, you won't have many flying squirrels. Few things are tastier to a cat, and on the ground or roof, they are easily caught. In the morning all you will find of the squirrel is its flat, gray tail.

A bat patrols our light each night, swooping past two or three times a minute, making clicking sounds as he captures a moth, homing in on it by sonar squeaks. (The powder of moths' wings probably absorbs much of the sound, providing less location-finding echo for the bat.) But early the next morning is when the big feed is on. Insects resting in the grass or on nearby trees are the delight of a wonderful assortment of birds. At daybreak there are brown thrashers and catbirds hopping through the grass below the light, along with robins and flickers and bluebirds, chipping sparrows, song sparrows and clay-colored sparrows. I had been reluctant to install the light, preferring that the moon alone light up the darkness. Now I am not so sure. The light is the easiest, most dependable bird feeder I know.

As I have already indicated, summer feeding of birds and animals has entertainment value, but something more. I know of no easier way of interesting children and adults in the world around them. They see how important food is. They're more likely to listen when I suggest that they plant shrubs and trees that will carry wildlife through the critical days of winter. They are more likely to believe me when I say that half a dozen ruffed grouse feasted at one time on the fruits of the Red Splendor crab apple that cling all winter to the branches and that during a late spring snow, my Sundog crab apple fed seventy-five robins for almost two weeks. (This year there won't be any left for the returning robins, because right now two magnificent deer—one a six-point and the other an eight-point buck—are eating the apple drops. I wish you could see them as they paw the snow, sending showers of white above their backs, then nudging it forward with their heads and antlers. Though deer are hunted relentlessly in our area and are therefore never tame, these two seem unaware that we are watching from a window not fifty feet away.)

❦

Food is important, winter or summer, but so too is habitat: living room, sanctuaries for nesting, resting, and escape. Most homeowners are quick to put up birdbaths, but what birds need far more than a bath is a home. The big mistake that homeowners make when they buy a place in the country is to police up every inch of it, cutting down dead trees and burning logs, cutting and burning brush, bulldozing it level into lawn. Then they wonder why they have no wildlife. What should they plant? Probably the very shrubs they eradicated.

What is there about a dead tree that men can't endure seeing it stand? A dead tree is home and sanctuary for a dozen kinds of wildlife; a hollow one is even better. Either dead or alive it is a sanctuary to be preserved at all costs.

Last winter my brother Robert, tending the ewes in his sheep barn at dusk, almost stepped on a big furry object beside the watering tank. He pulled back in surprise. The patch of fur stirred. A head slowly raised to look at him, and in the half-dark he saw the robber's mask of a raccoon.

"Ah, bandito!" he exclaimed. (It's hard not to talk to a raccoon.)

The animal slowly got to its feet and staggered away, groggy in its state approaching hibernation. Robert couldn't decide whether the animal was seeking food or refuge, but because it was so thin, he set a plate of calf pellets, flavored with anise, in front of it. The coon promptly fell to eating, and continued even when Robert stroked its back. For the next few days, Bandito— who proved to be an old male—lived among the bales of hay in the barn, following my brother about like a dog.

But a villain lived in the barn, an old ewe determined to stamp the old coon out of existence. She did, too, one cold night when the coon was probably sound asleep.

Had there been hollow trees nearby, the old coon would never have needed to seek shelter in a barn.

Not long ago, wood ducks seemed threatened with extinction. Then central heating arrived. No longer were old hardwood trees felled for firewood—not even in rural America. Sound trees, those without hollow centers, were still logged for their lumber, but the grizzled old veterans weren't worth it, and so survived. And in their commodious cavities wood ducks found nesting spots. Laws that forbid shooting wood ducks anywhere in the United States undoubtedly helped, but I believe that fuel-oil dealers did more for the wood duck than conservationists.

If you have been lucky enough to watch a pair of wood ducks in their search for a nesting site you will better understand their predicament. The cavity must be big. It must be within a quarter mile or so of water, and with woods nearby. Finding such a home isn't easy.

Eugene Hester, a North Carolina zoologist, has had a continuing project of helping wood ducks. Shortly after he and his father nailed up a section of hollow log to a cypress in their eight-acre pond, they had takers. The second year, with five nesting boxes, they had six nests —one in each box plus a second brood. They kept on building more nests: 12 x 12 x 24 inches, hinged at the top for easy cleaning, with four-inch holes and with five inches of sawdust in the bottom. The seventh year they had eighteen boxes, and averaged a nest to a box. This, they figured, must be the absolute limit that their pond could take. But for fun, they put up a dozen more. Early in February the ducks started coming up from their winter in Florida. Some boxes were used twice, others went unused. Often several ducks used the same box. One such hatched twenty-six out of thirty eggs. Other wildlife used the boxes, too: flickers, beautiful hooded mergansers, and screech owls, besides starlings, honeybees, squirrels, and opossums.

"Rather than fight them," says Gene, "we put up more nests."

The total crop of wood ducks during their tenth year, in the thirty boxes: 27 nests with 387 young!

So leave your gnarled old trees alone when you're warming up that chain saw. If you must saw something, to justify that expenditure to your good wife, take it out on sound trees.

Hands off that fallen log, too, especially a hollow one. It is a way station for frightened coons, possums, rabbits, mink, weasels, and foxes—almost all of America's small mammals—plus living quarters for some. Trees may not be better dead than alive, but to birds, standing dead trees may be, and after falling to the ground, they are for animals. Soon beetles will begin their excavations beneath the bark, and their click, click on a still evening or night is something a child will long remember. Moles and voles will come to feast on the insect life that begins to collect in profusion. Chipmunks and squirrels will stuff the cavity with winter food. As the tree begins to decay, mushrooms sprout from it. The rich moist decaying wood is an ideal nursery for trees and for certain plants which the most expert horticulturist finds difficult to germinate and grow. No one to my knowledge has ever grown rose moccasins from seed, but the red squirrel can and does, burying an entire pod in the rotting wood. Bunchberries take root and twinflowers spring up and take firm root before winter sets in.

And when spring thaws the woods and the log lies bare, perhaps a ruffed grouse comes to strut down its length and thump out his love call in the gathering dusk. I have tried dropping a big tree to give him a drumming log, but so far have had no takers. He seems to prefer a broader, rotting one.

I wish I knew why most humans feel a compulsion to haul away or burn a fallen log, mellow with moss and lichens. Maybe I should write my Congressman about it. Perhaps he could introduce a bill in behalf of tipups, too. They're the exposed roots of a tree that falls and pries up a crust of ground with them. The exposed earth below a tipup is often a nursery for exotic wild flowers like the pink lady's slippers.

If you can curb the arsonist in you, leave a few brush piles, too. They're like a running brook to a gold miner.

Any number of birds like to prospect around in them: wrens, catbirds, sparrows, thrushes, even warblers. More than that, they're an escape hatch. Birds feel safer with them around. If you see moving about in a pile of debris a house wren that's a little too small, a little too mouselike, check your bird book. It is probably a winter wren. Nothing attracts that elusive rare visitor more than a pile of sticks or an old woodpile.

Perhaps you can't stand a natural-looking, somewhat unkempt-looking place. Then why not manicure a part of your grounds into the golf-course look you cherish, and let the rest grow wild? Don't expect much more than robins on your immaculate lawn.

# 6 ❧ Swamp fever— worth catching

SOMETHING ELSE is in need of your help, even more urgently than dead trees and fallen logs and brush piles. That something is water.

Maybe our only hope of preserving America's water supply is to send all ditch-and-drain lobbyists into exile on the Sahara. And while we're at it, perhaps we ought to ship along all water-wasters—for a short stay, at least.

On the Sahara you'll see the respect—even the veneration—of some people for water. At a desert oasis, the well is the heart of the village, and from it in all directions goes the precious water: in jugs balanced on the heads of girls, or in buckets hung one at each end of a pole across the shoulder. The people come and go in an unending circle as the water moves out like blood in a circulatory system.

The well is understandably the hub, the social center, the Times Square of the village. When I told my host and translator that I wanted an audience with the villagers, it was beside the pool that we gathered and sat on the sand and talked until the sun set and torches were lit up.

In the desert sands of the Kharga, American engineers helped Egypt bore deep water wells that spouted thirty feet high when they came in. The water gushed down concrete sluiceways to begin watering what had been sterile, lifeless land for thousands of years. I wish you could have seen the way people gloried in those cool fountains. Boys leaped naked into the ditches and played like porpoises. Older men cried. No need to tell an Egyptian that a nation's water is more important than its balance of payments, its gross national product, or the size of its army.

Americans are beginning to care about scenic lakes. But few care about swamps and marshes that make up the giant reservoirs that keep streams and rivers flowing, and that prime the underground streams and rivers upon which much of America depends for drinking water. Most Americans abhor any water if it's not fit for drinking or swimming. In their view, streams with mudbanks are ugly, marshes are nothing but mosquito-breeders that must be drained and turned into useful land. And yet the place to start saving water is back in the swamps before it begins to move into brooks or creeks or whatever your region calls the first small trickles.

Here in northern Minnesota we haven't done very well by our water. Our Clearwater River was famous for its beauty even in the days when most streams ran pure. Early French explorers called the river Le Claire. There are still stretches where it glides along so clear you can look down through three feet of crystal water and see its bed of smooth, multicolored pebbles. This is all the more surprising because the Clearwater traverses sizable swamps, and there is mud along the banks where fine stands of wild rice grow almost as dense as sugar cane.

Canoeing down the Clearwater on a sunny day in June is a soft, silken experience. Often the only ripples are from broods of newly hatched mallards and teal and wood ducks that skitter into the weeds as you round a bend. Some of the downy youngsters plane like surf-boards, their churning feet kicking up small wakes. Once you set out on the Clearwater, you want never to stop. Each new curve promises a fresh outlook, new surprises: deer, muskrats, mergansers, blue herons, perhaps even a Canada lynx or moose. As it meanders north toward the Red River and eventually on into Hudson Bay, it passes through miles of bog.

This is where we have knifed a channel through the peat, forcing the beautiful Clearwater to become a ditch benefiting a few farmers—including my brother and his son—but destroying the waterfowl and marsh. Northern pike, some of them lunkers, used to revel in the pools and swirls. Now there are almost none. Ash and willows hung over the bank, dappling the water with dancing shadows. Limbs trailed in the current, making small eddies where minnows fed. Now those loops of the river are sealed off—stagnant pools almost devoid of life. The ditch, its once raw banks now infested with thistles and stinging nettles, hurries the muddy water along to the Red River. The stream bed used to invite water to stay awhile; the ditch is more efficient. Water moves so fast that the Red River and the cities along it are plagued with floods. And what is uglier than a river that floods? Willows are about all that can live along it; their branches sag with grimy debris like dirty clothes hung to dry. Few birds nest along it. There are no surprises along its banks; no gentians or lady's slippers or brilliant cardinal flowers.

The supreme irony of our drainage project is that just across the ditch bank the Department of the Interior has flooded three thousand acres as waterfowl habitat where Indians can take hunters for pay. The idea is a worthy one, certainly, but perhaps it is too much to expect bureaucracy to cooperate in such trifling matters.

The sad truth seems to be that almost nobody loves a marsh, or comprehends its crucial value in keeping alive the streams and rivers and lakes that everyone admires. Of all our habitats, swamps and marshes are in the most urgent need of saving. They are disappearing at heartbreaking speed.

Along the Atlantic Coast, salt marshes are being gobbled up by developers. Maryland is losing a thousand acres a year. Connecticut has already lost nearly half of her coastal marshes. And in the last ten years, Long Island has lost a third of her superb coastal marshes. First the marshes are converted into dump grounds and covered with garbage—because marshes have no spokesmen. Then those "eyesores" are *recovered* by developers who fill them with spoil, convert them into parking lots, shopping centers, marinas, and housing developments. And no amount of argument can convince most people that the public has lost out when it traded marshland for solid ground.

But some people who bought river-front cottages because they like to fish are beginning to wonder. "The fishing isn't so hot this year," they say, still failing or else refusing to understand that most fish—even ocean fish—need quiet bays to spawn in, where the emerging fry can hide from predators. It is said that two out of every three kinds of useful Atlantic fish—about two thirds of the value of the entire East Coast fisheries—are dependent on tidal marshes for their survival.

New Jersey farmers used to drive to the ocean with nets and haul home a full wagonload in just one day. The last commercial fishermen pulled up their pound nets several years ago. Ospreys that used to delight summer visitors with their air-to-water plunges are disappearing, too. My friend Joe Jacobs of New Jersey, a careful observer of wildlife, has studied ospreys for nearly thirty years along the same seven-mile stretch of New Jersey shore. Years ago ospreys used to come up with fish on nearly every plunge. Today they must make five or six tries before they succeed. Often they fail even then and return without fish to perch on a stake near the nest. Improved techniques of fishing, with radar devices, mechanized nets, and so on, have made it possible to gather practically all the menhaden, for instance, along the coast. Joe believes that lack of fish—as well as DDT—may be important in the decline of New Jersey ospreys.

Eagles, too, have all but disappeared from the New Jersey shores, where not long ago they were common. How long before the black skimmer—that marvel of grace and engineering that scribes the coastal bays with its long lower bill—gives way to the power boats racing through polluted and shrinking channels? The answer will come only from a citizenry united to save our marshlands. The states of Rhode Island, Connecticut, and Massachusetts have enacted laws to save their last estuaries, and several others have asked for federal funds to buy unprotected tidal wetlands. Rhode Island, to protect its thin vestige of remaining marsh, has helicopter patrols that watch the areas and levy fines against anybody who makes alterations without state permission.

Minneapolis residents have just concluded a battle over whether a small lake within a city satellite should be "improved" into still another place to swim, or left with its marsh and bog and surrounding brush intact, and dedicated as a wildlife and wild flower sanctuary where city children can keep watch on broods of ducklings, listen for the cries of coot and bittern and rail. Surprisingly, nature won out! Parents recognized that pools can be built for swimming, but that boggy lakes are precious, to be preserved for now and much later. The nature park has been fenced against dogs, and floating walks have been installed to permit close study of the marsh and its plant and animal riches.

Here and there are other small victories, the result of community action. A citizens' group in Douglaston, N.Y., roused several hundred people to protest filling in a hundred-acre tidal marsh off Little Neck Bay to make a parking lot and golf course.

But these are holding actions, temporary at best. We

can't rely on conservationists to save our wetlands. Urban developers are too powerful a lobby for even Congress to tackle.

There is no rhyme but there is reason for draining and damming: the simple game of vote-buying. You might check your Congressman's record in the game. Swamps and marshes are in for tough times unless the public at large begins to see the beauty in them.

Before you start a crusade to save swamps and marshes, you ought to learn to know and love them yourself. Fall is a fine time to cruise a swamp. Often it is drier then, and more important, you won't need to battle mosquitoes. You may find surprise bonuses: late blueberries, cranberries, and lingonberries. Spring is a fine time, too, if you douse yourself with mosquito-repellent and don boots, or far better, tennis shoes, and let the dark swamp water cool your feet. Taking the first step is the hardest. The second and third and fourth steps grow progressively easier. As soon as you forget your inhibitions about keeping dry, you'll begin enjoying the swamp. Soon you too will have swamp fever. Swamps are among the most exciting terrains I know.

The daintiest of all flowers grow here: the charming twinflower, its nodding pink bells only inches above the evergreen leaves and so fragrant that you look for larger plants for the source. Here too is the one-flowered wintergreen, waxy white bloom above a rosette of leaves, as well as foamflower, with stamens that make the six-inch stalk seem adrift with sea foam. Here the mosses are superb, each kind founding its own community under just the right conditions of light and moisture. Man knows next to nothing about the life of mosses and lichens. Scientists at the University of Missouri and elsewhere have found germ-inhibitors in moss secretions comparable to the antibiotics from molds. Sphagnum moss was put to use in World War II both for its antiseptic properties and its tremendous absorptive capacity, holding sixteen to eighteen times its weight in liquids.

In the openings in the bog grows a vine little thicker than a hair, set with dainty leaves that lie on the surface of the moss. In fall, its fruit—cranberries—appear on the moss as if they had dropped like hail out of the sky, and lie everywhere in small pools of vivid red. They are a pleasure to gather, and in good years you can pick sackfuls that will keep in the refrigerator much of the winter. Rarely you may find the mountain cranberry, otherwise known as lingonberry, a smaller, redder fruit which homesick Scandinavian immigrants (like my grandfather) used to import from Norway. Elsewhere in openings in the swamp may be Labrador tea, a fragrant shrub with leaves like leather, covered beneath with white wool, as well as pale laurel, which for a few weeks in May makes the swamp a cloud of pink. The most glamorous wild flowers in America grow in the marsh: the blazing cardinal flower and my favorite above all other wild flowers, the showy lady's slipper. In Minnesota we reckon the season in summer as either before or after pink lady's slippers are in bloom. They're that important to us. Big, dewy-fresh, they stand above the grass unreal in their size and splendor. Even prosaic people coming upon them in the swamp feel an urge to talk to them, to praise their beauty. I know so well what prompts them. Any wild flower that cares for itself, battling weeds and animals and insects without a single assist from man, somehow deserves commendation, and especially anything so big and stalwart.

In wetter parts of the swamp you may find yourself walking on a thick mat of roots and grass that actually floats on water. It is a hair-raising experience, believe me. The bog ripples like waves. You're certain you'll break through and sink out of sight forever. In terror you try to run, but it's as if you were in a dream, your legs only moving up and down. As you approach the tamarack tree that you think means safety, you see that it too is bobbing up and down.

I had walked on floating bogs from the time I was a child, but this one, covered with pitcher plants, seemed more dangerous than any others. My friend Bob Newcomb, one of the best naturalists I know, had taken me there to see the exotic flowers. The nearer we got to them, the more the bog waved. He could see I was frightened.

"Just keep away from open water," he said. It was an unnecessary caution. He went on to point out that under the grass is a network of roots so tough it would support several times my weight. As long as you avoid water or mud-holes you'll stay afloat.

More than that, you may even learn to enjoy it. The sensation is almost exactly like walking on a trampoline. Where the ground is firmer, but still covered with sphagnum, the feel is sensuous, like walking on a deep carpet. Even though you never come to feel easy on a bog, remember that the water below you is so much money in the U.S. bank, a reservoir that helps keep our streams fresh and clear and free from flooding.

The prairie marsh is another wetland in need of help. Of all the terrain in America, it is perhaps the most desolate to the passing motorist. Not even ducks or geese live here to excite the sportsman. Only an occasional red-tailed hawk comes looking for a dinner of toads. But stop and walk for an hour in the tall grass and you may find small grass blades studded with a violet-blue flower, appropriately named blue-eyed grass. Why should it thrive here and nowhere else? And how can it survive against its giant neighbors? A little farther on may be a fleck of yellow in a tuft of grass—a tiny star-like member of the daffodil family no taller than your finger. The whole plant would fit in a buttonhole. What brought it here, to struggle against sedges and reeds? I have taken it home to grow in a well-tended border and it died. It would have none of the soft life. Here and there are yellow lady's slippers with twisted brown sepals. Others are dainty white. On hummocks above the moisture are superbum lilies and blazing wood lilies. I can't help but think how they must have delighted the children of immigrant pioneers moving westward.

❧

If you have a wet corner on your property, you might consider creating your own pond with surrounding marsh. For fifty dollars or so a professional blaster will blow a hole thirty feet across and five or six feet deep, depending on the soil. The resulting pond can be a courting area for a pair of mallards, a pair of teal, and perhaps an all-summer home for a family of geese. Under the strict code of water-birds, only one pair of a species will use a small body of water, and both male and female will chase off other visitors of the same species. Yet they permit other species to use the pond for courting. Later, after the female is incubating, the males forget their hostilities, and gather like golfers in a clubhouse, amusing themselves with emerging mayflies, and taking flight only to race after a female who has left her nest to stretch her wings for a few minutes and forage. Once the young are hatched, the mother may lead them to a larger body of water or a marshy area where they feed amicably with many other broods. Meantime, the drakes are molting, and all but lose their ability to fly, concealing themselves in water weeds and bog edges until their flight feathers reappear. It is only during those few critical weeks of courting that each pair of ducks require a pond to themselves.

I wish I could report that my three ponds, blasted out of the marsh near our lake three years ago, were immensely productive of ducks, but I have no way of knowing, not having been there during early spring. I do see feathers on the banks, and the mud is packed smooth near the tree that I dropped into the water as a pier on which they can preen and sun themselves. My brother tells me that his own three ponds have a pair of wood ducks each spring, besides teal and mallards, and my friends report that their new ponds already are home to a family each of mallards and blue-winged teal.

Blasting is a highly technical job, best left to an expert. The explosive—a nitrate fertilizer mixed with fuel oil—is difficult to explode, even for the professional. My oldest brother, who has handled at least twenty tons of dynamite in the course of blasting out stumps and rocks and otherwise clearing 250 acres of wilderness, was unsuccessful with the nitrate mixture.

If your acreage is blessed with running water, you might call on a pair of beavers to engineer a dam and create your duck marsh. Check with your state game and fish department to see if they might be live-trapping animals from areas where their flooding is doing damage for release elsewhere.

Beavers are delightful anywhere that their flooding isn't too extensive. They quickly accustom themselves to humans, contrary to popular opinion. For years my father fed a beaver family with carrots and assorted tidbits, and though he made no effort to tame them, they came quickly when he approached the lake. I know of few more fascinating animals to watch. And yet for all their charm and value, beavers have few friends. Foresters dislike them because they sometimes flood a patch of woods. Farmers begrudge them the hay meadow they spoil. And game wardens resent having to enforce the bad trapping regulations current in most states. In Minnesota, a trapper can take ten beaver with one license. If he wants more, he simply buys licenses for his wife and friends. A big hide—called a blanket—may bring twenty-five or thirty-five dollars; a small one, no more than two dollars. A trapper has no way of keeping young pups out of his traps. Consequently, as many beavers are discarded as kept. Two other factors have contributed to a steady decline in population: the Connibear trap, which rarely misses, and the snowmobile, which leaves them no sanctuary, no matter how remote. Beavers can and should be harvested, but not exterminated. They should be live-trapped in areas where they don't belong and transported to places in need of their services. In the West, beaver pairs in boxes are being dropped by parachute into inaccessible places; they quickly chew their way out and start in damming small streams, minimizing the danger of downstream flooding as well as creating desirable habitats for a variety of wildlife. A single pair of beaver can do engineering work that would cost thousands of dollars of tax money, and their dams require no outlay for maintenance.

Their dams are a masterpiece of engineering. First they lay small trees and logs on the bottom, butt end upstream, and anchor them with mud. Then they stack more trees and brush and logs and mud on top. The dam must reach evenly from bank to bank as it grows. Eventually, the dam gets high enough to stop and hold water, and this is the marvel to me: It works! You know from childhood how frustrating it is to keep even the smallest trickle from washing away a dam. Consider a pair of beaver in the southern part of our county, who put in a dam two hundred feet long and fifteen to twenty feet high. The water trickles evenly across a vast stretch of the lip without gouging it. Nor does water undermine the dam and erode holes. Whenever I study a beaver dam I can't quite believe it.

Consider yourself lucky if you can find beavers for your property. Just one word of caution: remember that beavers, like all wildlife, need board as well as room. They can't survive without a sizable area of aspen, ash, and the like. And they don't differentiate between your prize trees and scrub thickets. So wrap your ornamentals with heavy hardware cloth or tin.

If you already have a duck marsh that you plan to keep in marsh, check with your county agricultural agent or state game and fish commission. Under the nation's wetland program, it is possible in some areas to leave such land in perpetuity for waterfowl, in return for a lump settlement. Many Midwest farmers are turning wet corners of their land into marsh, realizing that the opportunity to watch a flotilla of young ducks in convoy with their mother during summer is worth more than a few bushels of corn.

Some farmers have introduced Canada geese to their small marshes and induced them to nest in old tubs filled with hay and set on stakes above the marsh, safeguarding them from dogs and other predators. Geese that hatch in such places seem to prefer them to ground nests. The way geese adapt to new situations is a tribute to their intelligence. In parts of the West, they have taken to using osprey nests, some of them fifty to ninety feet above ground! Sportsmen there are augmenting the nesting sites with tubs and other platforms placed high in trees. The nesting success is high.

A marsh filled with waterfowl is a constant pleasure. I never tire of watching them drop in to decoys, and if game wardens only understood what I was doing, I would sit on a blind before season when the ducks decoy easily just to watch their wonderful twisting, tumbling acrobatics. Each time it is different. Sometimes they glide in smooth. Often they come in at a great rate, sideslipping left and right in a tumult of flashing wings.

Once in my life, watching blue geese gliding in to feed on the grassy marsh alongside James Bay in Canada, I saw a goose turn upside down and sail along on its back for two or three seconds, right itself for a second or so, then turn upside down again and continue gliding on its back for a shorter time, then right itself just before reaching earth.

I turned to my companion, Carroll Streeter.

"Cap, did you see what I saw?"

"Yes, but I don't believe it. I can't believe it."

Our story—when we had the courage to tell it—naturally brought scoffs, even though, years later, a photographer caught the same sight on movie film, and individual frames show the goose completely upside down except for its head. What function such flying serves puzzles me. Could it ease the muscles, as flipping on the back does in swimming? Or is it simply fun?

The latter, I am sure, would be my friend Ray Dankenbring's conclusion. Ray maintains that geese have more fun than people, and in his next reincarnation asks to be a Canada goose, the dangers notwithstanding, to travel the high air without worry over airports, limousines, and reservations, living in a climate of everlasting spring.

Did you know that waterfowl are reliable weather forecasters? When the barometer is falling and a storm is ahead, you can be sure that ducks will tell you by their short, restless flights. Another water bird is excellent: the loon. As sure as they take to the air—a difficult task for them—and start calling, look for rain or storm. Once in Canada the sky seemed full of loons, all calling. And that afternoon such a storm arose that my brothers and I barely made it back across the lake. Two young fishermen weren't so fortunate. The next morning the Mounties found their boat, the transom gone where the motor had been mounted. Later the bodies were recovered.

Ducks and geese are only part of the fun of having your own small pond or marsh. Muskrats may find a home there, and mink. Coons like the wetland habitat, and deer like the swamp edges. My own ponds are

ringed with the dainty hoofprints of fawns and of their
mothers' deeper prints. Nearby are deer "beds" where
the grass has been flattened by their bodies. The tips of
young tree shoots are nipped off, and all the jewel-
weeds, or what we call "touch-me-nots" are naked to the
stalk.

A marsh is a mysterious thing, a jungle in miniature.
Attached to the reeds just above waterline are the
cast-off skins of emerging dragonflies, which look indeed
like dragons and though empty, still seem evil and possessed of life. Just below the surface are tadpoles of both
frogs and toads coming up now and then to try out their
fast-developing lungs.

The sounds of a swamp are enchanting, and often
comic, from the bullfrog's threat, "Be drowned, be
drowned," to the silly whinny of the rail, reminiscent of
the nervous laugh of a woman who has trumped her
partner's ace at an afternoon bridge club. From the willows comes the lively drawl of the olive-sided flycatcher,
easy to identify from his whistled command, "Quick,
three beers!"

If your marsh has a sandy bank, a pair of spotted
sandpipers might choose to summer there, comic figures
whose tails bounce up and down constantly as they
search the banks for food.

Spring and fall, your pond and marsh may have visitors en route between Canada and Alaska and the Deep
South. These are the shorebirds, wheeling and turning
in tight formation like fighter airplanes, the sun glint-
ing from their wings as they pivot with astonishing precision. There are few more beautiful sights in all outdoors.

Some shorebirds are easy to identify. The busy
dowitcher probes the mud to his eyeballs with the
steady stitch of a sewing machine. The yellowlegs—
both lesser and greater—seem too beautiful and fragile
to be real; for generations men have attempted to catch

that beauty in decoys carved of wood. Bigger birds with stocky bodies that appear spring and fall are those celebrated travelers, the plovers, which winter in Patagonia and summer in the Arctic.

If your marsh is in the prairies, perhaps you might have visits from the avocet, a striking bird that God must have created in a jocular moment. Floating over your marsh may be a marvel of bird flight, the black tern, skimming like a swallow over the water, then pausing momentarily, treading air as it scrutinizes the fish life below. It probably won't nest in your pond, preferring to build its floating nest of reeds and mud in company with others on a bigger tract of water and marsh, but it will forage on your place, adding charm all spring and summer.

A visitor almost sure to find your marsh will be the killdeer, a big, bold plover who cuts short the tail of winter. Watch him closely with your field glasses as he forages. Notice how he vibrates the mud with one foot. For some reason this disturbance causes certain worms to surface. Killdeer are courageous parents, and masters of the broken-wing technique; no boy or dog or other predator can resist chasing after them, certain they can be caught.

Still another visitor to your marsh or pond may be the phalarope, which is the delight of women bird-watchers. There are three types of phalaropes, all of them dainty creatures a little smaller than a killdeer, that spin like a top on the water, as they make quick jabs with a slender bill capturing flies and small water beetles. What may endear them to women is that the submissive, plain-colored male handles all domestic chores including incubating the young, while the bigger, brightly colored female in the company of other females of her kind loafs away the sunny days of summer at some shallow pool nearby.

If you have no more room than a city lot, you can

still have your own bog garden where you and your children can watch the day-to-day life of the marsh. As simple a setup as a tub sunk to the rim will grow an assortment of sphagnum moss and cranberries as well as the pitcher plant, that flower so intriguing to children and artists. Its mahogany flowers rise tall above a circle of urn-shaped leaves with such grace that its form has adorned art work since the days of the earliest Americans. What fascinates a child is the way insects are attracted inside the hollow leaf by the sweetish sap there and, unable to crawl out past the stiff hairs all pointing downwards, end up decaying in the rain water that collects inside, providing a rich nitrogenous food for the plant.

Our family grew up alongside a homemade pool where we ate our suppers and loafed at noon for half an hour after dinner before returning to the field. We would lie on our stomachs watching the watery world of dragonflies and water bugs. For a summer or two we tried growing flowers along the edge, but they got in the way of our pool-watching. We had goldfish, of course, but they were disappointing. Like many an animal bred for beauty, they seemed tragically short of intelligence.

One day my father returned from fishing with a black bass of about a pound that he had accidentally caught. He hadn't intended to hook it, and now he couldn't kill it, so he put it into the pool and tossed in a grasshopper —which the fish grabbed and swallowed almost the moment it hit the water. The second or perhaps the third one it took from his fingers!

From the potato field, we had seen Dad ambling about the yard aimlessly, and we worried over what had happened to him. When we discovered he was hunting more grasshoppers we could hardly believe that a fish, just hooked and probably sore-mouthed, could accustom itself immediately to a pool not much bigger than a bathtub. Incredibly, it did.

In a day or two when we came to the pool with a frog, it would come up to meet us, and soon was leaping out of the water to grab it from our fingers. Its appetite was as unbelievable as its capacity. One day it devoured nine young leopard frogs in quick succession, only slowing down toward the end, when it would swim back below a lily pad to gulp. The hind feet of the last frog protruded for perhaps an hour before disappearing.

A pound and a half sunfish spent one summer in the same pool, and a dipperful of newly hatched catfish (or what we call bullheads) were a pleasure to watch another summer.

For children, a pool has marvels more absorbing than fish. Water striders race across the surface. Water boatmen skitter below, the capsule of air surrounding them flashing like silver. Snails carry on their slow-motion ritual of feeding and reproducing. Floating on the surface are tiny plants called duckweed, each one a leaf with a few dainty rootlets hanging beneath it.

When I say that you can have your own pond and stream—right on your own city lot—I really mean it. The pool in my yard is exactly the size of a stock watering tank. In fact, it *is* one, courtesy of Sears, Roebuck. And my waterfall, too, is courtesy of Sears. Yet wild things like it as well as the real thing. On hot days, the stream trickling over a few flat limestone rocks is an oasis for thirsty birds, even though the lake is six beats of a flicker's wing from it. Catbirds, robins, thrashers, siskins, bluejays, flickers, and warblers all come to drink and splash a bit, shaking liquid silver from their wings.

Quiet water is attractive to birds in summer. Running water is irresistible. My naturalist doctor, Paul Fluck, finds that for his bird banding, there is no better lure than water from a hole (or petcock) in a pail dripping into a shallow pan or crock on the ground. Almost everything from hawks to warblers seeks it out. Just try suspending your garden hose from a limb and letting a steady flow of drops fall into a pan. In hot weather, you'll have a steady pilgrimage of thirsty birds. But let me warn you, you won't be satisfied until you have a small pool with running water. Try a metal tank like mine. It's easy to install and takes no yearly repairs, as concrete pools do in our area of deeply frozen ground. A submersible pump costing around thirty dollars provides the running water.

My friend Carroll Streeter—a unique and thoroughly captivating blend, half gruff no-nonsense and half romantic—has built an elaborate series of small pools with connecting waterways in the back yard of his suburban Philadelphia home, and among my pleasantest memories of the East are garden parties beside those pools. At first the whole synthetic stream seemed pathetic, but you soon succumb to the charm of running water, the fish, and the rapids cloaked in shrubbery out of which the stream begins its course. What difference what causes the water to gurgle over the rocks? It doesn't matter. Nor does it matter to the birds who come to drink there despite the people. After dark when the toads begin to chorus, the place might be anywhere in time or space that you prefer—the Western prairies, the wilds of Canada, or a Louisiana bayou.

Having a pool and stream in the backyard isn't exactly conservation, but it is fun, and there's nothing wrong with that. At the rate we're polluting public waters, perhaps the only sweet-smelling streams will be fake.

# 7 🌿 The mystery of Mima mounds

IT'S OCTOBER in the marshy prairie—the setting for a mystery.

Take a look at that aerial view among the pictures in this book. What would you guess was the origin of those grassy mounds? They pre-date bulldozers and strip mining and even golf. There are thirty thousand acres of them out in a boggy area called the Mima Prairie south of Olympia, Washington, and they have been a conundrum to scientists for fifty years. The Chinook Indians used to gather for peace parleys there and their word for peace—Mima (pronounced my'ma)—is what gave the mounds their name.

"It's obvious that they're the graves of a prehistoric tribe," said the it's-obvious boys.

But when the curious clan started digging they didn't spade up a single skeleton or clay pot or arrowhead. The earth was loose and without a "soil profile"—the layers of clay and sand that record the centuries of wave and water action. The loose column of earth went down four or five feet through a thousand or more years of undisturbed soil. It was as if some animal had burrowed its way straight down.

Now pocket gophers do that, especially for their winter headquarters. They go two and even three feet down and throw up dirt as much as two feet above ground over their pantry of roots and bulbs. But the Mima mounds are forty feet across, and seven feet high. If it

were pocket gophers, they must have been giant ones—
and this was one theory advanced by scientists. Others
argued that pocket gophers don't favor wet ground like
that surrounding the mounds.

The puzzle grew worldwide, since there are Mima-
type mounds from Siberia to Patagonia, differing in size
but generally found on waterlogged soils. Frost action,
said the Russians, and that was a likely guess. Frost does
remarkable things to the tundra, breaking it up into
hexagonal patterns of haunting beauty. If you fly over
the tundra on the north slope of the Brooks Mountains
in Alaska you can see the same giant pattern, etched in
the peat and sphagnum moss like a giant comb of
honey, with the same faultless symmetry. In other places
the frost makes squares and other polygons, the causes
not well understood by students of the Arctic. Frost
might well have helped shape the Mima mounds, but it
couldn't account for the thorough mix of earth and
gravel.

Perhaps generations of ants might have done it. Or
was it carplike fish, eons ago, nosing deep in the gravel
bottom of a prehistoric lake after a buried treasure of
worms or plant roots? Or might it have been a buffalo
wallow from more recent times? All these theories were
advanced in scientific journals.

Fascinating as Mima mounds have been to the researchers, they are nothing but a nuisance to farmers.
Leveling the ground for agriculture generally costs too
much, and most of the prairie has been used to pasture
cattle. Only the ubiquitous bulldozer has been able to
destroy the magic of Mima mound prairie.

In northwest Minnesota are comparable patches of
virgin prairie that have gone untouched by the plow because they were too wet to use without costly drainage.
This too is in Indian country near such villages as Mahnomen (the Chippewa word for wild rice) and Waubun (morning). The Waubun prairie is a dismal-

looking wasteland of bluestem and reeds and cattails, with here and there a scrubby patch of higher ground covered with willows and aspen.

But the University of Minnesota, searching for vestiges of prairie that had never been disturbed by man, saw its uniqueness, and in 1954 petitioned the state to set aside a section of 640 acres as a place to research, to explore the past, to catch a glimpse of the world as it was before man in any numbers began tampering.

In 1957 a blond young man named John R. Tester drove his battered Ford north of the village of Mahnomen and turned off in a farmer's yard where he stopped to ask permission to cross the fields to the University's prairie. It was mid-May and cold and he buttoned his windbreaker around his neck when he stopped the car and stepped out. It was a bleak outlook: as far as he could see, there was a sea of dead grass. Here and there, though, he began to see mounds like those on the Mima Prairie. They varied from ten to forty feet across but were only a foot or two high, covered with tall weeds—not much to excite a young man who had chosen the place as the subject of his doctoral thesis, "The flora and fauna of the Waubun prairie." Except for a few red-winged blackbirds clinging to the dead cattails, nothing stirred.

Two days later when he returned it was a different matter. The prairie was hopping with toads, big warty masses of protoplasm normally inert but determined now to reach the nearest slough as fast as their skinny legs could take them. Tester followed them to the water's edge and watched. The males faced the shore and floated, inflating the skin of their throats like ping-pong balls as they trilled their song, a high, tremulous trill that went on for a minute and even more. Tester knew that their nostrils and mouths were closed all the while they sang, and they could take a breath without stopping their song, yet he marveled at their endurance.

The song came from air rushing past tightly stretched cords in the larynx. He remembered how as a child he had cut a ribbon of rubber from an inner tube and held it stretched above his head as he ran down the street, the ribbon strumming a throaty song. The toad's trill came in much the same way.

All around him the males were singing. It was easy to tell the males by their thumbs, which were dark brown and swollen. But the toads had no way of differentiating sex except by trial and error. One big male would mount another male and cling to him until the under-toad would mutter a few chirps of protest and wiggle free. The female when mounted would remain silent and quiescent and as the male tightened his grip around her ample waist, she would begin to emit a translucent string of eggs as throb after throb of sperm came pulsating from the male in a cloud that enveloped the eggs. The spent females would move back to the shallows at the margin of the slough. The males would return to the chorus at the center of the pond and resume singing.

Aside from an occasional wandering raccoon and a pair of yellow warblers, there was little animal life that spring. Elsewhere on the Waubun prairie were yellow rails, little bigger than a day-old chick, birds so rare that ornithologists would make pilgrimages there to find them, men in pairs dragging a long rope between them over the grass to flush the birds for a fleeting glimpse before they dropped into the dense cover. There were not even yellow rails in the tract Tester had chosen to scrutinize. Almost nothing but toads.

These he watched minutely. He took six of them and carefully made a slit in the skin of their backs, and inserted a minute piece of radioactive substance underneath. The toads lumbered off, apparently unconcerned by the operation. With a Geiger counter slung from one shoulder, Tester could find them at any hour of the day and record their slow-motion existence on a detailed map. Most stayed in one area a few days and then moved on. Others were home-lovers, moved little. The average distance between the most widely separated points was only 565 feet. Some showed strong homing instincts, escaping a pen and hopping home, almost a quarter of a mile away. So the summer wore on uneventfully. Before long the redwings began to gather in flocks that would swoop down in gusts to rest on the cattails. There was a chill in the moist air.

Suddenly one morning the prairie seemed dead, and for a while Tester wondered why. Slowly he realized that his summer's companions, the toads, were gone. Nothing stirred anywhere. He walked to the border of a slough where he had last recorded a radioactive toad. No buzz from his Geiger counter. He tested one after another slough. This was where authorities said toads hibernated along with frogs in the mud below, safe from freezing. But there was not a buzz anywhere. He searched the prairie, crossing and crisscrossing the low marshy ground. Not a trace.

He couldn't help feeling more than a little resentful that his lone friends of the summer should leave him without a hint of where they had gone. And he saw his summer's work blasted. What kind of researcher was he, who failed to find the wintering quarters of an animal that spends nine months of the year in hibernation? Filled with that humiliating thought—and still burning with the infidelity of his friends—he made another search of the prairie. But there wasn't a trace of a toad. It was as if they had taken wing and gone skyward.

He was on his way back to the car, taking a shortcut over a Mima mound that was the highest spot on the prairie when the Geiger counter suddenly sputtered. Down a few inches in the loose soil below the weeds was a friend, awake but torpid with the cold. Not far off was another. Eventually he located five of the six, all of them in Mima mounds. His spirits soared. He found himself singing as he drove back into town. That night at the hotel he got to thinking: if toads hibernate, how could they escape the frost that reaches down some winters for nearly four feet? Could toads actually freeze and then come to life again with the spring sun?

Next morning he found a plastic tube at the hardware store and drove out to the prairie where he pushed it down like a stake alongside a buried toad. He could insert a probe in the tube that would relay back by wire to the Geiger counter the whereabouts of the toad during winter. The following week when Tester inserted his probe he found the toad had moved an inch or two lower, just below the frost level. All winter the toad moved deeper, always an inch or two out of reach of frost. As days began to lengthen in February and March, it worked its way upwards until in April it was only a few inches below ground. In May the snow melted and the sun and rain began warming the surface of the prairie, thawing the earth for an inch, then two inches, then three. Suddenly the warmth of the earth and sun met and the seal of winter was broken. Once again the prairie was alive with toads, hurrying to the unlocked ponds to sing their thin, insistent song.

Tester's discovery that toads do not hibernate, but stay active all winter, and in dry soil rather than marsh bottoms, failed to excite much attention outside the range of zoologists. Who could care about such an unlovely member of God's kingdom? But to Tester they were increasingly fascinating, and after he won his doctorate and started work at the University of Minnesota's Museum of Natural History, he continued his study, and for the next six years haunted the Waubun prairie.

What a marvelous mechanism was the toad's body that permitted it to dig down, sometimes four feet, when its own temperature was a bare degree or two above freezing! And what a column of earth a toad moved during that time—the equivalent of its own volume for every two inches as the frost descended, and again that same amount as it rose again during spring. All with nothing more than its rubbery feet and legs, and on food stored in its body during three short months of summer. What a triumph for the fat man of the amphibian world, squirming his way up and down through the chill soil!

Some toads he equipped with radio transmitters harnessed to their backs. And from these he learned that some were individualists, burrowing down three feet immediately and staying there until time to emerge.

For every piece of knowledge that Tester unearthed, new questions kept arising. Did toads use only the Mima mounds to winter in? He fenced off one mound with eighteen-inch sheet metal. On the side nearest the pond he installed a funnel-shaped catching trap. Alongside on the prairie he set up another. On that magic day when the earth exploded with toads, the Mima mound was seething with toads. None in the prairie trap nearby. Later in the month, the Mima trap was filled with juvenile toads from the past year's hatch. Still none in the prairie trap. At the end of May, when all the toads had emerged, he totaled the catch from the Mima trap: 225. Not one from the prairie trap. Another spring he fenced other Mima mounds, including one at the highest point of the prairie. Here he found the greatest winter concentration. Did they hop to the highest point of their toad's-eye horizon searching the skyline through the thin horizontal slits of their orange eyes? Or did they simply seek the driest soil they could find, soil that was easy to dig even if frozen? Or did they hunt the mellow earth of the Mima mound where digging was easiest? Why were there no Mima mounds in other places where the Manitoba toad is common? And why was one mound a hundred times more attractive to toads than another seemingly alike? Were there "families" of toads—what naturalists call populations—that grew accustomed to one wintering spot from tradition alone? Perhaps the old heads led the younger ones there.

On a day in fall when the first wild geese were flying over, Tester watched a toad as it started its downward journey. Sitting like a miniature Buddha motionless and unblinking on a Mima mound, it began to swivel its ample bottom back and forth. On the soles of a toad's hind feet are surfaces like rough sandpaper, and these wore through the accumulation of weeds like a corkscrew. In fifteen minutes of squirming, the toad was half buried. An hour later it had disappeared, with nothing but a soft mound of earth to mark its burial shaft.

Mima mounds were a logical place for toads to burrow. Could it be that they were the builders—not just the tenants—of the mounds? Tester can't remember when the idea came to him. It seemed so absurd at first that a toad could be in the earth-moving business. But if they weren't the builders, at least they could be maintainers of the loose, homogeneous mound. One mound less than thirty feet in diameter held 3,276 toads that burrowed an average of three feet deep—moving in a single year nearly four tons of soil!

Tester, true scientist, doesn't say that toads cause Mima mounds. Addressing a worldwide symposium of naturalists at Helsinki, Finland, he only postulated a series of possible causes for the mounds on the Waubun prairie: a combination of pocket gophers, blowing dust caught by the tall weeds, badgers digging out the gophers, and lowly toads. "Over hundreds or even thousands of years they may be a significant factor in formation of Mima-type mounds," he said.

The mystery may still be unsolved, waiting for your answer.

One of Tester's graduate students, Michael A. Ewert,

did a doctoral study of the seasonal movements of toads. He found that *Bufo americanus* (the American toad) was a slowpoke about starting to move in the spring, and often spent a day or more just blinking and peering out of the burrow before he emerged completely. One sat, hinder in the burrow, for fifteen days. Many stayed within fifty feet of the hole before traveling to the pond to chorus.

But once they got started, some were great travelers. One went 750 feet in a night—about a city block; another went 1,030 feet. But *Bufo americanus* was a piker compared with one *Bufo cognatus,* another species, which traveled over half a mile in a single night.

The average toad of either species had several favorite feeding spots the size of a city lot, staying a few days at each, generally moving at night. But as fall approached, they moved more often during daylight hours, seeming to seek a place to overwinter.

Toad 18, a male, made irregular circles in the general area of his wintering spot, moving during the day and retreating into the debris of grass and leaves at night. He hopped slowly, deliberately, a foot at a time, and searched small breaks in the litter, often backing into them and attempting to burrow. After four days of search, he found a ground squirrel hole and crawled in for the winter.

Ewert chuckled as he remembered what that wonderful observer of toads, Mary C. Dickerson, had written long before in *The Frog Book*: "The toad makes his house and enters it at the same time—a great advantage, it would seem. But he must back in, which must have its disadvantages, since he cannot be certain until he is thoroughly and snugly in that he is going to have a house at all; he may bump against a stone, or take a long tumble into a cellar, or, worse still, into a well."

Late in September, toad 11, another male, was exactly one foot south of its previous wintering site, peering at small cavities, backing into some, then emerging and passing on. Ewert caught it and placed it in front of its last year's burrow, which had been enlarged by a ground squirrel, but it refused to enter. But when he put it next to a spot he had freshly scooped out of the prairie litter to expose the humus below, it promptly accepted the help and squirmed out of sight. Toad 11 used the same general overwintering site for three consecutive years.

Ewert concludes that every toad is familiar with many landmarks in his territory, and remembers their location for at least a year. Sun, moon, and stars may help him keep his directions at night, just as they do with birds. But toads manage perfectly well when the sky is overcast, and hence must depend on memory of certain features of their home grounds themselves. What those are, Ewert doesn't say, but they must be something more than small nearby plants or even bushes, because many toads are still hunting their old winter sites after the leaves have fallen and the landscape changed drastically.

Whoever starts to study the lowly toad comes somehow under its spell. It is so humble, so bowed down with handicaps. How can the fat man of the batrachian world possibly move fast enough to catch a fly? Yet he does, and seldom misses. Advancing on his prey he has all the fluid grace of a cat stalking a mouse. But it is his sensational tongue that is his greatest tool. It is attached to the front end of his lower jaw rather than the back, and can flip forward a good two inches with incredible speed, trapping the fly in the sticky surface, and flipping it back past his toothless jaws.

Beset by an unsophisticated dog or other annoyance, he might first flatten himself against the earth where he becomes almost invisible. Or he might squirm down out of sight until the earth caves in above him. Or he might take to leaping, changing directions sharply at each leap, discharging the contents of his bladder as he goes. A dog foolish enough may take a toad in his mouth once, but never again. For a toad has a set of glands behind each ear that secrete a milky juice that will torture a dog for a good twenty-four hours. Except for snakes and skunks, which seem somehow immune, the secretion is poisonous to small animals. Toads don't produce warts in humans, of course, but the milk secretion, if rubbed on the mouth or eyes, can sting. Toads use that weapon only in direst emergencies, however, and Mary C. Dickerson says that in thirty years of handling toads she encountered only one toad that used it on her.

All in all, the toad isn't the pathetic, defenseless glob he might seem to be.

Pick up the next toad you encounter and get to know him better. He's not wet or cold, and unlike frenetic frogs, may settle himself comfortably in your palm. Look at his ears. You're actually looking at his eardrums, protected only by a thin layer of skin. He has, of course, no ear flaps to catch sounds—they'd cut down his speed under water. Look at the white skin under his chin. He looks as if he's panting at a great rate, and in a sense he is. He has no rib cage to suck air into his lungs. Instead, he closes nostrils and mouth and pumps air to them with a bellows-like action of his chin membrane. The same membrane is the one he inflates when he choruses, giving resonance to his singing. *Bufo cognatus,* sitting half-submerged in a spring pool, puffs his four inches of body into a giant vocal effort that will carry three quarters of a mile. That's almost the equal of a braying donkey! Tickle *cognatus* under the chin and he may give a performance, with sounds anywhere from squawks below middle G to startling, piercing cries two octaves higher. There is no describing the variety of toad sounds. Some species when alarmed quack like a duck, others scream, still others make birdlike chirps. The mating songs of species differ considerably, and may be all that keeps the species from interbreeding. (If you can't find a toad to sing for you, find a frog. A leopard frog makes a beautiful pet and will sing when you handle him. Pour water gently on his back and he'll purr like a cat!)

It is the eyes of toads that have fascinated mankind for centuries. Shakespeare wrote:

> *Oh mark the beauty of his eye,*
> *What wonders in that circle lie!*
> *So clear, so bright, our fathers said—*
> *"He wears a jewel in his head."*

Notice that a toad closes one eye or both, lowering them into the roof of his mouth as the lid flips over. When he swallows, his eyes depress in the same way, and the action may help him push food down his gullet.

Three or four times a summer, toads peel off every vestige of skin, including the covering of eyes and mouth, swallowing it as they pull it from legs, stomach, and feet.

Most of the summer, toads seem friendly, barely budging to keep from being stepped on. But during hot, humid midsummer weather they grow irritable, and hop off whenever you come close. Often during hot, dry spells in July and August, toads burrow into the ground for a summer's snooze called *estivation*—and a few don't bother to emerge, continuing on into their winter retirement. More often, after a hard rain, toads emerge suddenly, and it seems as if the sky must have rained toads.

For the young and young in spirit: a little excitement this summer. Gather a string of toad eggs and keep them in a jar or fish bowl. (Frog eggs come in masses rather than strings, but if you get frog eggs, it won't matter because the growth is much the same.) Don't worry about exhausting the pond's supply of toad eggs. An adult female lays up to twelve thousand.

Hold the eggs up to the light and see how much of the egg is yolk—the light-colored bottom part below the pigmented top. That yolk must feed the growing tadpole for sixteen or more days, because till then it will have no mouth. The warmer the eggs, the faster they develop. The dark top surface absorbs more of the sun's heat than a lighter color would. In a matter of hours after fertilizing, the dark upper portion increases.

Now with a magnifying glass you can watch lines form around the egg that look for all the world like those that mark a globe into longitude and latitude. Each day come surprising changes—a long groove down the back, one end of which will become the brain, the rest spinal cord. About nine days after the eggs are laid, the young wriggle free of the jellylike string and attach themselves to weeds with a pair of mouthlike "suckers." Not till the sixteenth day do mouths appear, but from then on the young feed ravenously on minute pond organisms. (Fish food or boiled lettuce will serve your tadpoles nicely.)

As a fold of skin begins to cover the fingerlike gills, the young tadpoles come to the surface frequently to gulp air into the developing lungs. Tadpoles can survive extremely low oxygen concentrations. To keep warm, they move to shallow water during the day and deeper water at night. The warmer they are, the faster their metabolism and growth, and the shorter their period of vulnerability to the water beetles, water tigers, leeches, herons, and ducks that love a snack of tender tadpoles.

Now begins that transformation that excites even the most prosaic. Legs start protruding, eyes enlarging, and inside the body more profound changes take place as the intestine shortens from the long loop of the vegetarian to the short gut of the carnivore. Now the young animal must rush to the surface periodically to expel a bubble of used air for fresh. Occasionally, he sits on the water's edge while the corpuscles of his colorless blood are traveling out to the long tail and returning with particles of it to feed the growing organs (all easily seen under a microscope). If a heron bites off the tail or a developing leg, a perfect new one quickly regrows.

Almost from the moment a toad leaves the pond, he looks old. Yet he doesn't reach sexual maturity until age three or four. No one knows how long a toad will live. One American toad is reported to have lived to be thirty-six until it was accidentally killed.

To me, toads seem like recruits from a Walt Disney movie, partly, I suppose, because their small, delicate hands have only four fingers like the dwarfs in *Snow White,* but perhaps even more in that they are so unhurried, so at one with the world, so willing to take life as it comes.

Many researchers say that toads learn faster than frogs and react more quickly to new stimulations. Some scientists believe that though they have shorter memories than mammals, they can learn just as fast. Toads fed only once a week learned the hour of feeding after thirty or forty weeks. And yet toads are hoodwinked by the same ruse they play on their predators. A caterpillar confronted by a toad curls up and plays dead, and the toad, which won't eat anything that doesn't move, goes on.

The earthworm, though, has never learned that stratagem and goes on squirming as a toad creeps up cautiously ahead of it, so as to swallow it head first, then lashes out its tongue and starts pulling, the worm backing up with all the power of its coiling muscles. A slippery worm isn't easily dislodged by anything— man, bird, or toothless toad with nothing but a sticky tongue and dainty hands. The lucky toad will succeed in cramming the wriggling dinner down deep enough so that it won't crawl out, but after he's done so, he'll probably wear a dyspeptic look for a long while afterward. It's apparent he doesn't much care for the slime that coats the earthworm. Nonetheless, he is no gourmet.

Anything that moves is fair game, and school children have fed bird shot rolled towards toads until they were heavy with the lead. As you might expect, toads need little change in diet to satisfy them. I have watched a toad sit for hours below an oak tree, feasting on a column of ants that kept moving up and down past him in never-ending bounty. Other observers report two- and even three-day ant dinners.

Whatever he does, a toad seems to do it with pleasure. In Nature's passionate, often violent struggle to survive, the toad is the placid summer visitor, the quiet philosopher of balmy spring evenings and gentle summer rain.

Get the record *Voices of the Night* from Cornell University and listen until you recognize the toads and frogs of your area. Then when you stop the car along a stretch of marsh you will hear voices you never before noticed—songs that were being sung in Jurassic days, millions of years before the songs of birds were heard on earth, singing the haunting mystery of eternity.

# 8 ❦ How to hunt deer successfully—every time

THE LAST TOAD has squirmed his way out of sight. The wind has an edge to it as it whips off the last leaves of autumn. The woods stand deserted. For many this is a sad time of year.

Softly if not suddenly there are big flakes coming down, the first of the season. It is then that deer hunters —those evil people, enemies of nature—start growing restive.

"Tracking snow by morning," they'll say as they gather at the corner café for talk over coffee.

❦

Whenever I start talking about deer hunting, my friends smile. Some of them even laugh.

"Tell about Stud Run," they say. Stud Run is a place in the wilderness of the Rapid River below the Canadian border that I fear I have made famous.

It was late in November that my brothers and I were setting out to drive deer to our city friends who were "posting" on a cut-out line a quarter mile away. I was waiting for the signal to begin when I heard a light tramping sound coming from a grassy slough just ahead of me that contained a single clump of willows. It could hardly be a deer, I thought, because my brother Robert had crossed the slough only a few minutes before.

Suddenly a big buck jumped from behind the willows and came quartering toward me down a thin arm of the slough. Though he was intermittently screened by brush, I could see flashes of him—a tremendous animal that held his rack back over his head, his chest thrust forward like a proud stallion, running rather than jumping down the grassy path. It was a magnificent sight. It never occurred to me till he was gone that I had a high-powered rifle in my hand, and that the reason I was out in the woods was to shoot it, at deer, and especially a big trophy deer.

I called to my brother. "One went between us out of the drive!"

He was still in earshot.

"Why didn't you shoot?"

"Because you were in the way!"

"Don't worry about me! Just shoot. We need the venison!"

I started to move forward. I wanted to see where the big buck had been lying. Again, a rustle up front. I paused.

Again a buck leaped to his feet, one as big as the first, running down the same grassy path, holding his rack as proudly as the first. Again I marveled at the splendid big body and muscular grace and the blue of the rich, thick coat. His big white flag signaled goodbye as he leaped into the thick brush about the time I came to my senses.

"I saw another one!" I shouted. "Ran down the same path by me!" And then, taking the offensive, I added, "Why don't you keep out of line so I can shoot?" There came a rumble of disgust from my brother's direction.

And then from the willow clump a third stag came charging across the opening and down the swale, more majestic than even the first two, rack proudly held far back, racing but not ruffled. I jerked my gun to my shoulder and aimed at the slots in the brush, but there wasn't the right opening for me to fire. I didn't, but I shall never forget the grandeur of those animals, assembled for some reason in a stag party during rutting season. Nor will my brothers ever let me forget.

Each time after I fail to shoot, I have misgivings. I grew up in a family of hunters—six sons and a father, all with deer licenses. Seven deer went a long way toward providing our winter's meat. We hunted deer for the sport of it, and yet we were always conscious of the need for a big supply of venison.

More than that, in us as in every hunter there was a primordial urge to blend somehow with the beauty and grace of the deer, to see it up close. I don't believe it's an urge to kill or even possess but to know and absorb the beauty of the animal. If a deer were to stand still so that a hunter might admire it the way a botanist does a wild flower, there might be little deer-killing. Most hunters aren't bloodthirsty or even vain of their reputations as hunters. Their delight is in the chase, in trailing a sage old animal, circling ahead of it to intercept it, and surprising it, hoping somehow that it will be too wise to be fooled, admiring it all the more as it eludes them. Most hunters will understand what I am saying, will recognize the conflict between hoping for success and hoping the animal will escape.

In most hunters I know there is a genuine love of wildlife. In general, it is the hunter who hikes into the woods during midwinter to cut down aspen for deer food. It is the hunter who blasts out duck ponds and seeds wild rice.

Perhaps our cat has something of the same feelings. He had been lying in wait for a red squirrel that burrowed the most amazing subway system through last night's snow from tree to feeder to tree. Now that the cat has caught and killed him, he sits bored beside the body. I think I know something of how that cat feels, and so perhaps will many hunters. It is the desire to know and understand and be at one with wildlife that is basic to them. A person who can watch deer or ducks or other wildlife on his property during summer rarely cares very much about shooting them.

I have tried "hunting with a camera," but found it a farce. While I struggled with light readings, focus and aim, I lost those moments I might have captured on memory's film, sharp and vivid to call up at will for the rest of my life, without the encumbrance of projector or screen. I say let professional photographers capture the thrilling sequences for Disney footage.

I have shot a dozen or so deer, mainly when they stand so long that I eventually remember my responsibility to other members of the hunting party. But my deer hunting is literally that—I hunt for deer rather than shoot them. I comb the woods to find the places they frequent, where the bucks scratch the velvet from their itching antlers, where they paw the earth in the passion of the rut.

Once I waited in a tree above such a scrape, and almost immediately a buck came to the hollow, stood on his hind legs and slowly waved his head back and forth for several seconds, returned to all fours, then repeated it again until I accidentally snapped a twig under my foot. What prompted him to stand erect, I cannot guess. I have never heard of anyone else who has observed it.

Following a fresh deer track in the snow is a sport above all others. Here the animal has been jumping. What scared it? Was it coming my way and saw, smelled or heard me? Apparently it wasn't much frightened, for it soon settled down to a trot and before long was walking. Here it has paused to turn and watch its trail. Now it has leaped and gone on. One or more of its senses tells it I am following. This time it runs a longer distance. And now the track ends completely, as if the animal has taken wing. I am flabbergasted. Scrutinizing the tracks I see that the animal has doubled back on its tracks, stepping carefully into each one so that I am completely deceived; then, watching me come, has leaped to one side off the trail, throwing me off completely. After a while I find its jumping tracks. I continue once again until the jumps subside to a trot and then to a walk.

Once it appeared to go downwind to see if I were still following. Satisfied I was not, it has taken to feeding. I can tell by its meandering tracks much easier than by the clipped-off twigs that it is eating. Its circling means it will bed down. I look ahead for a dense thicket, a fallen tree, or the shelter of a spruce—all places where it might now be lying. I inch along, feeling rather than looking for a place to take my next step. I keep watch on two or three likely clumps of brush, swiveling my head slowly. Crash! A big doe leaps up from behind a stump much closer than the places I was scrutinizing. Two bounds and she is off. She has won this little game.

Had I shot her, I would have felt satisfaction, but of a different sort, an atavistic response, the kind you get when you gather and bring home wild strawberries or blackberries or plums.

What I am saying is that hunting deer and shooting deer are two different sports, and that I much prefer the first, as I believe most seasoned hunters do.

How do you hunt—not shoot—deer?

The first thing is to equip yourself with woolen shirt and pants, all red if you go hunting during season. Wool permits you to move quietly, something that cotton or synthetics won't permit. Until you find a track, you go still-hunting. This means moving slowly upwind through a patch of brush or woods, pausing for five minutes or so as you approach each new opening that offers a new look ahead. Walk quietly across the opening and look for a new vista. Wait for ten minutes if you feel you're near game. I've watched some deer stand motionless as a statue for twenty minutes. More often they spook and run, after freezing for a few minutes.

Other wildlife will stand rigid so long as they know they're not seen. But once your eyes are directly on them, they flee in panic. Three of us, hunting turkeys in the Pocono Mountains of Pennsylvania, walked past a fallen log unaware of a big gobbler crouched there. Just as we were passing him, up he rose, gobbling and flailing the air and brush until he cleared the treetops, then soared like an airliner across the valley to a timbered ridge.

I was perched bow-and-arrow-hunting for deer, one time in a small white pine, when I heard a flock of turkeys approaching. I was screened completely by the long needles. But the instant my eyes caught sight of the lead hen, she saw my eyes on her, and after a startled pause, took off in what I can only describe as a turkey-trot— calling an alarm as she went. I can't believe she saw much else of me but my staring disembodied eyes.

A tree is a fine place to watch for deer. Deer don't seem to look above them and they can't smell you, since the warmth of your body moves the air up. Kinglets come to look you over, and sit just out of arm's reach, their golden crowns bright even in November. Chickadees move in, and sometimes alight on your cap. Red squirrels cast aside their fears and sniff at your boots. A screech owl or barred owl might come and perch nearby, eyeing you curiously. You feel like a Mowgli among his friends. During cold weather, though, a tree perch quickly becomes unbearable, so better return to the ground. In the Vermont woods I have run across old car bodies hauled and left by hunters. These would make comfortable watching places, though hardly esthetic ones.

If you still-hunt properly, you'll see deer. Moving quietly, then pausing, is a deer's own style, and often one will mistake you for another deer and approach closer for a look. All you will know of its proximity is a sudden snort, as startling as a hit on the head. Don't bother to look for a deer that has snorted at you. Nearly always it will have sighted or smelled you, knows your location exactly, and is heading for the other end of the forest.

One evening in September, just after the first frost, I heard a strange call coming from the grove behind my home in Minnesota. Was it a hawk calling after dark? It seemed to come from a height. Could it be a calf or sheep? It was too high-pitched and strident to be a cow. My brother and I circled the grove. The sound stopped, then recurred after we had returned to the house. It was part whistle, part bleat, part bird call. Not until a friend returned from Alaska with a deer call did I know that we had been listening to a deer, something few hunters have ever heard.

I have tried repeatedly to call deer, with records and with a variety of homemade and store-bought calls. Not once have I had any response, even from deer grazing in sight of me. Something is wrong with every device I have tried, even one that a friend of mine used to call in two bucks in Alaska within five minutes of the time he started calling. I have tried rattling a stick against brush to approximate the sound of a buck thrashing a small tree, but without success, although some of my friends have brought out deer that way.

Away from home I have had better luck at calling game. In southern Nepal, in the magnificent jungle just below the foothills of the Himalayas, I was driving by jeep along a forest trail when ahead of me stood a sleek, dark nilghai, so big and fat he seemed more hippo than antelope. He crashed into the dense brush. I stopped the car and listened. Presently he started calling—a low grunting sound. I answered. And so did he! We kept up a dialogue as he started circling. In all modesty I must say I was magnificent, to my ears at least. The big antelope approached the road. I got my camera ready but he flipped across the road too fast for me. He continued circling from the other side now, coming closer and closer. Had I known that a nilghai buck can be dangerous when he charges, my pulse might have beat even faster. Our conversation grew quicker as he came closer. I could even hear him breathe. And there he stood, just out of sight. I decided to get out and stand on the hood to snap a shot. The instant I opened the door, he leaped away and I saw a flash of blue-gray as he returned to the jungle. Perhaps even without calling, he would have circled to look me over. But I choose to think it was our conversation that kept him there.

In your hunting, with or without gun or camera, make sure you have a compass so you can go without worrying about being lost. My friend Pete Leet, an inveterate card player and hunter, suggests a deck of cards instead of a compass.

"It's easy," he says. "All you do if you're lost is sit down on a stump and start playing a game of solitaire and someone is sure to come up and show you your next play."

So much for deer. Other creatures of the winter woods will charm you, too. Whenever I am truly lost, it seems, I hear an animated conversation not far off. I can almost distinguish the voices of my friends—but not quite. The words don't quite come through. The sound is a little too raucous, too. Slowly I realize I am listening to a pair of ravens deep in some intimate conversation. The effect is uncanny, and makes me shiver. They seem to be talking of Stygian things. Now and then they laugh. It is hard to tell where the sound is coming from. Occasionally they fly over and give the sound of a bell ringing. Why can't I ever listen to ravens when I am not worried about finding my way home?

There are other voices in the deep woods—the Canada jays, which light in a tree a few feet away, looking for a handout, associating the sight of man with food. Woodcutters call them lumberjacks or whiskeyjacks and feed them table scraps. If a cabin door is open the bird will fly in, help himself to bacon or eggs or bread and fly out. Hence another of his names: camp robber. As children we liked to visit my father's lumber camp and when the cook wasn't looking, we'd open the kitchen door and let the whiskeyjacks in.

If you listen in the deep woods away from camp you might hear one of them singing, slow and often sweet, interspersed with croaks and whistles. Canada jays sing most in midwinter, and nest in January and February. Snow may cover the brooding bird, but no matter. The male keeps his mate well fed. There are strong family ties among camp robbers. In May, a fully grown youngster, slaty gray all over, slammed into my car as I was driving past a swamp. I stopped and started backing up to identify the bird. Two adult jays were already sitting at the side of the dead bird.

The winter woods at times may seem lifeless and empty. But look closely. Watch every flick of action. There, right beside you, may be a weasel, so white that all that betrays him is the black of his tail. Sometimes in dim light it seems I must be watching a big cricket hopping over the snow. What vitality!

After dark in the Poconos one November I saw a mouse searching through the fallen leaves, moving straight toward where I sat. Only it wasn't a mouse, but an infinitesimal bird, creeping rather than walking to within a few inches of my foot. It was the tiny winter wren, smaller than the house wren, and capable of some of the most intricate singing in the bird world.

Listen closely to the sounds of winter. On a still, cold day the noise you are sure is a deer stealing past is actually a mouse, foraging in a brush pile. So silent are the woods at times that the smallest sounds seem magnified. Squirrels in winter often make more noise by far than deer. A ruffed grouse is another noisy one, and going to roost at night it often snaps twigs that you feel sure could only be broken by some big animal.

Sometimes the sounds of midwinter are startling.

Two tree trunks rubbing against one another in the wind make long wails and moans. Now and then a basswood or maple splits in the intense cold with the sound of a rifle.

How lucky for wildlife that trees do crack open, for rot will probably begin and the hollow heart that eventually forms will be a fortress for many a beleaguered animal as well as home for raccoons, flying squirrels, wood ducks, and honeybees.

On a night in January anywhere in the United States listen for the call of the great horned owl, that magnificent hunter who nests in February in some second-hand crow or hawk nest, and broods during the snow and cold of subzero winters. Its best-known call is like a distant dog barking, pitched around middle C. But it has an astonishing variety of chuckles, growls, and screams. The owl I kept for a time would close his eyes and whistle a soft, contented song when I stroked his back feathers or scratched him under the chin.

All of a sudden on your winter walk the snow will explode at your feet and out will come a ruffed grouse—a startling experience. Grouse are said to dive into soft snow a foot or two to escape cold nights. I have never seen them do it, but on several occasions I have seen them erupt a few feet ahead of me from an otherwise placid snowbank.

You can see much in winter that is hidden in summer. Hornets' nests loom up big and dark. Take one home with you and study its exterior and interior design. Don't worry about hornets inside. There aren't any. Only the female lives over winter, and she lies hidden in some sheltered spot.

Winter is the time to look for birds' nests. They stand out sharp and clear. There is no harm done in gathering them now. Except for hawks and a few others, birds almost never use their last year's structure.

My prize nest is a yellow-throated vireo's, which Headstrom in his fine field guide to nests describes this way: "Cup-shaped; of bark strips and plant fibers; lined with finer grasses; beautifully adorned with lichens and cocoons held in place with caterpillars' silk and spiders' webs; often placed in an oak tree." My hummingbird nest, a dainty jewel held together with nothing stronger than spider webs, is forty years old and survives after having been passed along rows of children in all the rural schools of the county for each of those forty years. Another gem is a wood pewee's flat nest that looks as if it grew out of the oak branch it rests on.

The goldfinch nest is an architectural triumph. Mine is made out of nothing more substantial than thistledown and wool, and appears to be floating above the branch it rests on, yet it is strong and firmly attached.

Certainly the worst nest I own is that of the crested flycatcher that nested one year in my purple martin house. I had promised a surprise to my nephew Dan, who held the ladder for me while I climbed up and brought down the contents.

We were both surprised. The nest was simply an accumulation of rubbish and feathers as I had expected. But scattered through it were the mummified remains of five half-grown nestlings, probably the result of our town's mosquito spraying.

Dan's surprise was the snakeskins looped around the grass and feathers. Why does the bird always have a snakeskin or two in its nest? he asked, eyes alight with that wonder which is the sacred gift of childhood. It did no good to say that nobody knows for sure, that sentimental people who like to believe that birds think like humans say that the bird hopes to scare away snakes from its nest. But few snakes crawl a tree to the heights that crested flycatchers go to build their nest in a hollow trunk. The snakeskins give no warmth or durability. Why then? he repeated, knowing that grownups possess all answers, if only they will offer them. Once again I had to disappoint him. We counted the skins. The nest had five of them, the most I had ever found. But no amount of skins could guard the young against man's insecticides.

There are pleasant souvenirs to bring home: the seed pods of wild roses, called rose hips, which never seem so vivid as in midwinter; shelf fungi; the leaves of ferns, some of them green in midwinter. I like the thickened stems of goldenrods, the swollen home that forms around the larva of a wasp that inserts its minute egg into the stem's interior.

Winter is the time to study the leaf-scars of trees—the belly buttons that mark the attachment of last summer's leaves. The nut trees especially have fascinating scars: puckish faces that differ by species enough to differentiate trees by leaf-scars alone. Children, with their sharp eyes, will delight in studying them, and may be moved to start a collection.

In the most frigid weather I have found snow fleas, no bigger than a grain of wheat, hopping on the snow. How their body juices can stay thawed is a conundrum. What they are feeding on is another mystery, although during maple-tapping season they like to dip into our buckets of sap.

During a snowstorm and on intensely cold days few creatures, unless disturbed, are moving about; most lie in their burrows or in the shelter of a brush pile or clump of grass, or among the dense branches of spruce and cedar. But on the first warm day there is a frenzy of activity.

Just look at the pawprints. Here is the delicate lacework of a pine mouse out prospecting after new food sources. His trail is a necklace of intricate white. Perhaps a weasel has gone by, his tiny paws leaving twin dots some eighteen inches apart; he was a big one, and in a hurry, too. There is rare beauty in tracks, and mystery. Following them is like solving a puzzle or reading a whodunit. Once you find the animal, the spell is gone. You can follow the animal with your eyes. There is no more wondering about his mission. Now it is all escape.

A light fall of giant flakes covers your jacket. And what hunter is there who can help but pause to look at them, holding his breath to preserve them a moment longer.

There is a way of preserving them, using a plastic called Formvar dissolved in ethylene dichloride. The Monsanto Company, Bircham Bend Plant, Springfield, Mass., supplies a sample free just for writing. With a supply on hand, next time the big flakes fall, go outside with a piece of glass the size of the slides for your projector, and a piece of dark cloth, both of them well chilled. Put a drop of the chemical on the glass with a glass stirring rod or something like it, then wait for fine specimen flakes falling on the cloth. Touch the flake you want with the rod and transfer it onto the drop. The flake will sink into the solution, leaving a permanent imprint in plastic. Leave the slide outdoors until the flake "sublimates" directly into the air. Then you'll have a transparency you can project onto a screen. Experts can tell from the makeup of a flake the kind of weather it encountered on its long journey down to earth. You can preserve the beauty of a frosted window pane, too, by painting or pouring a thin coat of the solution over the frost, letting it dry, and then peeling it off. Certain kinds of clear plastic in spray cans are said to work too.

There is pattern to winter as in no other season—in snowflakes, in animal tracks, and in the filigree of black limbs and twigs of branches against the winter sky, like the screens carved of alabaster in a Persian mosque. The spiked tops of black spruce become the spires of Notre Dame. There is pattern, form, and meaning.

Each dark rock that protrudes through the snow is a solar stove warming a multitude of creeping and crawling things below and beside it. Beneath the snowy mound in the marsh is a warm, snug muskrat family dining on the roots they stored during summer. And deep below the snow of what seems to be a lifeless earth are sleeping things—bloodroot and wild ginger and yellow bellwort and giant trillium, and here and there a chipmunk quietly dreams in that state of nirvana akin to death, waiting only the restless winds of spring to bring him back to life. Quiet, restful winter and the glorious spring that inevitably follows are all I need to know of resurrection. I cannot understand them, but I know they exist.

If a deer has slipped by me in my reveries, no matter. My kind of hunting is always a success.

# 9 ❧ A word for the condemned

ON A NIGHT IN WINTER I stood on the back step of the machine shed where we lived for a few years before our big house was built and looked out over the moonlit snow of the fields. The air seemed jagged with tiny icicles that pierced my light shirt and made my skin tingle. Suddenly a sound came across the snow from the pasture, a series of woofs that rose in pitch and tempo, then deepened into a single throaty wail like the beginning of an air raid alarm, then trailed off into space. I reached for the door behind me; my heart started thumping. I had just heard a timber wolf! The wail seemed powerful, and nearby; yet I knew he was beyond the pasture gate, at least a quarter mile off. For long moments the sound hung suspended like a jet trail in the thin cold air.

I have heard that same kind of lament: in the cold fury of John L. Lewis and again in the voice of Martin Luther King crying out against the odds of black existence. The timber wolf, too—through no other fault than that he was born—must battle for survival until he draws his last dying breath.

Twice again I have heard the timber wolf like the cry of the damned. Even far off his voice is magnificent, a lonely call more sad than angry, and deeply personal, speaking of lost hopes and disappointments and soul-weariness. It is a mistake, I suppose, to read all this into the call of the timber wolf. Perhaps his wail is a rallying call to assemble others of the pack. Perhaps it is what Konrad Lorenz calls a "displacement activity"—something an animal does to release its energy when another activity goes wrong. Anthropomorphically speaking, I like that idea. How often I have felt like lifting back my head and howling: at bureaucracy, red tape, racists, and especially at negative, do-nothing pessimists who masquerade under the name of "realists."

Students who have studied wolves minutely still can't explain a timber wolf's wail. The yap it makes when it returns to the den with food is something else, much like that of the coyote or brush wolf we used to hear nearly every afternoon as we were sitting in the grain field eating lunch. That was a happy yapping, joined in by the young for a few excited seconds. We could almost see the parent lugging in a rabbit, proud of himself, as the young fawned and twisted and curled, waiting for the first grab.

In northern Minnesota no subject—including politics—generates quite as much heat as the timber wolf. Conservationists say there are only a few hundred left in the United States, outside of Alaska, and that nearly all are in Minnesota. They say that the timber wolf preys on old and ailing wild animals, for the most part, and therefore helps keep the deer herd healthy. Careful studies of the ecology of Isle Royale in Lake Superior prove that both timber wolves and moose are necessary for the well-being of one another—at least on that 44-by-8-mile island. Farmers and many hunters are furious at such a suggestion. They point out that sheep raising needs no such balance, nor does the deer population, and that coyotes and wolves ought to be killed off by any means: trapping, poisoning, or shooting. The voices of dissent to such a view are feeble in this area.

The first timber wolf in the memory of this community was a killer, unfortunately. He must have strayed south from the Canadian wilderness during the 1930's when timber wolves were unheard of. My friend Algot Wicken caught him in a snare near Itasca State Park, headwaters of the Mississippi, but the snare broke loose from its moorings, and the wolf went free. The noose remained so tight that the wolf lay in the swamp for days, choking, until he lost enough weight to breathe. Algot tried in vain to catch him, both by snare and trap, but from that day on—through what seemed like some divine prescience—he avoided snares completely.

His tracks in the snow might show where he came catapulting down a slope, then stopped dead still just as he would have entered the noose. He made foraging circuits about thirty miles in diameter that took about a week to complete. Now and then he would be seen, pausing before he crossed a road. Wonder of wonders, there was steam coming out of a hole in his neck. The buckle of the snare must have worn a hole in his throat! He came to live primarily on deer, according to trappers and hunters who took his trail, and in a week was known to have killed a dozen. It appeared sometimes as if he waited on an uprooted tree along a deer trail, then leaped on them and broke their backs.

Posses were organized to hunt him down, but he always eluded them. Radio stations broadcast his journeys. A reward was offered. One inhabitant of a work camp, walking home by moonlight after a night of drinking, found himself being trailed by the wolf. He lit matches as he walked, faster and faster, and when his matches ran out he took to walking backward, with such preoccupation that he is said to have fallen rear foremost over the doorsill of the camp. Once a farmer in his pickup suddenly found the wolf running easily beside him, looking in at him without a sign of fear. He must have been big, folks said, because he broke through the ice that held a 200-pound man. Of such is the fabric of folklore. Many of the stories were undoubtedly true. But maverick or crippled animals are a poor indicator of the habits of the average.

In the Red Lake area in northern Minnesota, the tracks of a pair that I have been watching for several years indicate that they spend much of their time hunting beaver. In the winter they might well prey on deer, but it would seem that snowshoe hares would be far easier to catch during their periods of cyclic abundance.

It is going to be hard to find a compromise between agriculture and conservation. What I tell my farmer friends (and relatives) is that compromise for the sake of the common good is the very nature of democracy, and that—like it or not—the public will eventually demand and get protection for timber wolves and perhaps for coyotes, too. Because for every one farmer today there are ten nonfarmers, and many of them are nature-minded. And if predators force farmers in one area out of sheep, there are plenty of other places here and abroad that can grow sheep. How much better if sheep and cattle growers themselves propose their own solution that might be acceptable to a majority of Americans, yet permit them to continue farming? How about creating sanctuaries in which big predators were given priority over livestock production?

The Red Lake area in northern Minnesota might be such a sanctuary. It is a vast, swampy wilderness of tamarack and black spruce and cedar, interrupted by long sand ridges that mark the beaches of old glacial reservoirs. Only the Everglades, and perhaps the Great Dismal Swamp and Okefenokee Swamp, may be bigger. Roads follow the sand ridges and old ditch banks that date back to a time when the area was farmed. From these small roads you might with rare luck see a wolf—the only place this side of Alaska where this is possible. Timber wolves wouldn't necessarily stay within such an area. In fact, naturalists are finding that they range a hundred miles and more in their ordinary travels. But farmers could be compensated for their losses, and individual wolves that develop into livestock killers could be hunted down and killed. And so, seed stock of our magnificent predator could be safeguarded.

Such an arrangement would not satisfy certain hunters.

The same impulse that causes the most domestic, hearth-loving cat to turn tiger seems innate in many of us. Like a cat, we feel impelled not only to kill but to lug home our booty for approval. The bigger, the more ferocious the animal, the better. A timber wolf is still a prize, and confers on its killer a kind of proof of manhood. Apparently this is a trait of mankind no less real among sophisticated people than among the most primitive, who advertise their prowess with tiger teeth and bear claws round their neck. (So don't be too harsh with the boy who brings home a hawk on his first foray with a .22 rifle. He is obeying an age-old impulse. Your job—if you feel you must equip him with a gun—is to direct him to a rifle range.)

Coyotes and wolves have little chance against the snowmobile. So far they haven't learned—as the fox did quickly—that moving back and forth through fences tired out the pursuers. Wolves travel in a straight line toward brush and thickets, and are tired out and killed. A group of snowmobilers quickly surround a wolf and slaughter him. There is just no escape.

State legislatures will need to hurry through legislation to protect predators from snowmobilers.

In Michigan, shooting a wolf can get you a fine of $100 and up to ninety days in jail—penalties pretty hard to bring on, because the state has only about fifty wolves left. In Wisconsin, a wolf-killer can get up to six months in jail—again an unlikely penalty, since there are probably no more than twenty-five wolves left there.

Some states protect the black bear, realizing he is a fine citizen and a rare natural resource; other states permit him to be shot any time, anywhere, on sight. I think I know what prompts men to rush home to fetch their rifles whenever they see one. It is the chance to overcome the villain of our childhood, the terror of our dreams, and thereby vanquish that lingering fear of the dark which most men in their candid moments will admit to. I have beat the bushes to oust a mother bear and her cub from a thicket in our pasture while my brother waited with a rifle from the vantage of a lumber truck. Which of my emotions was uppermost I don't know: hope for success, sympathy for the bear, or downright fright. There had been no question about whether or not to go after the bear. It was doing no harm, but it was a bear, and all of us had grown up anti-bear.

Just how would you try to chase a she-bear with a cub? If I moved quietly through the dense brush, she might catch my scent and run, yet she wouldn't know my exact whereabouts and be able to ambush me. If I made a prodigious racket, she might be frightened and keep her distance. Then again she might wait for me, knowing exactly when to rush me. It was growing dark, almost pitch dark in the densest parts of the woods. Involuntarily I chose racket, singing and shouting and barking, wondering what sounds are most frightening to a bear. Suddenly—a stone's throw from me—there came a muffled thrashing of brush as the she-bear and cub decided to run from the violent creature that had invaded their woods. They escaped, and so did I. Later that summer my brother and I again went bear-hunting, this time at night to a cornfield where we could hear the bear twisting off ears and husking them.

"See, here's his trail," my brother whispered as we stopped at the edge of the field. "Look how he's knocked down the fence. Let's wait for him here and surprise him." I whispered that I'd be glad to surprise him from a tree, that I'd rather the bear wasn't too surprised.

"No, we've got to lie down on the ground, to keep our silhouette low. A bear holds his head so low to the ground he can see anything above two feet or so, especially at night against the skyline." That meant lying prone.

"What's the matter, you're not scared?" my brother said. "You've got a gun." Then he promptly fell off to sleep. But sleep was not in me. I'm clumsy with a gun. I can't find the safety and sometimes not even the trigger. And I know no bear would wait for me to find them. I could feel him swatting the gun from my hands. As long as the snapping sounds continued, I felt fairly easy. But there were long spells of absolute silence—from the cornfield, that is. My own heart was pounding so loud I knew I couldn't hear a bear's soft footfalls. The quiet from the field persisted for what I knew must be an hour. I awoke my brother and told him.

"OK, you wait here and I'll chase him out to you," he said.

I protested that he was a better shot, that he should wait and I'd chase. I circled the field quietly and entered from the far side.

Once again, I found myself torn between making a prodigious racket and stealing quietly through. This time I did a modified yipping. How I wished I had clipped that coupon ten years before that would have sent me the secret of throwing my voice! Now I could only swivel my head as I shouted and hope that my exact whereabouts would be at least blurred a little. Now and then I listened for a rushing sound. None came. So I went on deeper into the pitch darkness of the field, spraying my voice around me like a garden sprinkler. Still no bear. The nearer I came to the fence where my brother lay the surer I was that the bear would suddenly take some kind of action, and the louder I yelled. But no bear. Sometime during the night he must have left by another route.

"Look," I told my brother, "I'm glad he's already left. I feel more bear than human right now. That guy hasn't done a thing to bother us. Why do we hunt him?"

And my brother, who is an honest man, couldn't answer. Even years later, after a bear had killed a dozen of his sheep, he still didn't become a bear hunter. He respects them, and feels the same kinship I do with them: like us, bears love the forest, picking wild berries, fishing for big, fat suckers just as the ice leaves the lakes. They too get carried away by the excitement of the sucker run and slap out far more than they can eat, just as we sometimes do. And when their compulsion to eat comes upon them in late summer and fall, believe me, we know the feeling. On a cold midwinter morning, sometimes I think of the bear snoozing in some hole below a tipup, who needs only to yawn, roll over and go back to sleep for a few more weeks.

Minnesota in 1971 declared the bear a game animal, protected all year except during an open season. Praises be!

Other outcasts of nature I like too. Bobcats and lynx have the dignity of all cats, but unlike the lazy domestic kind, care for themselves and thereby earn the right to wear their cloak of dignity.

Hawks, too, have that same independence. They need fear nothing but man and are therefore not furtive, as most other birds must be. A hawk can fly unafraid, and unharried except for an occasional nesting blackbird. They can light on a topmost branch and peer out over the countryside at leisure. Around their nests they are fearless, sometimes attacking an intruder, and making an easy target for a boy with a gun. Like wolves and bears, hawks are considered proper targets in most states, and hitting one is a mark of manhood. Hunters used to justify shooting them because of the chickens one or two species occasionally stole, but with almost no more chickens grown outdoors, they talk now about the way hawks kill wildlife, carry off lambs and even babies, depending upon the degree of listener and lecturer intelligence.

The fact is that each of the fifteen or so kinds of hawks has quite different foraging habits. The dainty sparrow hawk, hovering above a hayfield, is waiting to pounce on a grasshopper or perhaps a mouse. Only once have I seen it catch a sparrow. A pair have taken to nesting in my grove in a tall aspen stub hollowed out by woodpeckers, and their busy wheeling and hovering and calling to their young are delightful. During migration time, the sharp-shinned and Cooper's are here, and the birds at the feeders are alert, spooking at every passing shadow.

It is true that sharp-shinned and Cooper's both feed on smaller birds, but what few people realize is that most of those small birds may already be weakened by disease. The sharp-shin that swoops down on a flock of house sparrows may appear to be diving at the lot of them, helter-skelter. Actually, he is after a single bird that he may have been chasing half a day.

Occasionally a hawk follows a bird right inside one of Paul Fluck's banding traps and may partly eat the bird before discovering that it is trapped. Almost invariably the remains of the bird indicate that it had been sick with a disease manifested by swollen or ulcerated feet. Other healthy birds in the trap will be untouched. Naturalists who have spent all their lives in the field testify that bird-killing hawks are important to keeping down diseases that might otherwise become epidemic.

The larger hawks, which feed on mice, ground squirrels, and rabbits, are exciting, beautiful birds, too. One summer a pair of magnificent goshawks stayed in the vicinity, swooping over the fields, dive-bombing and banking, then speeding like an arrow through the thick trees. It seemed incredible that they didn't crack up against limbs. I was walking my fence line in the middle of a patch of woods when I realized I was near their nest. They screamed and perched, watching me. And there up thirty feet in the crotch of an oak was the nest, about three feet across. Returning a month later, I found no trace of either bird. A neighbor—who has since moved—had killed them both, telling me how hard they had fought for life even lying on the ground. It was like the loss of friends; part of my pleasure that summer was gone. No goshawk has since returned.

Another superb hawk is the big, courageous red-tail, soaring almost out of sight in the clear sky, only now and then flashing the red of his tail as he banks on an upcurrent of air. So keen is his eyesight—equal to our own with 8-power glasses—that even at that height he can spot a ground squirrel. The hearing of some hawks is equally remarkable. Try out the hearing of a marsh hawk next time you see one. Hide yourself in a clump of weeds or back of a ditch bank and wait until he is downwind. Then suck the back of your hand, making a few small squeaking sounds like a mouse. Now sit still. The hawk seems to disappear, but actually drops just above grass height and homes on that sound with such accuracy that he will seldom miss your location more than a foot or two.

The speed of hawks in flight is thrilling. Most birds are fairly slow. Sparrows, wrens, and flycatchers rarely do above twenty miles an hour, and the bigger ones—grackles, robins, meadowlarks, and water birds like herons, gulls, and pelicans—generally keep between twenty and thirty miles an hour. Faster flyers are flickers, mourning doves, and starlings, which normally do between thirty and forty miles an hour. Still faster are ducks, geese, and common barnyard pigeons that rocket along from forty to sixty miles an hour. But the peregrine falcon in a power dive goes at twice that speed.

The place to see the real speed and grace of hawks in

flight, swooping and sailing, is during migration, spring
or fall, along some mountain ridge. The sight is unforgettable. The most famous observation point is at
Hawk Mountain about seventy-five miles above Philadelphia. Here the warm rocks of the mountains send up
air currents that push the birds skyward. They can mi-
grate along the ridge without moving a muscle, simply
by inclining their bodies downward, wings partly folded
like the paper planes we made as children. As you
watch, small specks in the sky grow larger and a shout
comes up from the other spectators scattered among the
rocks. In a few seconds the birds sweep into view, their
bodies and wings frozen, immobile as the sacred falcons
on the tombs of the Pharaohs. One by one they sail past
in silence, tense and rigid like skiers racing down a
slope, and you all but feel the exhilaration of the wind
in their faces. Their aerodynamics as they ride the up-
currents is a marvel to watch. Sometimes one of them
peels off and lets the current hoist him aloft. Another
might bank and sail back. Another might plummet out
of sight in the tangle of greens that clothe the moun-
tainside. Some days the birds skim over the mountain
top so close that observers feel the rush of their wings.

Early in the fall come the broad-winged hawks. Later
the red-shouldered and red-tailed hawks follow. From
time to time there are eagles, both bald and golden.
Only fifteen years ago, hunters shot them by the
hundreds in the name of sport. Now some of the same
men are watching with binoculars. Hunters, I repeat,
aren't necessarily lost souls. Hawk Mountain, as well as
nearby Bake Oven Knob, is now a sanctuary.

Less well known as observing posts during fall migration are the shores of the Great Lakes, particularly the
heights above Duluth. Here broad-wings—five hundred
and up to a thousand at a time—arc across the sky like
the Milky Way. Periodically they spiral upwards in what
hawk-watchers call a "kettle," riding strong thermals

from the warm water below. Up and up they circle in tighter and tighter spirals until they seem to boil out of sight. Hawks practice this kettling during summer whenever they find such thermals. Now it's the real thing and you can sense the excitement, even though you can barely see them with binoculars as they flash in and out of the clouds. Eventually they peel off in level straight flight, gliding on without effort to the next thermal. An occasional eagle moves with them, as well as ospreys, redtails, sharpshins, sparrow hawks and a rare peregrine.

Get yourself to a nearby hawk-watching post in September, along with a thermos of hot coffee and sandwiches. The best posts are nearly always windy and cold, and if the day is right, you won't want to leave till dark. Hawk migrations are among the most exciting sights in all outdoors. For the best hawk-watching near you, consult Olin Pettingill's *Guide to Bird Finding East of the Mississippi,* or its Western equivalent.

Let us hope that before it is too late, hawks are given nation-wide protection. We need them for the sake of a balanced ecology, but even more for their singular beauty and the touch of wonder they add to a cloudless sky as they appraise the world from high on soaring wings.

Even nation-wide protection may not be enough. The bald eagle, though carefully protected, continues its sharp decline. I was never more conscious of the loss than a few weeks ago when I returned to northern Manitoba to fish with my Cree friend Neal Cook, who loves bald eagles.

"What do you do with our eagles in the States?" he asked. In the area around Cedar Lake where we fish, thirteen pairs nested last year. This year only a single pair returned!

Revisiting Japan a few years ago I stopped to see my friend, Umeko Akahane or "Miss Plumblossom," who owns and operates the delightful Akahane Restaurant in Tokyo. I was surprised and a little disappointed that she no longer kept falcons. They used to sit in wicker cages below the eaves and at night when she moved back small sliding doors, you could see them from indoors, blinking in the bright light. Before the war Miss Plumblossom had been the premier woman falconer of all Japan; her uncle has been chief falconer to the Emperor. Now she had turned her birds loose. She tried to tell me why.

"They are too beautiful to be in jail," she said in her fragile English. "They love freedom too much." I quite agree.

Owls, too, are favorites of mine. Bold, self-sufficient, and dignified, they enforce a nightly curfew on small birds and mammals. I know most of the owls quite well, except for the barn owl, whose breeding range doesn't extend quite as far as northern Minnesota. I did learn to know one barn owl pretty well, however. It was a blind bird (detached retinas) that had become a permanent resident of Paul Fluck's bird hospital.

"This is the bird that gives deserted houses such a bad reputation," Paul said, tipping the bird upside down for a moment and causing it to wail and moan in supernatural agony.

"He's light, mostly feathers," Paul went on, handing me the bird. I was clumsy and missed, but not the sightless bird, which snapped shut one needle-sharp talon on my middle finger, and from the instant tingling sensation I knew he had reached the bone. You can't pull away from such a grip (remember that the next time you get in an owl's clutches). What you do is extend the owl's leg to the limit, then unclasp each toe. Next day when my finger swelled to dangerous proportions, my doctor phoned a surgeon.

"Here's one you won't believe," he said, describing my predicament, and the cause.

"Had one exactly like it last week," was the response.

I was hurried home to bed, where I was not to get up even to eat until the swelling subsided. Owls are immensely appealing to most people, especially the little saw-whet and screech owls. But the big horned owl—which makes off with an occasional ruffed grouse, pheasant, or domestic turkey—is unprotected in many states and often shot by hunters. What a shame for such a gallant bird!

My favorite of all owls is an Arctic visitor that appears in midwinter every five or six years when the supply of lemmings is low. I was playing Santa Claus at my nephew's home one Christmas Eve and had just emptied the sack and delivered a final ho-ho-ho when my nephew offered me a large cardboard box. "And now we have something for Santa Claus to take back to the North Pole," he said. Pulling my white beard out of the way, I looked inside the box to see a magnificent snowy owl, almost completely white, with only a few brown flecks, therefore probably a male. The big bird winked a knowing eye at me as if he could see beneath my mask.

My nephew had found him, unable to fly, that very evening and had brought him inside and fed him a handful of hamburger. The bird had promptly eaten the meat from his hand, carefully searching the palm and around the fingers for stray shreds. Here was a bird from the treeless Arctic, a habitat like few others in the world, which had immediately adapted to a brand-new situation in a radically changed environment.

Even though helpless, there was no terror in the bird, no wild attempts to escape, no threatening gestures. Perhaps hunger had dulled those reactions; except that the bird continued to be tame, even when—well-fed—he sat in a pasteboard box that I carried aboard a Northwest Airlines flight for Philadelphia.

"What do you have there," asked the stewardess, "a kitty?"

"No," I said, surprised that she could sense that my

box held anything alive. I didn't know—and didn't want to ask—whether or not the airline would permit such a cargo in personal luggage.

"Is it a doggy?" she asked. "No," I said.

"Then what is it?"

"An owl," I said.

She turned and left. I promptly fell asleep. I awakened with the feeling that someone was hovering over me, and there was—the hostess, waiting for me to awaken. She was practically breathless with excitement.

"You *have* an owl in that box!" she said. She had gone back to look in on the pet animal, bending down to peer with one eye into the hole I had made (directly through the "o" of MONARCH to escape detection). She found herself eyeball to eyeball with something big and fierce and unknown. Yet she was so intrigued that she opened the top to get a better look, and her delight with the bird summoned almost everyone in the plane for a look, including pilot, co-pilot, and navigator—all the while I slept. Not only had my owl and I escaped CAA regulations, we were something of celebrities—I think—as we left the plane.

The pilot suggested we submit a testimonial to the home office: "When a snowy owl flies east, of course he flies Northwest."

At a New Year's Eve party on our return to Philadelphia, the owl was a featured guest. He sat on the edge of the hors d'oeuvres table in profound dignity all evening. I warned people that his talons could tear out eyes or pieces of flesh, and that he should be studied at a distance, but they ignored my cautions, stroking him under the chin, which he loved, closing his eyes and murmuring a soft whistle.

As we left the party, descending in an elevator, a new operator was on hand. He was startled at first, then recovered.

"Where are you taking him now—to an all-night movie?"

I had hoped that the owl would recover full use of his wing so he could fly free—something he never did. Yet he didn't seem to mind his handicap or the restraints of apartment life.

Experts in bird behavior give owls a low rating in intelligence. But if adaptability is the best single criterion of brain power, I would say the experts are amiss. My owl took to life indoors better than most cats or dogs. When I gave him free rein in the evening, he liked to stand by my chair and watch television—the more action the better. Westerns were his favorites, as they were mine, and his head would follow along with stampeding cattle and galloping horses. When I would leave for work in the morning he seemed to scrutinize my face, and on my return would flap his wings in what seemed to be pleasure.

Keeping a captive owl is something I would never suggest. Owls are dangerous, first of all, and more important, they need their freedom. I tell the story of my snowy owl to demonstrate my belief that owls are wise, and to help engender respect for yet another of our predators that help make our world the exciting spaceship it is.

Man, the greatest predator of all, should admire his fellow hunters who make their living without guns or nets or fishhooks, with only talons and beak and incredible speed and daring. The true friend of nature is one who respects and loves it all—hunters as well as hunted.

To such a friend of nature, even the starling has his good points. He came into his own about the time that America seemed about to be swallowed up by Japanese beetles. Tirelessly, he patrols the lawn, jabbing with his bayonet beak and looking down the hole with eyes that are attached at each corner of his mouth. Sighting down

ABOVE: The larvae of moths like this one each spun half a mile of silk in my living room. Growing moths is a delight for the young and young in spirit. *Chapter 4*

PHOTO BY HARPO DEXTER

BELOW: A master at masquerade. When you're small and tasty, you need to look dangerous. Those eyes are not eyes, the mouth no mouth. No part of his head is visible here. *Page 238*

PHOTO BY KARL H. MASLOWSKI

ABOVE: Some birds, like some people, prefer a crowd. Here cormorants—and one blue heron—etch a Japanese print on the sky at our Agassiz Refuge.

U.S. FISH & WILDLIFE SERVICE BY C. J. HENRY

RIGHT: A tern in a courtship rite above Red Lake has dropped a fish to its mate, who has caught it in midair, and will ascend and return it.

RIGHT: Our Canada geese—the *maxima* strain—like people and talk with them by voice and neck movements. We hope they prosper when released in our northern lakes. *Page 99*

BELOW: This box is one of thirty on a farm which produced 387 wood ducks in one summer. *Chapter 5*

PHOTO BY JACK DERMID

LEFT: Killdeer in a quandary: Should she stay to shield her brood, or fly off with the evidence that draws crows? *Page 102*
BELOW: The crested flycatcher, which decks its nest with snake skins. Bold and cheerful, it's a lively guest. Our pair hatched a brood, which succumbed half-grown when our village sprayed. None have returned. *Page 131*
PHOTO BY JACK DERMID

All these love bogs and swampy lake edges and need them to survive, but their pleas go unheard. Developers and engineers have the money, the power, the votes. *Chapter 6*
PHOTO BY WALTER H. WETTSCHRECK

ABOVE AND RIGHT: My favorite habitat. To enjoy it, you need a boardwalk, boots, or a pair of feet that don't mind getting wet. *Chapter 6*

BELOW: I can't quite believe a beaver dam. Beavers hold back acres of water—without axe, wheelbarrow, or shovel—so easily they spend much of the time just enjoying life. *Pages 97–9*

LEFT: A riddle: What formed these mounds —forty feet wide by seven feet high—that dot 30,000 acres of prairie? *See Chapter 7*

ABOVE: A ruffed grouse spent the night here. To escape cold (and pursuing predators) it often plunges into soft snow. *Page 130*

BELOW: Reading the news: The snow is a late night extra of who's in town and what's doing. *Page 132*

LEFT: Eyes glowing, a deer feasts on apple drops outside our window. A tissue in the eyes acts like a mirror to reflect additional light onto the retina. *Chapter 8*

ABOVE: Man demands a villain, and here he is, damned because he shares man's taste for fresh meat. Except for Alaska, the timber wolf is almost extinct in the U.S. *Chapter 9*

RIGHT: Cubs at our Itasca Park. I feel akin to bears. They too like fishing, blueberries, and just plain eating. Only bear mothers and park panhandlers are dangerous. *Chapter 9*

LEFT AND ABOVE: A fearless mother, this weasel defended her young, then moved them to safer quarters. An occasional one comes in winter to the feeder by our back door. *Chapter 10*

BELOW: Though an accomplished robber, he trails a long clue. *Chapter 10*

PHOTO BY HARPO DEXTER

America's evangelist for nature is Paul H. Fluck, a pioneer in nature education. BELOW, in his nature center on Grand Bahama, he shows the lizard whose tail is food for migrating killdeer. *Page 62; Chapter 14*

FREEPORT, GRAND BAHAMA PORT AUTHORITY, LTD.

ABOVE: This muff of needles—a witch's broom—is a limb gone berserk. Its seeds produce genetic dwarfs. What singled out this one limb in an entire forest? *Page 234*
BELOW: The twin spires of this spruce keep precisely in step with each other. How does one tip—by fibrous roadway, a hundred feet away—signal the other? *Page 235*

the rifle-barrel of his own beak is a trick only the starling can perform. As far as usurping nesting boxes of martins and bluebirds, this is easily remedied. Simply set out enough homes for everybody. Then set out to bury your prejudices against starlings. You'll find them more interesting than bluebirds, I believe.

One summer I heard what sounded like a flock of chickens off in the distance, with roosters crowing occasionally, and I was glad for the sounds. You hardly hear a good crowing rooster any more. For several days I wondered whose flock it might be, until I found that the sounds were coming from my old walnut tree. A male starling was singing there, and his mimicry was so perfect I could not have recognized it until I saw the source. How it could make several sounds simultaneously I have never been able to understand. A starling's mimicry of other birds, though often whispered and soft, is remarkably accurate, and suggests their close relationship with the mynah bird of India. A fledgling starling, confined in a home in Philadelphia so that it never heard other bird songs, suddenly began speaking in complete sentences with such clarity that few in an audience which listened to a tape recording made by my friend, George Reynard, could believe it wasn't a human speaking. I have heard an occasional starling mimic a policeman's whistle. Most commonly starlings mimic the calls of birds they feed with in the country: meadowlarks, killdeer, and sometimes robins.

The intelligence of starlings is all but legendary. Paul Fluck tells about a pair that found a hole in the siding of the old Nature Education Center building at Washington Crossing. Sometime just before the young were ready to leave, the nest must have fallen down inside of the wall out of reach of the adults. From nowhere, Paul says, a flock of thirty to forty starlings appeared with such squawking that he went to investigate. As fast as they could, all the birds were bringing in twigs and bits of brush and sticks and dropping them into the hole. Paul could hardly believe what he was seeing. Before dark the space between the studding was filled with debris and the young, keeping atop of the mounting pile, emerged. Animal behaviorists warn us not to ascribe this reaction to intelligence, but to a "built-in response" to a situation—whatever that means.

Other birds that have few advocates include the house or English sparrow: street urchin, roustabout, scrounger. During my growing-up days we shot them, tore down their nests, risking our lives to get at some in the topmost recesses of our big barn—for no other reason than that they were dirty and usurped the martin house. It never occurred to us, I think, that we might have put up other martin boxes. Besides, I suppose, children—like childish adults, too—must have villains to hate just as much as heroes to worship. And the sparrows provided that villain.

Once we tore out a nest under the eaves above a martin box, and promptly the sparrows returned, eyed their loss, entered the martin box and threw out the nestling martins, one after another, before we could stop them. "Built-in response" or revenge, it mattered not to me. From then on, we redoubled our anti-sparrow crusade with a fury matched only by the great Chinese national bird-eradication year, when no bird was permitted to alight in peace over the whole subcontinent.

A couple of years ago my farmer brother was feeding grain to his sheep on a subzero day in January. I remarked that the sparrows were eating up his grain.

"They're welcome to it," he said. "Any little bird that is willing to stick it out in the cold with me is my friend." They brightened his long winters, he said. For the first time, I came to look on sparrows as something besides nuisances. I say there are prospects for erasing prejudices in anybody.

It is surprising how many prejudices and misconceptions still persist. "Swallows carry bedbugs and lice," you hear people say as they knock down the mud cups of barn swallows and the marvelous earthen jugs of cliff swallows.

"They're so dirty, too," say others. And it is true that the floor below a barn swallow's nest does get spattered after the young are big enough to perch on the rim of the nest and void over the edge. When the nestlings are smaller, the parents, like many other birds, bring food and then snatch the fecal sac which often immediately follows a feeding, flying off a short ways to drop it. A board below a barn swallow's nest will catch the soil. There is of course no defense against the clouds of cliff swallows that a colony under the eaves of a barn can generate in a summer. But a flock of five hundred or so keeps my nephew's entire farmyard completely free of mosquitoes while nearby farmyards are engulfed in them. Yet many farmers continue to knock down the nests.

There is one swallow that breaks down the hostility and even the indifference of almost everyone. That is the effervescent, eternally optimistic tree swallow.

Two of my good neighbors along the lake bought a fog sprayer—a gadget that unfortunately is both fun to operate and effective—and sprayed their grounds prior to a weekend of visitors. Within two or three days all the young tree swallows in five nests were dead or dying, as well as a nest of crested flycatchers and another of phoebes. To remonstrate was useless. Who cares about birds at a time when mosquitoes are killing you? Such a response is only natural for anyone without an affection for nature, and no amount of argument, letters to the editor, or what have you will change it.

What I did was take a couple of tree swallow boxes over and tell them where to install them. Make sure they're low so you can look in on the mother bird while she's sitting on her eggs, I said, and so you can watch the young ones grow. Visit them every day, because they grow so fast you need to enjoy them the few days they are here. Both boxes got occupants: bluebirds in one and swallows in the other. There has been no spraying since. People's viewpoints can be changed, though seldom by argument. Someday soon I shall tell my good neighbors that the birdhouses were not gifts of generosity but of pure self-interest.

Just what are predators, anyhow? Should we call swallows predators? They're just as determined, fierce, even savage in their hunt for mosquitoes and gnats as hawks or owls or wolves. It is part of the divine plan of ecology that swallows feed on flying insects, and wolves on rabbits and deer. There is nothing else they can do.

At this moment, word comes that someone has sighted a mountain lion in the Red Lake wilderness, and a friend has come to tell me he has just seen one cross the road ahead of his car outside of Itasca Park.

"He was half the width of the road," he said, "and flowed across it."

What excitement for those who love all nature. Even if we never see them, the prospect that we just might enriches our lives.

The true lovers of the outdoors have an appreciation, if not always an affection, for all living things and for their role in the drama of existence. Such people may even be hunters, knowing that some species can be harvested without loss—and should be—so that the remaining populations will be healthier and less likely to starve. They know too that other predators besides man perform a real function in preserving the health of a species and preventing its periodic overabundance. To such friends of nature, the call of a wolf on a frozen night is assurance that all's well with the world.

# 10 🌿 More birds at your feeder

SIX MILLION FAMILIES are feeding birds during winter; bird-feeding companies can barely keep up with the demand. The figure might be even greater. I'd guess that for every bird-watcher, there are probably three who feed birds. The trouble with getting a true count is that feeding birds isn't something the average man will own up to.

"My wife is feeding birds," says the guy who has driven a hundred miles for a bargain on sunflower seeds by the sack. Feeding birds still isn't the manly thing to do. But that's going to change. First, because new-model feeders are coming out every year, like new car models, and that's bound to trap the guy who must by nature be out ahead. Second, there's "science" now to feeding; certain seeds, such as Niger thistle and safflower, that are still hard to get may draw your neighbor's birds to your own feeders. Women have always fed birds, moved by the maternal satisfaction of providing for a family. Now men will take it up, and admit to it, for less unselfish reasons.

There are four good places for feeders: outside the kitchen, bathroom, bedroom, and dining-room windows. With a daily circus just beyond the kitchen window, the sink won't seem so dreary. And with early birds at your bedroom window on gray winter mornings, or at your bathroom window as you brush your teeth, you won't feel quite so much the martyr, seeing others up and about. If that sounds contrived, just try putting some feeders there and see.

We seldom eat a meal all winter without looking out on outdoor diners, so close they seem to be eating at our own table. And believe me, if anyone needs an inducement to eat—which unhappily I do not—birds at the feeder ought to do it. There's no toying with their food. In fact, they're so enthusiastic that you can't help but feel grateful for your own victuals, grateful that you are free of that gnaw of hunger that compels an unceasing search for food over acres of icy bark and crusted snowbanks.

Most seed-feeding boxes aren't worth putting up. Some with glass sides give birds promise of food but little more; they don't self-feed as they are intended to. They offer no protection against wind and give no room for more than a single bird or two at a time. Birds need elbow room. They don't crowd like chickens or hogs at a feeder. You almost never see them sitting wing to wing on a wire or limb. They need room to take off swiftly without batting their wings against a neighbor. And yet, few birds feel safe if they are all alone at a feeder. Flock feeders, especially, won't stay long without others around them.

For this reason, the best seed feeders are big. The one outside my living-room window is four feet long and almost a foot wide. A dozen evening grosbeaks can eat at once, while a hundred others wait their turn in the trees. When the grosbeaks are through, the crossbills come; these beautiful, amicable birds feed almost wing to wing. A feeder outside our kitchen window is three feet long, and overflow crowds of grosbeaks, besides chickadees and nuthatches, feed here.

Siskins, sparrows, juncos, and goldfinches prefer feeding on the ground, which is fine until snow comes. After that you can feed inside a big cardboard box lying on its side, which will be free of snow and sheltered from the wind. Off from the house a hundred feet or more I keep a square tub or a plastic wastebasket on its side filled with corn for the bluejays, to keep them from hauling off expensive sunflower seed. I don't begrudge the jays their daily bread, but when they spend all day gobbling up sunflower seeds and flying across the lake to hide them in rotting stumps or even snowbanks, then I call a halt. I like my food eaten on the premises. (Where rats are a problem, better feed well off the ground.)

The best seed feeder for those who want lots of action and who don't mind a somewhat unsightly structure outside the window is one made with a window screen for the floor and a storm window a foot or two above it for the roof, held up by four strong posts. Rain and melting snow can drain through the screen, and the roof keeps out most of the snow. You can use another window as a windbreak on one side. The trick is getting the window attached strongly enough so the wind doesn't tear it loose. I pound down a metal fence post at each corner, and run a long screw through a hole in the post and into the wooden frame of the window and screen. Where snow isn't much of a problem, you can simply use the screen.

Suet feeders are simpler. All you need is something to hold the suet out of reach of dogs. A mesh onion bag is as good as anything. I use chicken wire tacked to my pine trees in the form of looping baskets where dozens of chickadees, woodpeckers, and nuthatches can feed at one time. Some say that a bird's foot or tongue will cling to metal during cold weather, but I have never seen it, even though there is hardly a winter in northern Minnesota that it doesn't get as low as 45 degrees below zero.

There are dozens of tricky little suet feeders on the market, all of them fine for winter feeding if you don't mind the messy job of replenishing them every day or so, smearing peanut butter or suet into tiny holes. Co-

conut shells filled with suet are attractive, and so are big pine cones. But as more and more birds start coming, you'll want increasingly bigger feeders.

Woodpeckers, nuthatches, titmice, and chickadees seem to prefer a vertical feeder, but for warblers, bluebirds and most perching birds, you need a horizontal one. Paul Fluck uses a cedar log which revolves on metal pins and is supported horizontally between three-foot posts. He gouges out holes an inch deep to hold suet. When starlings are around, he can rotate the log so the holes are underneath out of reach. As many as fifteen downy and hairy woodpeckers use it at a time. At other times there are kinglets, Carolina wrens, brown creepers, nuthatches, flickers, and myrtle warblers, and in spring as many as twenty warblers of many kinds have used it at once. During a siege of continued sleet and snow, seventeen bluebirds fed on it, and it may have been all that kept them from starving. All summer, orioles, catbirds, and chats feed on it, for a year-round total of thirty species.

Now for the food you use to stock your feeders. Kidney suet is probably the favorite of birds, but with so many people feeding birds today, most of us are content with any beef suet. A little meat mixed through it won't hurt. In fact, chickadees prefer it now and then for variety's sake. Just make sure there's none of it in your feeder when warm weather comes. The fragrance gets pretty high. Stocking the suet feeder costs little or nothing. Feeding seed-eaters is another matter.

Birdseed has become a big business. Around Washington, D.C. alone, more than five thousand tons—worth a million dollars—is fed every year. One North Dakota wholesaler ships out the equivalent of 350 freight cars of birdseed a year.

The prime food is sunflower seeds. Bluejays will gobble up forty or fifty at a time until their fronts bulge like a Wagnerian soprano's, then fly off to hide them in some secret savings deposit. Sunflower seeds aren't easy for most birds to crack. The bluejay hews away at it like a woodsplitter. The crossbill, for all his fancy equipment, can barely manage. Watch the nuthatch. He'll wedge it into a crevice of bark while he hacks at it, returning to the same crevice with one seed after another until the bark gives way. Only the cardinal, grosbeak and purple finch can manage sunflower seeds simply, and they do it with such savoir faire that other birds look clumsy. A European cousin of the grosbeak can even crack open olive pits!

If you really want to play Santa Claus, crack the sunflower seeds. There's no easy way I know, but a rolling pin works. For coaxing birds to eat out of your hands, there's probably no better bait than sunflower meats crushed into small bits.

You can save considerably on sunflowers by buying the small-seeded kind, by the sack or in 100-pound lots. Buy buckwheat if you can; it's almost as good and generally costs quite a bit less. Flaxseed attracts some birds. Few seem to care about wheat or oats or barley. Corn, either whole, cracked, or on the cob is popular with jays, titmice, cardinals, and red-bellied woodpeckers. Millet and sorghum are fine and inexpensive. Birds much prefer white to red millet.

In states where it is legal to sell "screenings"—the broken kernels and weed seeds that are a by-product of mills and elevators—you can feed these, preferably after baking in an oven to destroy germination. A variety of sparrows, finches, redpolls, siskins, and the like will flock in to screenings.

In the process of making peanut butter the germs or hearts are extracted, and these are worth trying to get hold of. At 20 to 25 cents a pound they're a good buy. Peanut butter itself is a top food for a great many birds. But have a care about feeding salted peanuts. They kill birds.

There are dozens of foods that birds like. Dog biscuits pulverized with a rolling pin make a fine food. Nutmeats of any kind are good, and if you have an accumulation of black walnuts in the fall, save and crush them for the winter feeding table. Pumpkin, squash, and cantaloupe seeds attract some birds. My window ledge feeder holds a smorgasbord of odds and ends. It's fun to see how birds vary their diet, given a choice. Sometimes there's a run on suet-peanut butter mix. Another time it might be cornbread leftovers.

Most popular with a number of birds are doughnuts. To thwart squirrels, we string them on a wire one above another and suspend them from a branch. It's not long before only a thin white skeleton of the doughnut remains. If you can buy stale doughnuts, that's great. We can't. All we can get are fresh, homemade ones. It's not easy to put those voluptuous goodies—still warm—out onto a cold shelf. I tell myself (sometimes between bites) that the chickadees need them more than I.

Now for the feeding secrets—the tricks that will lure your neighbor's birds to your yard. Peanut hearts, buckwheat, and canary seed will do it. So too will safflower seed. Niger thistle will draw goldfinches like a magnet. Don't worry that it will start a weed problem. Attempts to grow it in California for its high protein and oil content all have failed.

A secret ingredient of cage-bird feed is the seed of a member of the lowly cabbage and turnip family with an exotic name: gold of pleasure. For generations, old hands at canary breeding used it to gloss up plumage and promote singing. It does the same for wild birds, Paul Fluck tells me. Goldfinches color up and sing. So do redpolls and cardinals. It's expensive and hard to get,* but a little should last a long while. I know my

---

* Your dealer can order it from Knauf and Tesch, Chilton, Wisc. 53014.

sack will. In ten months of testing, not one bird has eaten it. But I'll keep trying.

Some reputable students of nature discourage winter bird feeding, and say in effect that it corrupts the native self-reliance of wildlife, that a natural diet is better, that birds around a feeding station are more exposed to disease due to crowding, and that birds accustomed to feeders are likely to starve when people forget to feed or grow tired of it. That point of view is one that can't be quickly dismissed. Feeding certainly dislocates a great number of birds.

Yet I notice that the fall flocks of evening grosbeaks don't come to the feeders until they have exhausted all the nearby swamp maple and box elder seeds. Friendly little crossbills, so tame they often sit on the feeder when you replenish it and even allow themselves to be stroked, desert the feeder periodically to feed on spruce cones, clinging to a twig upside down like little parrots, or holding a cone in one foot while they pry open the scales for the seeds. In the coldest part of winter I find chickadees out foraging among the aspens when half a dozen of their favorite foods are waiting for them on a shelf only a few blocks away. I think that the hunt for food must sharpen the appetite. The same love of the hunt and of discovery may run deep in birds as well as in man. I can't believe that winter feeding will turn our birds into helpless panhandlers.

The danger that people will begin to feed and then stop is minor, I think. I have yet to find anyone who— once infected with the winter feeding bug—gives it up. If a person forgets now and then, the birds are sure to remind him, chirping and twittering outside the window or from a nearby tree. And if they do find some householder with a sudden attack of parsimony, they flock off to another, more generous supplier. Most experts believe that winter feeding permits more birds to escape starvation during the critical coldest months when natural food is likely to run low. Roger Tory Peterson says that feeders saved at least a million birds in Britain during the cold and snow of 1963. Other professionals, including those in federal and state Fish and Wildlife agencies, recommend winter feeding.

It is altogether possible that evening grosbeaks, titmice, and redpolls may build up very large populations, and whenever you get heavy concentrations of any wildlife at certain points there is danger of disease. But with more and more people feeding, using large feeders, there need be no congestion at any one point.

It is true, too, that feeding encourages some birds to winter farther north than their usual range, and without continuous feeding, these would be in trouble. A bird's metabolism is so rapid that many can barely keep alive overnight. Hummingbirds can't, except for the fact that they go into a kind of hibernation every night, their metabolism dropping to one twentieth of normal. The poorwill of California actually hibernates from November to February in rocky niches in the walls of canyons, its temperature dropping from 100 degrees F to 66 degrees F. Owls can live through the long winter nights of the far north because they mostly forage at night. But for most birds, winter and winter nights are critical. They must have full crops when night falls. Cardinals in Minneapolis, for instance, seem barely able to survive the long winter nights of the north. They are usually the last at the feeder in the evening and the first there in the morning. It is likely that birds have a physiological northern limit based on their metabolic rate and body food reserves.

In their search along roadsides for sand and gravel, many birds get killed by cars. So have a little sand in a pail or on your feeder.

Paul Fluck believes that birds looking for water probably die from drinking the antifreeze residue along the highways. In a single day a man outside Philadelphia found thirty-eight dead goldfinches along a short stretch of road. If this was the cause of death, it's apparent that birds need water in winter. The new waterers heated by electric cable are said to be effective and enjoyed by birds. I wouldn't know. My own birds eat snow and rather seem to enjoy it, gulping down big beakfuls between courses at the feeder.

The time to start feeding is early in the fall, at the time the whitethroated sparrows are arriving to scratch the first fallen leaves at the edges of your lot. If you wait for the juncos, your neighbors will have lured the birds away, and it will take longer until they find your feeders. If you have trouble getting them started, begin with your feeder next to a bush where they usually perch. Birds feel safer near such a getaway. If you don't have such a spot, pile a few limbs nearby, stand up your discarded Christmas tree, and resolve to plant arbor vitae or forsythia or dogwood there in spring.

Don't worry if at first you get no more distinguished visitors than starlings and house sparrows. Birds draw birds. Simply put up enough feeders so everybody can get a chance, shy ones as well as bullies. Starlings, despite their notoriety, are worthy visitors and possessed of some of the best brains in the bird world. Keep a couple of extra feeders stocked with bread for the starlings at the back of your property and your small birds will have the grain feeders to themselves.

Squirrels will come, generally. If they eat too much to please you, buy or borrow a Havahart trap that will quickly capture them alive and unharmed. Take them out several miles away to a patch of oaks and release them. Or you can put metal collars on the posts of your feeders. A piece of spouting may be the right size to fit down around the post.

Now then, how do you keep birds from killing themselves when they hit windows? One of my bachelor friends, an otherwise cleanly fellow, has one answer. He never cleans his windows. They're not particularly hard to look out of, but to the birds, they must seem practically opaque, because since he hit upon the strategy, he hasn't had a single bird fatality. Before that he was plagued, especially by ruffed grouse. Sometimes they would crash through one window and out through another on the other side of the house. More often he would find them lying dead inside.

I have seen other ideas offered by people who I feel sure have never tried them themselves. Put up a stuffed owl at the window, or an imitation one. If it kept away birds, wouldn't it also keep them away from a feeder? Another: Cover the window with chicken wire.

Now then for the Davids system, which is clearly and obviously superior. Simply position the feeder right outside the window—the nearer the safer. Birds will hit it occasionally, but not with much force, whereas birds that spook at the feeder when it's twenty feet or so off strike the glass at killing speeds. From the time I moved my big feeder to within five feet of the picture window, only a rare bird has been killed, although many strike the window, and a few leave feathers at the impact site. Sometimes I feed all along the eight-foot window ledge, and the window lights up like the footlights of a stage with the bright yellows of a dozen grosbeaks.

There's another advantage in feeding so close. Starlings and bluejays are generally too wary to come this near; most other birds grow accustomed and eventually don't mind the movement inside.

There are frustrations to bird feeding. Try as I may I can't induce the big, splashy pileated woodpeckers that nest on the back corner of my property to come to my feeders. One of them came on Thanksgiving Day and started hacking at a crack in a pine tree twenty-five feet from the picture window, while a houseful of people watched. And when he momentarily retired to the swamp, we hurriedly stuffed the hole he had been working on with peanut butter and suet. Returning, he cocked his big red-crested head, gave a few experimental raps, then shifted a few inches to the side and began hammering. I've crawled up a ladder to stuff suet in the hole in an elm tree where he works now and then, but again without success. I have finally given up. That woodpecker is like some people I know: lusterless, prosaic, who wouldn't think of trying anything new. I prefer more venturesome woodpeckers and people.

Sometimes unusual birds come to feeders. An old lady in our county raised a pheasant that eventually went off on his own, but during the coldest weather returned to the back porch each morning where he would find a braided rag rug she had warmed in the oven for him, along with a tin of corn, bread crumbs and other assorted tidbits. One day he arrived with a ruffed grouse for company, and the two kept coming until spring.

Seldom is it possible to identify a single individual at our feeders. There are too many birds. The one exception was a one-legged chickadee that fed one winter with us, balancing with ease on the feeder ledge. Occasionally a bird is identifiable by missing tail feathers, but these soon grow out.

The excitement comes when a visitor arrives from afar. Now and then a boreal or brown-capped chickadee comes far south to dine for a few weeks with us. And for most of one winter we had visitors from the Rockies—a pair of gray-crowned rosy finches that fed with the grosbeaks. Only once before have they even been seen in Minnesota. I tried to get photographic proof, but taking pictures out the window, with strong backlighting from the snow, is difficult.

There is other unscheduled excitement. Now and then a flying squirrel comes to feed at night outside the window. And a raccoon fed all fall at a feeder beside the kitchen door. How he learned to extricate food from the feeder is hard to say. The feeder is a wide-mouthed three-gallon glass jar on its side held in place by a metal strip around the middle that is nailed to a wood strip suspended from the eaves. There is a hole less than two inches in diameter in the metal cover. The idea is to provide a feeder for chickadees and nuthatches that jays and grosbeaks can't get into, and it does that just fine. But the contraption didn't stop the coon. Balancing on a narrow oak railing, he reached up nearly three feet, thrust his paw through the hole and extracted the doughnuts inside. Every night, generally around midnight, we could hear him raiding the feeder. Sometimes he would set the hanging feeder into motion like a pendulum. Whether or not he swung it intentionally, doughnuts at the back out of his reach would slide forward. Never a night all fall that the feeder wasn't emptied. We're waiting now—the feeder stocked with doughnuts, his favorite food—for the rattling sound that means he's back with us. Will he bring friends or family and demonstrate the strategy of a midnight doughnut foray?

On rare occasions a weasel glides up the trunk of the pine that holds our basket of suet and spends the morning tugging at the fat, flinching when a nuthatch comes to feed. So white is the weasel's winter pelage against the suet that all I can see of him are his bright eyes and black tail-tip. He seldom returns. There is no adventure, no fight, no passion to a lump of suet, and a weasel's whole life is one of violence, whether mating or food-gathering or escaping the great horned owl. A mink fed at a friend's feeder in Minnesota, but it too didn't return.

A snowshoe hare standing on tiptoes fed one winter from a table feeder two feet high. The snow was deep that winter. Along in February a starving bobcat came up from the swamp, leaping through the soft snow directly to our back door where he cowered, shivering either from fear or hunger or both. I wish I might say that he climbed the tree to eat suet, but he didn't. Sometime during the night he must have returned and caught the snowshoe hare and eaten him on the spot.

Do you see why I say bird feeding is a great sport?

Right now as I'm writing, it is mid-April. Yesterday the tulips were six inches high and the chionodoxa in bud. This morning I awoke to a white world. A foot of wet snow fell during the night, and it is still falling. There are birds everywhere. The place looks like a chicken yard. At least fifty fox sparrows, caught in the storm, are scratching for food, singing between mouthfuls their glorious spring song that puts any caged canary to shame—a carefree, casual song of slurred whistles, each bird with its own distinctive melody. How strange it seems that during a blizzard almost as violent as I have known, the air should be filled with music above the gusty blasts of wind. We open the door occasionally to get the full sound. The only other places I have heard them are Alaska and northern Canada, to which they will shortly travel.

A cloud of juncos has descended and is feeding everywhere—on the suet, the doughnuts, the peanut butter, on the granules of corn left by the squirrels after they extracted the oily germs. Another fifty purple finches are here and there at the feeders, as well as half a dozen song sparrows and an occasional tree sparrow, jaunty in his red cap and black stickpin. Three pairs of rusty blackbirds are at the corn feeder, and two redwings. Above them a bluebird is singing. Add to that our old friends at the feeders: fifteen bluejays, twenty chickadees, six nuthatches and as many hairies and downies, twenty-five redpolls and that many red crossbills and evening grosbeaks.

The biggest surprise is the robins. At the back doorstep, in a space no bigger than three feet square, are twenty-five robins crowding wing to wing, defying what I have said about a bird's need for elbow room. They are eating chunks of bread and discarded sprays of bittersweet. I have never before looked down on a nearly solid mat of robins, a mosaic of red and black. Periodically they swarm on three clumps of wild rose out front, tugging off the berries, then fly to a crab apple that has provided them with food for the last ten days. Now and then they spook and are gone for fifteen minutes, and I have just found out why. Hidden in the dark of the spruces, only sling-shot distance from the front feeders, is a falcon—either pigeon hawk or peregrine, I can't quite see—and when he makes a sudden pass, the birds scatter. Can you see why a feeding station is a lively place?

If you have children, put up a feeder at once. They will be fascinated. They will learn compassion and maybe a sense of responsibility. If you have a spray-happy neighbor, give him a feeder, install it and stock it. It will be a better argument against indiscriminate mosquito-spraying than the most vigorous harangue. If you have a shut-in parent or friend, by all means set up a feeder outside his window. The parade of birds will be more compelling than a television set. On a frosty morning the grosbeaks will swarm in, their head feathers and nostrils white with frost from their freezing breaths. How can anyone be depressed with such perky, energetic companions?

There is hardly a place anywhere in the United States that won't draw birds. My friends, the Paul Flucks, lived for years in the very heart of a New Jersey village, as they say, "halfway between the post office and the jail." They had feeders outside their first-floor, second-floor, and third-floor windows. Catbirds, thrashers, cardinals, and most kinds of sparrows came to feed on the flat tin roof outside their second-floor kitchen, where they caught and banded six thousand birds.

A friend of Paul's who used to idle away his spare time in bars when he was out traveling was laid low with a heart attack. Over his protests, his wife put up a feeder outside the window. Soon he was watching the bird traffic, and asked her what the yellow-and-black birds were.

"Evening grosbeaks," she said.

He paused a moment. "I'll bet we have more of them than most places."

He was hooked. Within a year he was feeding a garbage can of sunflower seeds every day, and as you drove past his place even with the windows of the car closed you could hear the racket of his grosbeaks.

"And to think," he told Paul, "that I could have had this fun all my life!"

# 11 🌿 *My favorite nature-fiction*

So far in the slow roll of the seasons, we have all but ignored the plant kingdom. There are pleasures here as varied as among birds and animals and insects. There is opportunity, too, for students of science to make significant discoveries. But before you begin, as any thorough-going scientist knows, you must "survey the literature" on the subject. To this end, I invite you to start with the fiction.

🌿

At six, I fell victim to a language—the perfumed, altiloquent language of the seed catalog. Long before I encountered the terse drama of "Run, Jack, run," I was sounding out the words of a more alluring piece of fiction: "Stocks, sweet smelling, ten weeks, 1 pkg. 2¢." Postage would take another 2 cents; I could manage that. So I gambled, and planted them on my birthday, May 15. I studied the calendar: their day to smell would be July 24. June loafed past and most of July. On S-Day, my stocks had just broken ground. From that year on, my reading has improved, but not my stocks, sweet smelling, ten weeks. I water them, fertilize them —even show them the calendar—but they sit, unmoved, unperfumed, till frost mercifully strikes them down.

The next year I tried one package of rhododendron seeds with even less to show, and in my third, one package of eschscholtzia, not so much that I believed they'd grow as that I had learned to spell the name. The year was triumphant. The brachycome was a sheet of blue; the pansies were a rich velvet. But success hasn't deepened my love affair with seed catalogs as much as failure.

Let others grow carrots and peas and turnips. I'll grow the salsify, Mammoth Sandwich Island "with the savory goodness of oysters." I'll grow the garden almonds. I'll grow the beans with yard-long pods. I'll grow the squash packed full of spaghetti. I mean I'll keep on trying. Last year my package of peanut seeds— Jumbo Virginia—gave me two pallid, frightened-looking little nuts. My very own "basement crop of mouth-watering mushrooms, postpaid $2.59 pkg. complete with growing medium" gave me exactly one mushroom. Seems a little high for horse manure.

Don't think I'm complaining. I wouldn't have it otherwise. There's even a practical value in failure—as everyone knows who has found himself with wheelbarrow loads too many of tomatoes or cucumbers or summer squash.

If all the apple trees I plant were to grow, I'd be swamped. Every year as the catalogs arrive I see vistas of Fireside and Oriole and Prairie Spy, this one for eating "out of hand," that one for cooking, others for winter evenings. I have an allergy to apples that gives me a headache, but no matter. Each spring I order a batch. Years ago I used to space them a careful twenty-five feet apart, but now I dig them down side by side almost anywhere. It's a kind of ritual to spring, because I know they won't survive a Minnesota winter. And if they do, they face a hungering horde: mice at the grass line, rabbits at knee height, and above that, deer and curculios and small boys, while below ground, pocket gophers gnaw at the roots. It seems that all the world loves apples. Maybe—just maybe—if I planted a whole acre, would there be enough for us all?

As a boy I hid my passion for seed catalogs from even my closest friends. It was too tender an emotion to risk their jeers. Much as I longed to spell eschscholtzia for them, I knew that they would never understand the limpid language of the seed catalogs—a romance language of rainbow-hued adjectives, where superlatives need superlatives, where candor is a sin, where the tense is always future, the number is never less than armfuls or bushels and the mood imperative: Plant now. Thrill tomorrow. And there are no ugly words like b**tles, aph*ds, or mild*w. So I dreamed alone in catalog-land, where flowers bloom profusely on long-stemmed stalks superb for cutting, continuing until frost, with blooms the size of dinner plates.

It wasn't until college that I learned I needn't hide my weakness. George Washington himself in between chores at Bunker Hill and Valley Forge probably mooned over seed catalogs. He was the first in America to grow alfalfa, I knew, but no history book had ever told me the more important facts, that he was a pushover for the luminous language of seeds. Every year he thanked a British firm for its catalog "which I have had much satisfaction in perusing. In publishing so useful and beneficial a work, than which nothing, in my opinion, can be more conducive to the welfare of your country . . ." He would order "8 bushels of holy clover and 8 bushels of what you call velvet wheat, of which I perceive you are an admirer," then entreat the ship's captain "to keep the seeds in the cabin, or out of the ship's hold, at any rate, as they never fail to heat and spoil when put there." The ship would spring a leak and the seeds sprout. He wrote a friend, "Nothing is more to be regretted than to sow seed that does not come up." Mr. Washington, I know exactly what you mean!

Other heroes felt the same lure of plants. John Quincy Adams commanded his consuls to send him seeds of all promising plants. Benjamin Franklin even smuggled out of Italy seeds of upland rice (which turned out to be a bust), introduced the Chinese tallow tree, and something else called rhubarb. The Lewis and Clark expedition, some historians say, was actually planned in a seed house by Jefferson, largely because of his engrossing interest in new plants.

So to all fellow catalog lovers, forget your embarrassment. You're in league with the great. And if your gardening doesn't always equal your dreams, remember the summer at Mount Vernon when Our Founder himself planted limes and lindens sent him by Governor Clinton of New York, horse chestnuts from "Light Horse Harry Lee," lilacs, mock oranges, magnolias, hickories, yews, pawpaws, locusts, crabs, service berries, catalpas, and four bushels of holly seed. The spring was a scorcher and Mr. Washington couldn't be at home to water. When he returned, he set down in his diary: "Most of my transplanted trees have a sickly look. The small Pines are entirely dead. Almost the whole of the holly are dead. Not a single ash has unfolded its buds. In short, half the trees are dead and declining."

He didn't blame the seed catalog, as John Hancock's uncle Thomas did in a letter that concluded: "P.S. The Tulip Roots you were pleased to make a present of are all dead as well."

Now then, here was history that meant something. I scoured the library for more. It was a seedsman named David Landreth who set up shop a few blocks away from Independence Hall in Philadelphia, and whose catalog blazed a purple path for all to follow. His plants were growing "in the household gardens of the Emperors of Austria and Japan, the Kings of Spain, Portugal, Italy, Greece, Belgium, Wurtemberg, Sweden, the Sultan of Turkey, the Pope of Rome, and the Vice-Roy of India." Perhaps even they dreamed as they read of hybrid rhododendrons from England, a wondrous peach with a free stone, a fabulous new flower from Mexico called the zinnia, not to mention cardoon, chervil, nasturtium for pickling, scurvy grass, and spinage. Each catalog served up new temptations: "strawberries red or yellow" in 1790; Virginia green grass, the "talk of all visitors" in 1795; orange trees "found growing along the Osage River by Lewis & Clark," in 1808; "the first really white potato ever grown" in 1811; a fruit "to embellish the table," the tomato, in 1820; and corn for humans "as sweet as sugar" in 1830.

There was history interwoven in the catalogs. Passenger pigeons came to roost in the Landreth nursery in such numbers they snapped the limbs of his trees. And to save a horse-powered threshing machine from destruction by jealous laborers he had to mount armed guards every night. During the Civil War people were enjoined to plant chicory as a substitute for coffee and okra as a substitute for paper pulp (a fine idea to my taste!) Landreth catalogs sold lawn rakes for 5 cents a tooth, ran testimonials both signed and notarized, carried poetry and essays on such topics as "The Moral Influence of Flowers."

"When we began," wrote Landreth, "we had but little idea of what awaited our little messenger. But now it is 600,000 strong!" It surpassed the Bible in distribution.

Throughout the world, other catalogs have been sending forth messages of hope and beauty. The Peace rose in a German catalog is described as "best alles"; in Danish it is "underbar" and "fantastik"; in Italian it is "grossissima" and "magnifica." The hybridizer who actually created the Peace rose, Francois Meilland of France, described it to me with a shrug of his shoulders: "She's all right, but too steengy with blooms." I'm glad that plant breeders don't write seed catalogs!

Only once in world history has the language of the catalogs ever faltered. It was in 1872, when one catalog (which shall be nameless) described bachelor buttons as "showy in a rude way," and mignonette as "destitute of beauty but delightfully fragrant," and with shocking realism enjoined asparagus growers to "take a dung fork and dig in manure."

As one who has invested more time and money than most in the pages of seed catalogs, let me give the novice a few tips on mastering the language.

You'll see something listed as "a gem for the rockery." Once I ordered a bluebell like that and when spring came I couldn't find it. I walked back and forth over the wet ground, finally traversed the area on my knees—and there it was: three leaves and a bloom an inch high that I had mistaken for a gum wrapper.

"Good for naturalizing," you read. This is the kind of plant your neighbor gives you, that gallops through the iris and even smothers out the weeds.

"Not a rampant grower" describes a climbing hydrangea that goes by the whimsical name of petiolaris. "It clings to any wall in sun or deep shade, giving big snowy whorls of bloom all summer; can be kept to any height." Five years ago I ordered petiolaris and dug it down carefully next to a shingled wall in the mellow loam it preferred. I watered and waited. One season turned into two and Pete just sat there, sprouting only a few leaves. The third year I urged him onward and upward with a stake pointed at the shingled wall he was to bedeck with snowy whorls. The fourth year I threatened to douse him with gibberellic acid, and last year I did. Pete thrust a cautious finger along the ground and under the shingles, a vine that shriveled as I retrieved it. Some day my house may be the envy of the block but don't rush over just yet, for hydrangea petiolaris is truly not a rampant grower.

There are many ways to read a seed catalog. I take mine to bed and dog-ear the appropriate pages. First page: giant $F_1$ marigolds, expensive because hand-

pollinated. I crease that page. $F_2$ hybrids, cheaper
because they're the product of a love-match of $F_1$'s out
in the field, unassisted by man. I crease that page. Trip-
loid marigolds, sterile mules that bloom desperately
all summer trying to reproduce. "To obtain seed, we
have to make crosses each year. It's very expensive."
What matter the cost, I snort, rising to the bait. The
page is already creased, so I give it a reverse bend. Next
page more marigolds: dwarf double, extra early double,
petite and pygmy. I can get along without them. But
look: a tetra ruffled red and two all-America winners. I
dog-ear that page and go on. What—still-more marigolds? Carnation-flowered, gold-coin series, sun giants,
jubilees! I turn off the light. All night, squadrons of
marigolds tramp through my dreams, led by David
Burpee in shining armor in quest of a snow-white marigold.

Reality sets in when the box of seed packages arrives.
Marigolds are fine, but do I really need a dozen kinds?
"Will sow 50 feet," a package reads. Multiplied by
twelve, that will be a tenth of a mile of marigolds—not
counting the plants I'll probably pick up at the super-
market.

Our ancestors must have had a tough time making
out their orders. A century ago one catalog had 1,300
kinds of pears, 900 apples, 300 grapes and 300 peaches.
And listen to just a few of the goodies in colonial days:
in pears, Chair's Choice and Stump the World; in
apples, Red Cheek and Maiden's Blush. Some of Jefferson's orders bore the mark of desperation: "Apricots, I
leave to you to fix on three or four of the best kinds;
sugar maples, all you have; bush cranberries, all you
have." That's all right if you have a Monticello.

Jefferson, by the way, would have made it big as a
seed catalog writer. His garden diary, which he kept for
nearly sixty years, is often pure poetry: "Purple hya-
cinth begins to bloom. Puckoon flowers fallen." Then

he would go on: "No occupation is so delightful as that of the garden . . . some one (plant) always coming to perfection . . . the failure of one thing repaired by the success of another. . . . Though an old man, I am but a young gardener."

The lure of the catalog is hard to explain. It's a call to explore, a jungle safari, a backyard Everest to scale just because it's there. George Washington wrote his favorite seedsmen: "As I am unacquainted with herds-grass, send one pound of that seed also, for an experiment." Reason enough for Mr. Washington.

Among my most recent experiments was the loofa, a vegetable sponge from Egypt shaped like a giant cucumber. "Makes the world's best bathtub backscratcher," said the catalog. I was delighted to find the seed. I have owned a loofa ever since my days in the army; it never wears out. I told all my friends I was growing loofas for them. "Notch or file seed and soak overnight to speed germination." That done, what the directions didn't say was to wait and wonder, if not pray. Autumn came and with it my loofas emerged, shivered and fell back to earth. My itchy-backed friends will get their loofas from a pharmacy where I found them for sale. Someday, though, I'll try again.

Ever since a trip to Japan I have searched for a catalog of the radishes and strawberries you meet up with there. As you eat shrimp tempura you dip each golden morsel in a tiny saucer of grated radish. Food indescribable! And at lunch when you order a fruit sandwich, you can't believe your eyes, for the same slice of strawberry goes all the way across and peers out both sides. Each strawberry is as big as a tomato!

Like many a great moment, success came unexpectedly. Along with a shipment of burpless cucumber seed from a Japanese importing firm came a catalog listing both treasures. The strawberries were sold out for the season but the radish seeds came and they grew. In fact, they were soon the size of baseballs, and before long, footballs. Along the way I sampled one. It was like biting down on a porcupine. What to do with them? I had bushels of them, too good to throw, and my customary neighborhood dispersal system I knew wouldn't work. So I called in my friends and offered a few slivers as hors d'oeuvres.

"Whatever are they for?" said one, gulping his drink to dampen the fire.

And all I could answer, tears in my eyes from the shred I had swallowed, was "They're great with shrimp tempura." I didn't pass off a single radish.

I was all set to order the giant strawberries when I happened to talk with a Japanese who knew just how the fruit was grown. "We plant them on a hillside among big rocks, where the spring sun warms them." So far so good. "Keep them covered with glass or plastic so they won't freeze." Well, I could still manage. "Then we feed them on—what you say—night soil." There my venture ended.

It wasn't until last summer that I tried those ten-foot-tall tomatoes that you pick from a stepladder. I put up a fence only head-high; no sense yet to alert the neighborhood (which my tomatoes would soon be the envy of). The vines grew fast, but they wouldn't climb on anything but the ground. Every day I lashed them to the fence where they slumped like a child asleep with all his clothes on. I nailed extensions to the top of my fence. Long before harvest I was up on the stepladder struggling with a forest of vines. A neighbor came over and called up to ask why I wanted tomatoes that tall.

"So I can pick them from a ——." I caught myself. "So they won't touch the ground and rot." He shook his head slowly. How could I explain? A man of reason is no real gardener. It takes a poet to understand why you climb a ladder to stake tomatoes that you later need a ladder to pick.

# 12 🪴 The lowdown on plants

EVERY MORNING at seven a bank of fluorescent lights snapped on in my bedroom window in Philadelphia. Suddenly it was spring. Under the lights, flowers bloomed profusely. Outside grimy snow might be lying on bare rooftops, but inside it was always spring or lush midsummer. For less than thirty dollars I had my own indoor greenhouse, one I would recommend enthusiastically for anyone who:

> likes to grow things;
> likes to experiment;
> needs to get away from the city;
> likes to grow flowers but can't;
> has nothing but a north window;
> can't get around except by wheelchair;
> wants to impress his neighbors and office-mates;
> is bored with himself.

A garden under lights beats the outdoor kind in several ways. You can control the climate precisely. By setting plants on a tray of wet pebbles you can have a steaming jungle. Under such conditions you can start seeds that refuse to grow outdoors. It is obvious that flowers in fall and winter are more appreciated than during the spring and summer. But the biggest plus for me is that in winter I have more time to watch the growth habits of each plant, the effect of light and heat and humidity. I can learn to know each plant as an individual and learn about its appetite, whims, and table manners.

The first plants I tried were gloxinias. I bought a package of "tigered, spotted hybrid" seeds and planted them in a shallow plastic tray filled with nothing other than rotted wood that I scooped out of the heart of a hardwood stump, then wet thoroughly. The seed was like so much brown dust, and when I planted it, I felt like Merlin of old scattering magic powder over the dark earth. It seemed incredible that there could be life in anything so small. Miraculously, within ten days the soil turned green with young plants and in a matter of weeks, fat, furry little plants began to crowd one another for elbow room. Then began a program of expansion that kept me bringing home clay pots from Gimbel's and Woolworth's every few days. Soon I needed a second fluorescent fixture above the first, and still the gloxinias kept growing. A few weeks later I got a third fixture and installed it still higher in the window. And then—within three and a half months after sowing the seeds—the plants started blooming, each one different from the last, but all big, ruffled giant blooms at least two inches across. Some blooms lasted only a few days. Some plants grew tall and leggy. Others sat and concentrated on blooming. Under fluorescence, some blooms glowed like neon lights, much more striking than in plain daylight. Every morning there was at least one new plant in bloom. The best ones I potted up and brought to the office and got rid of them that way. Reluctant as people are to take a plant not yet in bloom, it was amazing how ready they were to take a blooming one.

If the plants slowed down in growth, I had only to mix a little fish emulsion fertilizer in the water and they spurted. Once a week feeding was good; twice was better.

Under seventeen hours of light a day, the plants

never stopped blooming. After two years, when I tired of them, I lopped off the tops and put the tubers in the refrigerator. Other plants were crowding for light, namely cinerarias, those big lavender daisylike plants that only florists seem to grow. Mine came with all the gusto of a garbage truck and soon they too needed a pot apiece. They lapped up fertilizer with the same abandon as the gloxinias. Even before they bloomed they were magnificent with big maplelike leaves that were purple beneath and heavily furred. But when hot weather struck—as it can only in Philadelphia—one after another plant started to collapse as if it had been burned, every leaf falling limp and black. My Taylor's *Encyclopedia of Gardening* said that cinerarias need a night temperature of 50 degrees or less and a day temperature of no more than 60. Heat prostration—that's what ailed them! I left my air conditioner on all day and even though the cold blast showered over them they prospered. Those I sent home with friends, however, generally died within a day—which didn't altogether displease me.

I grew outdoor plants, too, under lights. Petunias that had always before damped off or grown pale and spindly now got sturdy and squat and began blooming. Going outdoors was no shock to them; they already had been getting almost constant light. A package of coleus seed gave hundreds of plants. They came up like strands of green paint across the planting tray and grew phenomenally. For a few weeks it seemed they would all be plain green, but soon they took on the reds, yellows, purples, and variegated coats that make the plant so rewarding. I tried the most exotic plants I could find in the catalogs, some I had tried to start since childhood, without success. They grew luxuriantly and so I had plants to give away that friends had never heard of, and took only grudgingly: plume poppy, a giant with big cabbagelike leaves; the beautiful fiery wild flower cursed with the name of butterfly weed, which few of my friends would take home; cardinal flower, another magnificent wild flower; and double platycodon, another whose name was against it.

I tried different kinds of lighting tubes, but could see no difference among them. Flowers seemed to do better with natural daylight to boot, but they prospered in a closet and in the basement without any sunlight. My brother's basement, however, was too cold or airless or both.

I wish I could say that my experiments added to man's knowledge of plants but I fear I cannot. I can only say that if you want some fun this winter, get a fixture and get going. Keep the lights three or four inches above the soil after planting and move them up only enough to let the plants grow. They won't burn. Fluorescent light is cool. There's little to read on the subject that will help you. Books on the subject tell you almost nothing beyond what I have set down here.

The whole matter of plants and how they grow is wide open to the amateur scientist. Despite the thousands of years man has tended plants, only recently are we beginning to understand them.

Roots, for instance, can't discriminate between good and harmful elements. Certain locoweeds take up enough selenium, which they store unable to use, to kill animals that feed on them.

Scientists say that fertilizer sprinkled on the soil is mostly wasted, either because it gets bound to soil particles and therefore grounded for the season or else washed down below the root zone. Putting fertilizer two inches below the seeds was more efficient. Roots reach it within two days but tended to concentrate there, making them subject to dry weather. Fertilizer placed two inches below and two inches to the side took a week for the roots to reach but gave a better root system. When fertilizer was three inches below, seedlings didn't respond for three or four weeks.

The fast and efficient way to feed is through the leaves. Up to 95 percent of certain nutrients are absorbed that way compared with 10 percent through the roots. If we could figure the right way to feed crops through the leaves we could bypass the waste of strewing fertilizer on the ground—a colossal saving.

On Cape Cod several years ago I saw the most luxurious rose garden in my life, and its owners gave credit to foliar feeding. They experimented to see just how much dissolved food a rose would absorb through the leaves without burning. The leaves never did burn. The plants simply kept growing faster and blooming more heavily. The only bad effect they found was that the neck of the bloom couldn't support the weight of the flower.

Orchardists are already foliar-feeding phosphorus and potash and especially the expensive ingredient nitrogen in the form of urea. Only calcium of the major nutrients must be applied to the soil since it doesn't appear to travel downwards from leaves to roots. Foliar feeding is something you might experiment with. Gloxinias and cinerarias that I fed through the leaves spurted in growth.

Now for a closer look at plants. Their table manners are far from dainty. They absorb food through every inch of their surface. Not just the leaves take it up, but twigs, fruit and even flowers do. So does the bark. Dormant fruit trees in California and Oregon sprayed with fertilizer made better fruit the next year. And here is a bigger surprise: the bark picks up fertilizer even in midwinter, at temperatures below freezing. Using nutrients tagged by radioactivity, scientists can follow the flow through the plant. Zinc moved in midwinter about two feet in a day.

A plant relies on two transportation systems. Its water system is made up of xylem (zy′lem) and its food system of phloem (flow′em) cells. (I offer those terms for no other reason than that you can use them to impress your friends, and that they roll nicely over the tongue.) When a rabbit or mouse chews off the bark completely around the tree exposing the wood, the phloem cells are destroyed and the tree is "girdled." The xylem cells that permeate the rest of the stem still function, because they are little more than tubes for conducting water (and dissolved minerals) upward, and so the tree lives for a year or two on food stored in the roots, then dies when the roots are starved out. In some plants, like the Virginia creeper, the xylem cells are simply tubes uninterrupted for a yard or so, and water poured in at the top will run out the other end. More often they are shorter, and water moves out through thin parts of the wall. For a while in spring before the leaves are out, the roots exert a slight pumping action that forces sap upward, but the big force that moves water upward—along with the raw materials for plant growth—is the suction created as water is evaporated through the leaves. The action is like a siphon. In the case of a tree, this means that tons of water must be sucked up through miles of roots to heights seventy and eighty feet above ground. On a good summer day, one big elm may give off as much as 150 gallons of water. A big birch may give off 90 gallons. No wonder big trees are such excellent air-conditioners. It's not so much that they keep off the sun as the refrigerating effects of all that water evaporating. If you doubt this, just notice how much cooler it is crossing the treeless Southwest deserts whenever you pass between alfalfa fields. A cool breeze seems to move past.

Phloem cells are a thin layer of inner bark, and through their pathway go food particles, either down to feed the roots and store food there or upward to feed developing twigs and flowers. In summer and fall, trees and shrubs begin storing food, mainly as starch, in their stems and roots, ready for next spring's burst of growth.

To make room for that storage, the roots keep on growing and do so in some cases long after frost and in the case of deciduous trees perhaps all winter as long as the soil temperature stays at 45 degrees or above. One researcher reports growth at 35 degrees when the land lay blanketed in snow and the thermometer hovered around zero. Fall planting may therefore be better than spring in that it gives roots a chance to establish themselves before the great upward suction of spring drains away their energy and moisture.

Pine trees store great quantities of food in their roots and stem, since they make nearly all their growth in the first six weeks of spring. Aldo Leopold, the Wisconsin naturalist whose *Sand County Almanac* is a modern classic, points out that you can read the cash balance of a pine tree's bank account by June 30 of each year. If the terminal shoot has a cluster of ten or more buds, the tree has salted away enough sun and rain and energy to make two or even three feet of growth the following spring. If there are only four or six buds, the growth will be less.

To complete your course in botany, let me tell you about the cambium layer, the fragile collection of cells that appears like a thin syrup under the tree bark. This is mysterious stuff and altogether remarkable. The inner cells grow xylem, the outer grow phloem.

The rate of flow of sap differs. It moves slowly through phloem—a few inches to a foot an hour—and fast through the long xylem tubes. In young bean plants sap moves through xylem at 60 feet an hour. In elms the rate is 125 feet an hour. That's 2 inches a minute. No wonder that an insecticide injected into the tree will cause bark beetles (which spread Dutch elm disease) to start falling from the lower branches while you wait.

The rate of sap flow is crucial. Too fast, and a plant or tree might bleed to death if cut off near the ground. As it is, the plant seals itself off before that happens. Scar tissue forms, and new sprouts appear. Yet the flow must be fairly rapid, because a plant has a big job to do in the few months of summer: draw enough water into its seed to swell and burst the coat and let the embryo emerge and punch through the hard crust of the soil, strike down roots to both anchor and feed itself, thrust up a sturdy stalk to compete against its neighbors for a place in the sun, construct a factory of leaves to manufacture food to send down to the roots, enlarge the stem and send up supplies to the buds and flowers, then throw its all into reproducing and ripening the seed. On top of that, it must repair damage by insects and disease.

The morning glory outside my window is moving up its stake six inches in a single day. I feel sure I must be mistaken. I measure it. In twenty-four hours it grows more than six inches, and now is waving about beyond the end of the stake with a rotary movement peculiar to vines in search of support. I can almost fancy I see the movement. In the garden, a squash tendril feels my finger, and in just twenty minutes begins to coil around it!

Even so, a plant seems serene, viewed from outside. But inside its stem and leaves and roots, there is a frenzy of activity.

At Cornell University I watched the activity inside the root hair of a living peanut. It was like looking down at a superhighway choked with traffic. Tiny particles were gliding along the center lanes, slower ones along the edges. Sometimes the slow ones got caught momentarily on the shoulder of the highway, then broke loose and moved on. Some particles were big and transparent, others small and granular. All jammed so tightly together and jockeyed so endlessly for position that it might have been lower Broadway during noon hour.

Most food materials moving along with the particles were heading toward the leaves to build them up. During fall, the traffic in phosphorus moves toward the seed. Magnesium, too, travels toward the seed from its temporary summer storage in the leaves. Looking down on the traffic disguises the complexity of chemical operations taking place. When urea—a compound of nitrogen, oxygen and carbon—is absorbed into the leaf, an enzyme specifically for the purpose splits it. The nitrogen part combines with hydrogen in the plant moisture to form ammonia, which travels along the plant's sap highway. The carbon and oxygen combine into carbon dioxide, a food constituent of plants. Other carbon dioxide comes from the air and is repaid by oxygen. A full-grown pine gives off enough oxygen in its short growing season to keep one man breathing all year (or about 450 pounds). But it takes fifty such trees to supply the year's oxygen intake for a car, and a hundred for a big truck. You begin to see why people who care are worried about the oxygen–carbon dioxide ratio.

Some herbicides travel around the plant's sap highway down to the roots and are actually ejected from the roots before the plant dies, then taken up by the roots of another plant, killing it. Certain insecticides, too, remain unchanged in the plant, traveling constantly up and down the highway, remaining potent for weeks, killing off bugs and beetles as soon as they start feeding. Such bug killers are called systemics.

Even more remarkable is an antibiotic called Actidione developed by the Upjohn Company for certain rare diseases in humans. Someone in the company with more imagination than sense sprayed it on white pine infected with a disease known as blister rust, a complex organism that must spend part of its life on gooseberries or currants. The white pine recovered. In the past, all you could do with an infected tree was cut out the dead limb with its yellow needles and hope the disease didn't spread. But it generally did, or was reinfected the following year. And when the infection reached the trunk, the bark blistered and died, and a mass of pustules mixed with pitch to form an ugly, running sore. Eventually, when the canker completely encircled the trunk, the whole tree died.

A dozen years ago I found that most of the white pines I had grown from seed and planted around the yard were badly infected. In half a dozen of them the canker had eaten away all but an inch or two of bark. A few months more and they would have been brown. I slashed the bark above and below the canker as the directions then called for and brushed on the antibiotic. When I returned the next summer I felt sure that my sick trees had died and been cut down. There was no trace of the canker on any of the trees. I couldn't believe it until I found slight depressions in the bark which the tree hadn't yet filled in.

Acti-dione had made the cure. But far more remarkable, it has prevented reinfection. For how long? Some scientists say for ten years, and probably twenty, and maybe for the life of the tree.

What kind of mechanism is that? Is the chemical forever held in suspension? Or does it confer some unknown type of immunity which the disease alone cannot give? As far as I know there is no parallel in disease control and prevention. I have six acres of young white pine, badly diseased, which I am going to treat tree by tree—a laborious job but one I will do gladly, knowing that I shall need to treat them only once in my lifetime. (Acti-dione in a formulation for pine has been discontinued for lack of a sufficient market.)

For years I had promised myself that someday I would try grafting, but until recently I was always away from my place in Minnesota at grafting time. Once I made fifty bud grafts in August when the bark slipped away from the wood; only one bud grew. Then last spring I was at home in Minnesota just as the buds were swelling. I had the crisper of the refrigerator stuffed with twigs of exotic apples, plus big bundles in the freezer-locker. I read again the government bulletins on grafting. You can use rubber bands, grafting wax, or electrician's tape, the bulletins said.

Let me tell you, you can't. At least I can't. The rubber bands disintegrated in the sun. The electrician's tape I got was plastic and didn't stretch, so it didn't make a tight seal. I wasted half of my bundle of scions that the University's Plant Breeding Station had sold me. It wasn't until I talked with my friend Paul Tangjerd, our local self-taught botanist and one of the most rare human beings I have ever known, that I learned how to graft. Buy *rubber* electrician's tape, Paul said, and don't let the hardware store sell you the plastic stuff. Then peel off the cloth backing and stretch it tight around the spliced wood. Neither hardware store carried it, both insisting that the plastic was better, but Paul had an extra roll. So, I began, doing just as he had shown me. My tops (properly called scions) were too small to make the fancy notched unions that Paul prefers to make, so I simply made a slashing diagonal cut across it so that the cut section was a little less than two inches long, then made the same cut across the limb I was grafting it to (called stock). To make sure they matched in length of cut and thickness of twig I held them side by side, cut surfaces up. Getting a match isn't hard, but what the book doesn't tell you is how hard it is to make a straight slanting cut across a limber twig the size of a lead pencil or smaller. You can hold the scion on your knee if you are careful with a knife, but what about the stock? I cut as best I could, held the two cut faces together so the bark of one made contact as far as possible with that of the other, then bound them together tight with the rubber tape. That's all there was to my grafting. No grafting wax to worry about—and I do mean worry. The wax sticks to your fingers, your knife, and the graft, too, up to a point—the exact point when you try to withdraw your hand. Then it comes blithely along with you, carrying the scion with it. Of the many, many frustrating, infuriating experiences in the world, few can equal an encounter with grafting wax. If you have tried it and given up to preserve your sanity, try grafting this time with rubber tape. It's a pleasure.

I admit I get carried away with grafting. I feel like a surgeon making quick, decisive cuts, splinting on a new limb here, another there, holding the two sections between firm, practiced fingers so that the skin of each just matches, then coiling a tight bandage around the severed ends. I can almost hear the cheers from a gallery of interns.

I covered a Dolgo ornamental crab with grafts. Another crab had emerged from an old stump; it was young and growthy and its branches emerged at right angles to the trunk. It was exactly the strong scaffold tree to bear the weight of the exotic new apples that would soon be hanging heavily on it. I made grafts on the growing end of every limb. A Canadian apple beside the back door I settled upon as my smorgasbord tree. It would soon bear one of every kind of apple that grows here, and some that don't. A five-in-one apple tree? I'd have twenty-five in one! And so I kept grafting.

I bought a bundle of fifty seedlings from my friend Melvin Bergeson (who originated what to me is the most beautiful of all ornamental crabs—Red Splendor). I cut off the tops just above the roots and gave them new ones, then buried them in wet shavings in a tub in the basement. Paul Tangjerd had another bundle of fifty he couldn't use, so he gave them to me. And so I went on grafting all spring. The hardware dealer in our neighboring town from whom I bought rubber electrician's tape asked if I could do some wiring for him. Electricians' wages being what they are, I was sorry to disappoint him.

All of a sudden, out in the orchard there they were—fat green sprouts coming from my scions! I felt like passing out cigars. For the first time in my life, I had grafted. Some sprouts started flowering and set fruits which fell off, but it didn't matter. I could wait.

The plums I had set out on wild trees mostly dried up, but a few came, ample to satisfy me. Weeping birch twigs that I grafted onto wild birch started growing vigorously, then died. But the half dozen grafts from my glamorous French lilacs all started in growing here and there on the tops of a thicket of old-fashioned lilacs. Had I known that lilacs are so easy to graft, I suspect I would have beheaded the whole thicket.

In their excellent book, *America's Garden Book,* that doughty little crusader for beauty in the slums, Louise Bush-Brown, and her husband suggest other ways to graft. Cleft-grafting, in which you split the end of a limb and insert wedgelike scions, is a common one. I've had one successful graft with that kind. You can cut a slit in the bark of a tree trunk and insert a scion. You can notch, peel, pare, and bind together in any way as long as the moist cambium under the bark meets the host cambium. You can plant a desired tree alongside the host and graft them while they're growing—a true merger.

The book tells everything about grafting except what fun it is, and to my knowledge, no book has, even though grafting has been described since the beginning of the printing press.

For my future grafts, I am going to attempt more difficult ones: I want to splice apples onto wild thorn apples and fancy cherries onto wild ones. And when I can find a big, upright-growing cactus that stands stiff and strong, I want to top it off and insert a Christmas cactus on top to form a blooming cactus tree, the kind you sometimes see in Park Avenue florists' windows for 50 dollars. My gardening cousin who owns a greenhouse tells me that grafting cactus is easy. All you need to do is attach the scion to the sheared-off top of the stock with a common pin. Paul Tangjerd grafts pine trees, attaching a good-looking white pine that seems to be resistant to blister rust onto a seedling stock. Paul hadn't read that it is next to impossible to graft pine trees.

This grafting has a way of getting into the blood. Only God can make a tree, I'll admit, but the grafter can remake one.

I wish I could tell you how visitors gasp when they see my smorgasbord tree bedecked with Fireside, Prairie Spy, Redwell, Red Baron, Honeygold, and a host of others with names I love to roll across my tongue. But it is still too early. I wish too I could show you my piebald lilac thicket; that too will need to wait. But in this plant business, waiting is part of the fun. You can buy a new car, and the enjoyment begins to pall after the first ride is over. My new-model trees and plants will keep getting better, year after year as each spring arrives.

Hybridizing is the ultimate in creating new models, but that takes too much waiting to suit me. I spent a day with one of the famous hybridizers, François Meilland, whose Peace rose is acknowledged to be the world's greatest rose. He told me something of the art learned from his parents, grandparents and great-grandparents, all hybridizers who spent their lives cross-pollinating, planting, and waiting two years for the season's roses to bloom. To earn a living while they waited, they grew and sold cut flowers, and during the hard work of rose-growing, cutting blooms and all, both Meilland's mother and grandfather died from "rose fever"—a disease that follows repeated infection by thorns.

Two good roses—like two good parents—don't necessarily produce good offspring, Meilland said. Some inherit one good quality and no others. A few inherit all the weaknesses. Only the rare one combines the good traits of both parents. Linked to each good trait genetically is a bad one. Thus a highly fragrant rose is thorny. Rich yellows are poor growers. A rose that holds its petals well may not shed them at all, or not until they are unsightly. A rampant grower is a sparse bloomer.

A faster way to produce new varieties is with colchicine, a drug used in treating gout. Milton Arndt, a tall, lanky industrialist of Hightstown, New Jersey, showed me how he has produced dozens of new variegated-leaf geraniums. All you do is snap off the top of a plant and dust the drug onto the raw end. The top leaf will probably wither and die, but the next may turn deep red, the next red and yellow, and so on down the stem, each leaf a different pattern and combination of colors. It's amazing. Each leaf is an exact indicator of what the young plant will be that pushes out from the stem at the base of the leaf. About the time I was set to buy some colchicine and try it, Arndt warned against it. It can cause cancer, and did produce a skin cancer on his wife's face. So Arndt takes the longer, safer route of hybridizing, and in his search for parent stock has amassed several greenhouses full, from tiny windowsill geraniums with a rosette of leaves no more than six inches across to giants that never stop growing.

On a trip to Mexico in search of geraniums, he returned with a new enthusiasm: cactus. He brought so much cactus seed back with him that he promptly had to build a new greenhouse. One of his cactuses was a small one with yellow blossoms that never seemed to open. Just when did it open? He took it into the house to watch. As he and his wife were having shrimp cocktails the buds exploded open. Next morning they were closed tight. Again the next evening they sprang open. The time was exactly the same both nights: six-thirty. The plant seemed to have a clock inside it. At a cocktail party Arndt announced to a houseful of guests that he had asked a visiting cactus to perform.

Were their watches synchronized?

Then watch the little flower.

The countdown came. Faithful to the minute, the cactus burst open, to the amazement of the house.

Arndt made plans for the Philadelphia Flower Show. His cactus would be the hit of this early spring exhibit. He would propagate thousands of them—not to make money, of which he has far more than he ever needs— but to let everyone share the fun the little plant had brought him (and because at heart he's a circus barker). Arndt set out flats of the yellow cactus.

He had considered calling in television reporters for the first dusk that settled at the Flower Show, but reconsidered. He would first give it a try quietly. Even so, a crowd of exhibitors hovered around as the crucial time arrived. At six-thirty the cactus didn't stir. At seven, no movement. At seven-thirty the cactus seemed sound asleep. Nor did it open all night. Being moved into strange surroundings, he thought, might have been the trouble. But the next night the faithful little cactus still snoozed, buds held tight. Arndt sheepishly stowed his racks of cactus under a counter. Late at night, though, he had an idea. Perhaps the little cactus needed actual sun, not artificial lights, to set its alarm clock for the evening bloom. He took one to his hotel room and left it in the window. That night it burst open at the appointed minute. It was the middle of the week by then, however, and he trucked them on home.

How light can influence plants so profoundly is a question of absorbing interest to science. At Beltsville, scientists have found a substance in leaves which they named phytochrome, which reacts to light somewhat the way a color film does, even when it has been extracted and stored in a bottle. How this "electric eye" transmits the message around the plant causing it to respond is still a mystery, however.

Light can have profound effects on germination. Some seeds won't grow unless they have been exposed to light. H. M. Cathey, of Beltsville, found that 59 species from among 111 he tested germinate on the basis of temperature alone, including alyssum, carnation, marigold, and zinnia; light is necessary or helpful to 27 small-seeded plants like begonia, petunia, and snapdragon; total darkness is essential for good germination of 25, including larkspur, cornflower, and pansy. Does this help explain why some years none of your seeds germinate? Other experimenters found that certain seeds need light, but no more than 1/1000 of a second will satisfy. Plants appear to react as fast as animals to light. A green leaf forms complex sugars after being exposed to light for only one second.

What sort of a signaling system does a plant have? Nobody knows, except that it is remarkably efficient. On a hot, windy day, the cells that guard the evaporating jets on the underside of the leaf close in, shutting down the water output. An elm that would normally give off one hundred gallons a day, for instance, might shut down to only fifty. A sensitive plant reacts almost instantly to bumping. A Venus's flytrap snaps its jaws shut just as quickly when the proper number of hairs inside the leaf are touched. Consider this: when an insect walks inside that is too small to bother with, the jaws don't close; too big and they ignore it, too. What a splendid built-in computer the plant must have to react almost instantly to the proper signals!

Do plants feel pain? There's no way of measuring, just as there is no known method of measuring pain in humans, except subjectively. The worst toothache, the most excruciating backache just can't be measured by any device. A tree doesn't wince when I saw off a limb, but I confess that I do. After all, if the tree responds to a wound by directing formation of callous or scar tissue, it must sense something. My reasoning, I must admit, is something less than scientific.

# 13 ❦ How to lure kids

A CHILD WHO grows up with an affection for plants and flowers and birds and moths and predators can't help but become a feeling, understanding adult, sensitive to the needs of others and especially of the underprivileged.

It is difficult to interest an adult in nature. It is almost absurdly easy to excite a child with it.

❦

This is a chapter about little things—mosses and wild flowers and bugs and birds and mushrooms—but especially about little human beings, and how to inculcate in them a love of other small, helpless things.

"Let's find us a castle," says my niece, her four-year-old trailing behind her through the woods. "Here's one," she whispers excitedly as she bends over a stump, rotting and moss-encrusted. She gets to her knees to scrutinize it. The child follows suit, dropping to his knees and elbows, and cupping his head in his hands so he is only inches away from the emerald world of moss and small growing things.

"Here at the top must be where the king lives," she whispers, pointing to the fire-blackened wood. "And this is the road up the mountain where the knights ride. Now then, where do you and I live?"

The boy finds a hole in the moss that would be a snug house, he says.

"But somebody already lives there," says his mother. "See, this probably already belongs to a chipmunk. See where he's been shucking pine cones and eating them?"

They go on to find an unused cranny of the stump.

"Now then, let's go for a walk up to the palace." They hunt a path that is not too steep.

"But it's starting to rain," she says. "Where can we hide?"

The boy spies a mushroom and points to it excitedly, his voice rising. His mother cautions him to speak softly, because animals and birds of the forest are shy, and frightened by loud noises.

On the way up the road they encounter other travelers: an ant lugging a grub that the boy watches with fascination; a harvestman or "daddy long-legs" whose antics make the boy giggle; perhaps a centipede undulating across the path.

"Just look at the flowers that grow out of this fine lawn," she says. "Those are the flowers of moss."

The boy's eyes widen as he discovers a moss with a different kind of flower. He finds another and still another. He is transported. The thrill of that find may remain among the most exciting he will ever experience in his life. He has discovered the world of little things, which will enrich the rest of his life. Suddenly he sees ashy-gray lichens making lace circles on the stump. No longer is it necessary to weave fantasy around the stump. He is off on his own expedition into reality that is stranger than any fiction.

Here is a miniature forest of foxtail moss whose spore-bearing stalks flame up when you ruffle up a tuft of it and light it. The Chinese used those spores as gunpowder thousands of years ago. For the rest of the day there is nothing else in the world for the boy but mosses. They take home small samples of each kind to study and admire still further, and to identify, matching them with the pictures in the *Golden Book of Non-Flowering Plants.*

On another trip they might concentrate on flowers. Here is one with white petals that count up to four—just as old as he is—and with a circle of leaves below it that number six—his sister's age. This is the bunchberry, and what seem like petals are really sepals, the overcoat that protects the flower until it's time to open and attract the bees that pollinate it. The bunchberry's real petals are so small they wouldn't attract much attention from anything; the sepals must do it.

Here on the bunchberry's leaves are the droppings or "frass" of a larva that must be feeding directly overhead. With luck they find it. Flying past may be a Monarch butterfly that may have come all the way up from the Gulf of Mexico. Some Monarchs travel from Canada to Mexico and return—an 1,800-mile trip.

So did my niece introduce each of her four children to the world of little things, a world which many adults have never discovered, and now have no wish to. Nor did she stop with her own children. She has brought dozens of others to the country from among the big-city congregation where she is a parish worker. A few she has steered towards a specialty in science. And in most she has helped develop a compassion for small, helpless things.

Sometimes she takes a child on a listening trip. At first the youngster can hear only robins and frogs. Before long, his ear is attuned to the thin, shrill calls of insects. Now and then they might arise early to listen to the dawn chorus of birds. Sometimes she carries a portable tape recorder and together with the children makes a sound track of the trip. Later she replays it and asks the children to recall where they were at each point, and if possible to identify what they heard.

She has developed a game that is popular with sizable

groups of children. She gives each team of two or three a yard-long piece of string which they tie in a circle and place on a spot anywhere on the yard, then vie with the next group to see which team can identify the most things within the circle. Anything counts: air, granules of sand, weed seeds, ants, plants, and humus. The lists compiled by team secretaries generally surprise both children and judges.

It is easy to interest a child in the big, splashy side of nature—in deer and other animals, in fish, in trees and the more spectacular wild flowers. It takes ingenuity to focus his enthusiasm onto minute things. My niece finds that even in twos or threes, one child is pretty sure to distract the others.

So when you take your child on such a trip, take him alone. And after a seeing tour and a listening tour, take him on a smelling trip, keeping tab of the smells as you go. Flowers are the most obvious to record. But notice: is plum blossom any different from apple? Is evening primrose any different from water lily? Crush the leaf of a calendula. Its smell is indistinguishable from rhubarb! See if the odor of giant milkweed blossom isn't strongly reminiscent of lilac. The tall stalks of horsebalm, a mint, smell strongly of lemon. Domestic primrose root has the fragrance of licorice. Pine and spruce and balm of Gilead have fragrances all their own as far as I can tell. For a pleasant fragrance, look for the green ears of sweet flag in some marsh. Walking through the tall grass you will likely catch the strong smell of mint. There are many kinds, but all have square stems—something a child can learn to look for. In late summer, learn to know the fruit fragrance of mayapple, and the rich, nutty smell of filberts. Fall is a smorgasbord of smells.

In the course of your tour you may encounter the unmistakable odor of animal: something like the smell of a wet dog in the case of woodchuck, badger and fox, or a musky smell in the case of deer. Look quickly upwind and you may glimpse a deer. Often you will find a groundhog or a fox den. With a little encouragement and practice, your nose will lead you to many animal signs you would otherwise miss. The smell of animal at the hole of a den is almost as sure a mark of its use as are the remains of food, broken twigs and leaves and fresh tracks.

Take home samples of the most interesting-smelling plants, including that rank one, the carrion flower, whose odor of decayed meat draws flies from a distance. See if the folks at home can identify them all blindfolded. We seem to forget the lowliest of our senses, or make sport of it, and by failing to respond to it, gradually blunt the messages it tries to send us. I know a missionary with the Wycliffe Translators whose life was probably saved by her Indian companion, who smelled a venomous snake hanging from a limb above the trail. Perhaps our sense of smell has been permanently damaged by the pollution of the city, so that we could never smell a snake. I don't know.

Try a tasting tour, too. Many trees have distinctive flavors, most spectacular, perhaps, the black or cherry birch, which is wintergreen. Commercial oil of wintergreen used to be extracted from the twigs and bark. How does it happen that a tree of the hardwood forest manufactures an oil that is just about identical to that of the tiny little evergreen of the sandy softwood forests? Sassafras twigs have a pleasant medicinal flavor.

Night is a good time for a walk with a child. Sounds you would never notice by day come through clear; the snap, snap, snap of the click beetle in a rotting log is as regular as a metronome. With any luck you might find glowworms in the moist grass or another of the haunting sights in nature—chunks of wet wood that seem to be on fire, glowing with yellowish or greenish lights. This is foxfire, a name that fits the eerie glow. The lu-

minescence comes from a network of cobwebby filaments in the wood which are the vegetative part or
mycelia of a fungus whose fruit is the delicious honey
mushroom.

For a few weeks in summer, fireflies will be out, their
flashes signaling to one another their readiness to mate.
Several species may be flashing at one time, posing a
problem to a male on the prowl. The way he can tell
that a receptive female is of his own species is by the
time interval between her flashes. One common species
flashes at six-second intervals, and both male and female
continue flashing until they make physical contact. A
male who mistakes the beat or is over-anxious enough
to home in on a female flashing at a different beat could
be in for real trouble. A female *Photuris pennsylvanica,*
though mated, may continue to flash, luring in males of
other species, which she seizes and eats, adding protein
to her egg-laying reserves.

Along your night walk, your flashlight or the head-
lights of a passing car may pick out the glowing eyes of
a cat or dog. The eyes of most predators and of some
nocturnal animals have a tissue in the eye which acts
like a bright mirror, reflecting light back again through
the retina for maximum use of light, and giving them a
wonderful eye-shine.

Mosquitoes are out after you? Only one species, perhaps—if that knowledge helps. There are fifty or sixty
kinds, each with different feeding times and places.
Some wouldn't consider entering the house with you.
Others are mainly house-feeders. Some feed at dusk.
Others may rest motionless in the house until dawn
before they attack.

A walk in the woods is never quite complete, especially for children, unless you bring something home as
a memento. For those lucky people who see red, there
are strawberries, pin cherries, and red elderberries—and
no fruit tastes half as good as what you have gathered

from the wild. On the way back from chasing the cows
to the pasture, my brothers and I would fill our pockets
with wild gooseberries. Auntie, who was our mother out
on the farm, would make pies of any fruit we brought.
In a pinch, as little as two cups of fruit was all it took,
and how we struggled to find that much of wild currants or Juneberries or blueberries.

Picking wild berries was a favorite Sunday outing for
our whole family. Just once my father took his six sons
to pick strawberries. While he filled his gallon pail and
a straw hat besides, five of us came up with a few cup-
fuls each. He looked at us and shook his head. He knew
we had tried. He knew we hadn't eaten our berries.
Then what was wrong with us? He could never quite
understand that five of his six couldn't see red. He always thought we were fooling. He never did take us
strawberry picking again. It was different with
blueberries. In good years, we could gather tubfuls.
Blue was a color that shone bright and bold.

If you haven't gone berrying, do so. Until you do, you
won't know what a pleasure it is. Just make sure you are
on public lands. Some rural people still treasure their
berry patches—more than their cultivated crops.

If you haven't already been introduced to another kind
of food-gathering, permit me to do so right now. Mushroom collecting doesn't really belong in a chapter on
luring kids into an appreciation of nature, but where
else would I talk about this wonderful hobby?

Arm yourself with a good book on the subject. The
best one I know is a University of Michigan Press book,
*The Mushroom Hunter's Field Guide,* by Alexander H.
Smith. You might expect the beautiful golden mushroom on the cover to be one the author especially re-
commends. Actually, it is poisonous. Gradually, page by
page, you discover that the author is allergic to mush-

rooms; moreover he doesn't even like them! Nevertheless the book is most informative and in a macabre way amusing. My brother and I have read and reread it.

To those unhappy people who shudder at the sight of what they call toadstools, it is inconceivable that anyone should gather them as food. But once you begin with the safe ones—morels and puffballs among several—your interest widens. Next you try the shaggy-mane, that remarkable engineer of old highways that can push up its head through thick layers of asphalt, yet whose flesh is tender and delicate as well as delicious. Then you progress to tree funguses and chanterelles. By now you have bought a mushroom book and are off on what will keep growing year after year into one of your pleasantest avocations. My brother, an inveterate deer hunter, has become so engrossed in mushroom hunting that last fall he overlooked fresh moose tracks near a cluster of oyster-shell mushrooms.

His wife, too, is head-over-heels in love with mushrooms. At intervals all summer and fall the two hunt them and return home to match up their finds with the color illustrations in *The Mushroom Hunter's Handbook*. After their treasures are sautéed in butter, the two dine in solitary splendor (few of their friends care to partake). Now and then after trying a new species they have misgivings and awaken one another at night.

"You feel all right, Margaret?" my brother asks.

"Just fine. How about you?"

"Never better."

Then they drop on back to sleep.

One night, though, they must have eaten mushrooms that varied considerably from any of the safe ones pictured. Their house was dark when I stopped in, rather late, to see them. As I snapped on the living-room light, I saw a sheet of paper on the floor, a note scrawled across it:

"To whom it might concern. We ate mushrooms at 7:30."

A little startled, I called upstairs to them.

"Best mushrooms we ever ate," they called down to me.

My cousin Mae remains the most ardent mushroom-hunter of all. "The bad ones at least aren't habit-forming," she says, nibbling at a new species to check the flavor. "Besides, I'm so old," she says, "it doesn't much matter." This is not to be recommended, however, for any age.

There is hardly a human who can't give you a safe rule-of-thumb for mushrooms. One says: "All on rotting woods are safe." Another says: "All on rotting wood are poisonous." Still another says, "All fairy rings are safe." And another says: "Toadstools are poisonous." And what, you ask, is a toadstool? "Anything with a collar."

All of which generalizations are not only false but dangerous. Experts insist that there are no simple rules. You must learn to recognize each kind, just as you learn to differentiate apples from oranges from peaches from apricots from plums.

Picking mushrooms doesn't diminish their numbers a whit. The part above ground is the fruit with its fruiting stalk, like an apple with its stem. The body of the plant is all underground. A single elm stump in the yard of another brother who lives outside of Minneapolis keeps his family supplied with delicious inky-cap mushrooms all summer. At each new rain, a fresh supply emerges. In dry weather my brother has tried watering the stump to induce a new batch to arise, but so far without success. Yet, anticipating moisture, the stump sends up a fine new supply the day before it rains!

Morels keep growing in northern Michigan in the aspen woods, even though hordes of mushroom collectors have been harvesting them for years, traveling from as far as Chicago. Several counties offer maps of good morel grounds, so numerous are the mushroom-hunters. Children will appreciate the beautiful *Marasmius oreades,* which is commonly called fairy ring mushroom, though others, too, may form rings. It will keep on supplying food all summer, year after year, sending up its small yellow parasols in a slowly widening circle over the lawn. Long ago the first ancestor of the fairy ring scattered its spores about itself and began growing outward, and exhausting the soil nearby, kept pushing outward by spores or mycelia into a bigger and bigger ring. Experts estimate that the biggest fairy rings—over fifty feet across—are nearly four centuries old. At that rate even a small circle on your lawn may be ancient. Whether or not you gather them to eat won't matter to children. A fairy ring to them will always be a work of magic.

Besides plants and mushrooms, good mementoes of a trip, whether by foot or car, are rocks. As soon as you return, better paste a tag on each one, indicating where you got it, or you'll quickly lose track. Help a child find a suitable container for his rocks if he wants to start a collection. And if his interest wanes or is at best spasmodic, don't badger him. Your own enthusiasm comes and goes, too. The important thing is that all your excursions and explorations be pleasant.

Sometimes the simplest mementoes of a trip are best. Bits of moss that continue to grow in a dish garden or rose bowl will capitalize on a child's newly awakened interest. A fragment of bark or earth—in the style of Japanese haiku—can symbolize all of earth; a seedling spruce can be all of the world's forests; a saucer of water, the oceans of the earth; a rock, all the mountains of the earth.

Try sometime taking home a piece of wood with its

mosses intact. One such small stump I pulled from a marsh in late fall and kept in a shallow tray covered with a plastic cake cover. The mosses stayed as brilliant as ever. And slowly the stump's dwellers came alive. Delicate ferns began to unfold. Small flowers I had never seen before began to bloom. A dewberry vine began to flower. A few delicate gnats emerged from somewhere and perched on a small clump of sphagnum moss, that reminder of the age of coal. My stump gave us a daily walk through the swamp and a chance to become familiar with its daintiest inhabitants.

Some of the simplest mementoes of a trip were those Auntie brought back from the shortest of trips, often no farther than the barn. We would laugh as she came in with a few red clover heads in her hand, a few white clover heads, perhaps a wisp of redtop grass and an oxeye daisy. "Auntie, you're spreading weeds," we said. She would only smile and arrange them in a sugar bowl or a quart glass jar in the center of the table. It was amazing how sweet the room began to smell, and how pretty the plants looked that we would soon be mowing down and converting into hay. We couldn't help but study the red clover blossoms (which we insisted were blue) and the way the individual florets arranged themselves around the stalk. I doubt that any of us would have picked a handful of insignificant flowers the way Auntie did, but we came to look for them as the summer wore on. And we walked the meadows more carefully. (Much later, when I was taking basic training in the cavalry in Kansas in June, I could hardly bear to march through the prairie grass to the rifle grounds, trampling a variety of prairie flowers the like of which I have never again seen.) One winter Auntie slipped on the ice of the back step of our machine shed home, and the kettle of scalding water she was carrying spilled over her side and face and into her ear. For some months she lay in bed, and it wasn't until June that she could walk outside. She came back from her first little walk with a few wisps of grass in her hand.

"I didn't know I was in bed so long," she mused, almost to herself. "It was January when I fell, and now the grass is in bloom." To this day, none of us can walk through a pasture or weedy patch without looking to see if the grass is in bloom. Auntie bequeathed us many things, but among the best was her quiet love of little things.

Grasses have real beauty that children will be quick to appreciate if you pick a few stalks of each kind and look at them closely. Use a separate container for each species, and look at the grace with which they arrange themselves. Along the edges of a marsh in New Jersey I was struck with the diversity of grasses growing there one fall during duck season. Some were tall, dark-stemmed with weeping pendants of black seeds; others were strands of silver; still others were crisply erect golden plumes. I gathered a dozen kinds and fastened a small cluster of each kind to my apartment wall. The effect was arresting for the few days that the cellophane tape would hold them there.

The lasting memento of a trip afield with children is the living plant, carefully lifted and moved to your own wild-flower garden. I hesitate to recommend this. Too many people pull up a wild flower and plant it in a spot completely unsuited to it. Unlike tame flowers, most of which grow and bloom best in full sun, a large number of the most beautiful wild ones do best in shade. Many of them like rich soil with plenty of black humus; many need considerable water. Without these they just can't exist.

Nearly everyone who sees the pink lady's slipper—Minnesota's state flower—wants to take a clump home with him. Some people do, although digging them—except on your own property—is illegal in our state. The roots must be bought from a wild-flower nursery. Lady's slippers are not hard to transplant. In common with most orchids, the roots are big, simple, unbranched. The difficulty is that without the right rich, moist soil, kept acid by pine-needle mulches or chemicals, the plant gradually disappears. Yet with a little care, they come year after year and even multiply. My own clump, chopped out of the frozen bog at the end of my lake, now has 50 blooms. One small clump in rich moist soil beside a friend's house has spread into a patch with 150 blooms—a breath-taking sight. Why not try growing some yourself?

Flowers that like the deep woods will grow well in the shade on the north side of your house, particularly if the soil is rich. The big showy trillium will grow to perfection there, and to my eyes it is one of the most beautiful flowers in the world. If only I were a poet I could tell you about its snow-white purity and the casual ruffle of its petals, which turn pink as they age. My friends gasp when they see my bed of trilliums. In states where it is legal to do so, you can gather a few from the woods, taking care to dig the bulb. Show your child how almost everything about the plant comes in threes: leaves, sepals, and petals.

Wild flowers seem made for children; so many are novel in one way or another. There are the tiny pantaloons of Dutchman's-breeches, the yellow kernels that are the storage roots of squirrel corn, the remarkable canopy of jack-in-the-pulpit followed by the brilliant red cluster of seeds, and the strange cleistogamous seed pods of violets that push out of the ground long after the flower stems have died. Tell your children how Indians used the juice of bloodroot to paint their faces. The plant is easy to move and grow, the big dissected leaves are as picturesque as the white flowers. Wild ginger is another to intrigue children, with the spicy fragrance of its root and its whimsical blossoms. Who ever heard of a flower pushed halfway into the ground? Only ants pollinate it. Homeowners who are tired of prosaic pachysandra ought to try wild ginger as a ground cover.

By the way, pachysandra is an awful bore, I think. It just sits there, summer and winter unchanged, as monotonous as a brick wall. To me there is a time for living and a time for dying. I like plants that grow and flower and die. There is excitement in the way frost blackens a plant and kills the top. The awakening next spring is that much more exciting. All during spring the wild ginger leaves are flattened purses lying on their sides until one day when the ground and sun are just warm enough. Suddenly the little purses stand upright and the leaves unfold and grow to become the handsome heart-shaped leafy canopy of summer.

Other ground-cover favorites of mine are Solomon's seal, dwarf columbine, wild bleeding heart, bloodroot, and in mild climates from Philadelphia and south, lily-turf, out of which come miniature stalks like delphinium.

The wild-flower garden in a shady corner will be a pleasure for children from earliest spring when the hepatica pushes its bright bouquet of lavender, pink, or white stars up through the brown leaves until fall when bottled gentian blooms. Among my great favorites is yellow bellwort—which we as children called hang-downs. It combines a rich yellow with a luna-moth green leaf that appeals to my color-blind eyes, and its shy demeanor captivates me now as it did in childhood. The yellow lady's slipper is another with a Disney charm; the blooms seem like yellow shoes that Mickey Mouse might be wearing. There are at least three sizes: a miniature with dark twisted sepals, an intermediate, and a large one with slippers the size of golf balls. When the yellow slippers are blooming alongside wild forget-me-nots, the combination, though not exactly subtle, is one that hits me hard. The blue of Colorado columbine nearby is another pleasure, and so too are wild phlox I gathered in Virginia and prairie phlox. In July comes the stately turk's-cap lily, sometimes eight feet tall, whose scientific name, *superbum,* is appropriate. And though I would rather have conferred that name on the Canada lily, Linnaeus got there ahead of me. The nodding yellow bells of the Canada lily have the sinuous grace of adolescence. The petals never seem to age or wither and curve upwards with the same tilt as the temple roofs in Bangkok. Mine bloom outside an east window where they make a living picture, swaying in the breeze and flecked with sunlight coming through a few elm branches high above them.

In a sandy, sunny spot by the back door I have blueberries, bearberries and the splendid wild pentstemon growing, as well as two plants of the rare rose moccasin. Most botanists say it is nearly impossible to move, that rain splashing dirt on the leaves will kill it, but I have moved several, all of which grew and flowered. I have more trouble with transplanting that sand-lover, the golden puccoon.

Naturalists might decry the suggestion that you dig certain wild flowers and move them home. But I have found that inveterate plant-diggers are among the most ardent conservationists. In getting a plant to grow and thrive it is essential that you reproduce the right habitat —jackpine, prairie, marshland, or what have you—and this is no easy task. Anyone who does, comes to appreciate all types of habitat and the need for preserving them. To such a person the New Jersey pine barrens, for example, are no longer a dreary desert. Here grow the curly-grass fern, golden crest, and rare orchids found almost nowhere else in America. A swamp is no longer a scummy breeding ground for mosquitoes but the home of a host of delightful plants. I would strongly urge you to start growing wild flowers, both for fun and to help inculcate a love of nature in your children.

Plants in such habitats are only part of the excitement for children. The sandy spot beside your driveway may be no bigger than a dinner plate, yet here may be the hatchery where a parasitic wasp digs a tunnel to bury an egg alongside a grub or larva which it has stung into a stupor. Look in the sand for a funnel an inch or so across beneath which the ant-lion waits to pull down and devour an ant whose struggles to climb the sandy incline alerts the submerged beetle—a drama as absorbing as a television show.

The world of little things can be a magic world to children, and for adults a tranquil interlude between home and office, one that eases tensions and heals the spirit.

What a world this would be if all its people cared about helpless little things—plants and insects and animals and helpless humans, too.

# 14 ☙ A gathering of nature-nuts

IT WAS A magnificent July day in the Arctic, and I was tramping over the tundra at Point Barrow, the most northerly land in all America. The sun was just warm enough to dull the edge of a brisk breeze from an ice pack that had receded here and there a few hundred feet from shore.

The tundra was something I had dreamed about and longed to see since the time I studied about Eskimos in second grade. Here it was at last, and no disappointment. The tundra was a calico coat of miniature Iceland poppies, each plant no bigger than a boutonniere, yet crowded with fifty blooms each. Pussy willows whose dainty branches lay embedded in the moss pushed their catkins a few inches above the tundra. In small boggy pools red phalarope females loafed, while their drab mates brooded the eggs or tended the young. When I searched for the nests it was the smaller male who hovered about anxiously calling and leading me away. On the edge of a nearby lake I was suddenly met by a flock of spectacled eider ducks, and knew at once what they were from the big goggles that decorated their faces. There were shorebirds and gulls in profusion, plus old squaw ducks diving between ice floes and reappearing in precise formation, the way shorebirds wheel and turn in precision flight. From time to time a lemming scurried down a mossy channel. As I neared a slight rise, a pair of birds began screaming at me from high above, and I knew that I had seen my first jaegers. Other jaegers appeared with longer tails. The whole day seemed more dream than reality.

That night I was bursting to share with someone the excitement of my fantastic encounter with the Arctic. But who among the thousand Eskimos at Barrow would care about what I had seen?

I went to supper in Point Barrow's best and only restaurant, a small building sitting on the sand of the beach a stone's throw from the ice pack. It is owned and operated by Tom Brower and his wife, an Eskimo couple. Mr. Brower himself, a handsome, dignified man in reindeer skins, served me.

I couldn't keep from discussing what I had seen.

"You have a lot of birds up here," I said by way of opening the conversation.

"Yes," he replied, and went to the kitchen for the whale roast.

On his return I persisted. "I saw the first of what some people call jaegers—."

"What kind?" he asked.

"Well, I think they were long-tailed," I said hesitantly.

"We have all three—parasitic, long-tailed, and pomarine. What you saw was probably pomarine."

There was whale roast in front of me; much as I love to sample exotic foods, I can't remember what it tasted like. Nor do I recall what the reindeer tongue and muktuk were like. My interest in nature had found me a friend, one who spoke my language, and who told me about the bird and animal life of the tundra with the precision of a Harvard professor. The birds I had seen were only a fraction of the flocks that would soon gather, flying across the sand-spit at the very tip of Barrow, where Eskimos would soon set up tents and gather food for the long winter. Mr. Brower had collected bird specimens for the Smithsonian and the Museum of

Natural History in New York from the time he was a boy. His white father had come as a young man from Brooklyn, married a native woman, and begun the whaling industry, a story he told in a book worth reading called *Fifty Years Below Zero*. The day had been unforgettable. But sharing it with a fellow nature-enthusiast made the evening just as memorable.

A love of nature makes the whole world kin. I really believe that. Enjoyment of nature can be a solitary pursuit like Thoreau's. But sharing it magnifies the pleasure.

I have found in fellow nature-appreciators some of the most interesting people in my life—and the most dedicated.

❄️

Millions of older Americans remember the baseball star and evangelist, Billy Sunday, who converted thousands during his anti-sin crusades. The Billy Sunday of nature is a doctor named Paul Fluck, currently setting up a nature center at Freeport on Grand Bahama, off the coast of Florida, but who for twenty years at Washington Crossing, Pennsylvania, led what may well be the most amazing crusade in nature education in the United States. Every Saturday and Sunday all year long, crowds found their way down narrow, traffic-choked roads to the tiny sanctuary on the Delaware near the spot where Washington made his historic crossing, to sit on outdoor benches as the trim, brisk-speaking doctor described the bird he was holding—a magnificent cardinal, which only moments before was flying free through the sanctuary before being caught in a box-trap nearby. As Paul moved through the crowd giving each person a close look there would be gasps of admiration, even from long-time bird-watchers, few of whom had seen a live bird close up.

"Just look at that lipstick," he would say, pointing to

the bill. "And how about those red eyebrows—how long before you women use red eyebrow pencils?" He pauses while someone takes a picture. Then suddenly there is a flash of crimson as the bird flies off, mingled with cries of dismay from the crowd which doesn't yet realize that the escape was intentional.

The next bird is a bluejay riding comfortably on the doctor's hand. "Here is the real Johnny Appleseed, tree-planter of America. If all of New York City were to be leveled by some catastrophe, a forest would soon be growing there, planted by bluejays." He offers the bird an acorn, which it grasps in its beak as it flies off. To challenge the experts, he has a "mystery bird" for them to identify—perhaps a Lincoln sparrow, female indigo bunting, or house finch. Next there might be an oriole or an indigo bunting or a scarlet tanager, each one a splash of vivid color against the sky as they wing off over the upturned heads. There is something fragile and haunting about the performance, knowing that the tiny performers—borrowed for a few breathless moments—may soon be in some steaming jungle half a world away, still wild and free.

The astonishing success of his programs in Pennsylvania, in Florida, where he occasionally lectures, and in the Bahamas, demonstrates—as more than one visitor has remarked—that a bird in the hand is worth a hundred in the bush or in books or nature films.

Half of the visitors come without knowledge or even sympathy for birds or conservation. Only a few have binoculars. But for many who first see inches away the iridescence of a grackle or the jeweled eyes of a kinglet, a new world of interest suddenly bursts upon them. Some buy bird guides on the spot. Many return for the second lecture in the day. In Pennsylvania, busloads of school children came on Wednesdays and by appointment other days of the week. Celebrities from New York and Washington sat alongside boy scouts, campfire girls, foreign visitors, perhaps a class of crippled children. The blind came to feel the birds he held for them—the only people so permitted. During May at morning "bird concerts" Paul identified forty species that might be singing. The programs continued all winter, and many a crowd sat ankle-deep in snow. A total of half a million have heard Paul Fluck since he began nearly twenty years ago, and fathers who first learned conservation from him have brought their children to listen.

To date he has logged in 2,500 lectures—a staggering number for someone who is neither politician, teacher, nor preacher, and who until recently has done it all without pay.

"What's more," a friend said, "he's probably the only one who prefaces every speech with a mile run."

Whether it be in the United States or the Bahamas, fifteen minutes before show time he dogtrots around his entire circuit of wire box traps, since he refuses to keep birds captive more than a few minutes. He begins every talk a little breathless.

Backstage at every performance is someone who matches the doctor in dedication—his pretty, soft-spoken wife Jeanne, a registered nurse, who continues to bring in birds while her husband is speaking, to ensure an interesting variety, and whose overwhelming patience keeps alive many of the injured and fledgling birds the public insists on bringing them.

Nature education is a labor of love for Paul and Jeanne. For most of the twenty years in Pennsylvania they worked without pay, devoting every Saturday and Sunday to nature education. Once they had $12,000 in reserve for a dream home, but that disappeared long ago for the center, and for liver, mice, and mealworms for bird patients. Their only home is a narrow, three-story frame house where Paul conducted his medical practice after his days in medical school. The center itself is across the river, with headquarters in an old farmhouse. (During the first few weeks after Paul tacked up a sign NATURE CENTER, several cars pulled up expecting from the sign to find a nudist camp. He hurriedly changed the name to NATURE EDUCATION CENTER.) To free his weekends for work there, Paul specialized in ophthalmology, confining his office hours to late afternoon and evening.

Now that he has retired from his practice, he devotes his full time to nature work. In general, after an afternoon of lectures he continues around the trapline every half hour until dark, often with Jeanne assisting as he checks the eyes and general health of each bird with the same swift precision he gave his office patients. Then he attaches a band and releases it. On an average day of banding he walks seven miles and handles up to a thousand birds. Many are free-loaders, already banded, returning for food, some as often as 20 or 30 times a month. One downy woodpecker in Pennsylvania has more than 100 handlings recorded on its file card. Paul's total of 100,000 banded birds is equaled by only a few other Americans. Keeping the files current on this horde takes hours of laborious accounting.

Despite Paul's urgent pleas that injured birds be left alone—their metabolic rate is so rapid that bones mend within a few days and a bird hidden in the brush can often keep alive that long—injured birds continue to be brought to him.

The first such was Saucy, a bluejay whose entire bill had been snipped off. With a piece of cellulose that he held in place for half an hour Paul stopped the bleeding, but the patient seemed hopeless. Jeanne objected when he was about to put the bird to sleep.

"How can she eat?" Paul asked.

"We'll see about that when the time comes," said Jeanne. She tried spoons, tweezers, and all manner of coaxing sounds. But without success. Finally she tried chewing the fruit and raw vegetables and letting the bird pick the food from between her lips, in the manner of a parent bird feeding its young. It worked like a charm. So for the next three weeks she did this, at least a dozen times a day. Eventually the bird began eating mashed potatoes and milk by itself and the bill grew back.

Four orphaned bluebirds were next, and for the next two weeks Jeanne had to force four wriggling mealworms every twenty minutes—with a kitchen timer to remind her—down each of the four throats. A whippoorwill with a broken wing never did learn to open its mouth and swallow, and from September until May, long after it began flying through the house, it had to be force-fed mealworms five or six times a day. In the bathroom at the same time was a saw-whet owl rescued from drowning in the Atlantic by two boys in a boat. Over the years there have been close to two thousand such invalid birds from great blue herons down to "Bessie" and "Buzzy"—two ruby-throated hummingbirds. Last winter in the Bahamas I saw Jeanne feeding a jewel of a hummingbird—the Bahama wood-star—dipping its broken beak into a teaspoon filled with colored sugar-water as the incredibly long tongue flicked in the liquid. Paul himself has carried a flicker from anthill to anthill, has chased grasshoppers during summer and fall as special treats for his permanent house guests, a kingbird and a scarlet tanager.

Paul rescued the scarlet tanager as a fledgling from a tall white oak after its mother was killed by a car. At fifteen, Peanut is probably the oldest scarlet tanager in existence, and though he is by now almost naked of feathers, greets each new spring by sporting a few scarlet feathers over his bald breast. Currently, an oriole that refuses to stay outdoors resides on the Flucks' screened porch, preferring his meals inside at the table as they eat.

Wherever Paul goes, he builds ponds and pools and

marshes. With a wheelbarrow that Jeanne presented him for Christmas he hauled mud to stop up a small trickle in a secluded corner of the Pennsylvania sanctuary and after five years completed building a woodland pool where wood ducks each year bring off a brood.

His bills for birdfeed are enormous. At one time in Pennsylvania he spent 1,000 dollars a year. In 1955, when a late blizzard swept the Northeast, blocking roads for three days, Paul shouldered two twenty-five-pound sacks of feed and set out the four miles from his home to the center, sometimes through waist-high drifts, sleet stinging his cheeks. At a rivulet he saw about fifty famished robins watching for small morsels washing down the side of the mountain. A dozen starving bluebirds descended on the horizontal suet log.

"Conservation is like that," he says in the most cogent definition I have ever heard. "Conservation means simply taking care of nature."

His lectures to children have the simplicity and excitement of Hans Christian Andersen: "An Indian boy never ran around the woods hollering, 'Hey Mom' or 'Hey Pop' to call his parents. He made the sound of a screech owl. A little girl might use the voice of a toad. Two friends might call back and forth making the sound of a whippoorwill." Then he has them imitate the whippoorwill as loud as they can. He has them listen for a red-eyed vireo's song—"a robin's song chopped up in little pieces." He might bring out a wood duck. "This is the bird that taught Indians how to paint their faces." Then he tells about its need for a nesting box. Sometimes he holds open a woodpecker's mouth to show them the bird's incredibly long, spearlike tongue. Another day he carries out an opossum with a pouch crammed with tiny babies so small that ten will fit in a tablespoon. "We need to take care of wildlife the way you look after a baby brother or sister."

He has kind words for everything in nature. He holds

a cowbird. "This is the bird that invented baby-sitting," he says, moving among the youngsters. "Indians used to call it the buffalo bird because it followed the herd picking insects off their backs." He lets the bird grasp their fingers. "Just see how hard they could pull. They shake hands like a politician! Well, the buffalo bird couldn't stay long enough in one place to take care of its babies because the herd was always moving, so it laid its eggs in other birds' nests. And it still does."

A story from Ernest Thompson Seton's *Handbook of Woodcraft* has haunted him all his life. Seton told the story of a rich man who took three hundred boys from the New York slums on a riverboat up the Hudson fifty years ago for what should have been a glorious day in the Catskills. But even as the boat docked, the boys were reluctant to get off, and hours later when it returned, they were still at the dock shooting craps, smoking, and playing cards—all they knew how to do. The poverty of the lives of those boys—and of succeeding generations of Americans—appalls Paul.

Not one among all the hundred Philadelphia tenth-graders at the nature center could name the bird he was showing them: a robin. Not one knew a starling. Not one knew a maple leaf. Yet all seemed eager to learn.

"It's not enough to take people out of the city," he says. "It's not enough to set aside twenty-one million acres of national parks and twenty-two million acres for national forests if people don't give a hoot about them."

Paul believes the gulf between nature and the public is widening. A generation ago most children played outdoors every day or had an uncle or grandfather living on a farm where they learned about nature. "Today, TV is stealing away their love of the outdoors," he says. "A weekend of sitting at the TV set is normal living for millions of children."

He goes on. "Parents mortgage their souls for a place in the suburbs where their family can grow up. First thing they do is bulldoze out the wonderful trees and native shrubs and skim off the topsoil that was 500 years in building. Then after they're tired out from mowing lawns and fighting crabgrass, they come ask me what they should plant to attract birds and wildlife."

Former Secretary of the Interior Udall has stated: "Nature has had other friends—Teddy Roosevelt, Gifford Pinchot, and Aldo Leopold—but even they didn't surpass Paul Fluck in drive, determination, or fervor." Udall named him the outstanding servant of conservation for 1968.

Beyond his unrelenting crusade, Paul Fluck has added to the total knowledge of birds. A forlorn-looking turkey vulture, left on the porch at the Pennsylvania center one morning, set him off on a long study of birds' eyes. When Paul opened the door, the vulture walked in and seemed at ease in the dim light. The bird had cataracts and was starving. After that he began a systematic check of all the older birds coming to the center and found that many had cataracts in one or both eyes. For years ornithologists have puzzled over orioles, catbirds, or robins that are hopping around northern gardens in midwinter. Paul believes that such birds—if otherwise healthy—probably have cataracts not serious enough to interfere with short flights but enough to prevent their seeing distant landmarks essential to migration. To date he has found cataracts in the eyes of eighteen species, including two tiny hummingbirds. He feels certain that other birds are farsighted, others nearsighted, still others have astigmatism, but hasn't been able to figure a way to test them or fit them with glasses (which, knowing his ingenuity, surprises me).

What have been the rewards of all Paul's labor? Who else, he asks, has had the privilege of watching the light turn on in the eyes of nearly a quarter of a million children as they pet their first live owl? In thirty-three years of medical practice only nineteen people have written him letters of gratitude, but every year he gets a thousand from children and adults who got their first glimpse of nature on his park benches.

Once he asked a crowd of several hundred adults and children to name the animal he held—the smallest mammal in North America. There was no response. When he repeated the question an eight-year-old girl shyly raised her hand. "Pygmy shrew," she whispered. Paul was so moved he could scarcely speak. When he recovered, he said, "Our redwoods are safer and our whooping cranes and our very air, too, because we have children like this little girl."

Paul is full of plans for the future. First off, he wants real nature programs at our national parks. On a trip to Yosemite while vivid black-headed grosbeaks flew overhead among magnificent ponderosa pine, he waited eagerly for the evening "nature talk." Out came the director to announce the program—an evening of rock and roll! "That's not multiple use of our parks," he says, "that's multiple abuse!" With millions of visitors to the nation's parks every year, he is appalled at the wasted opportunities for conservation education.

He envisions a chain of nature centers, complete with motel and restaurant, where tourists can stop for a meal or overnight, watch wildlife and birds of the region at a feeder and wild ducks swimming on a pond, take a nature walk, and enjoy campfire talks at night. Such centers would soon be self-supporting.

"As long as conservation depends on handouts, it's never going to get to first base," he says. "Just how long could General Motors operate if it had to depend on volunteers?"

Paul's Washington Crossing crusade ended in tragedy when elm trees in an adjoining area of the park were sprayed with DDT. Visitors brought him hundreds of dead and dying birds: chickadees, titmice, woodpeckers, nuthatches, thrushes, even wood ducks—all birds that thousands of people had seen in Paul's hands. One was a thirteen-year-old hairy woodpecker, oldest of her species in bird-banding history.

Although Paul and Jeanne left Washington Crossing broken-hearted, so effective had their programs been that Bucks County now has several new nature centers and an Audubon Club with almost a thousand members. Moreover, a number of the three hundred nature centers throughout the United States trace their origins back to those Washington Crossing programs.

At the Rand Memorial Nature Center in Freeport, in the warm and sunny Bahamas, Paul and Jeanne continue their conservation programs, adequately endowed. Visitors from the north find Paul with a flamingo or a stripeheaded tanager or a smoothbilled ani in his hands. He has no need to trap them for his programs. They come in on call, five and up to ten species, to perch in the trees. Olive-cap and yellow-throated warblers dive down to take insects from his fingers. Pewees and kingbirds catch them in the air as he tosses them out. For the humid summer months when there are few tourists, the Flucks plan a nature program for Alaska, where they believe the most urgent work in conservation education remains to be done. But in the mail come requests from nature centers all over the world, as far off as New Zealand.

❧

There are other missionaries like the Flucks. Mrs. Ruth Fagen, a farm woman outside of Perry, Iowa, has given herself to the cause of introducing children to nature. She converted five acres of woods into a fairyland for children, open without charge all summer, where classes from surrounding schools can enjoy wild flowers and bird and animal life, listen to Mrs. Fagen's spirited lectures, and pore over collections of rocks, shells, nests, and fossils from local riverbeds. For very small children there are hundreds of her own ceramic creations: brownies and elves set along woodsy trails, hid in hollow trees, or suspended from overhanging branches. Like the Flucks, Mrs. Fagen feels amply rewarded just to be sharing with children what is often their first encounter with the outdoor world.

Mrs. John Aull is another such missionary. She and her late husband built a nature center outside of Dayton, Ohio, called Aullwood, and donated it to the National Audubon Society. The grounds around her own home, where she has induced wild flowers to grow in profusion, are also open to the public; when her "Miami mist" blooms, it covers the hillsides with a lavender froth. A main building at the Center houses changing exhibits of living plants and animals that are among the best teaching devices I have ever seen. And on half a dozen fertile acres at the back of the property is a meadow where wild prairie grasses grow as they may have in the days of Daniel Boone. One of them—called big bluestem or turkeyfoot—was found growing along roadsides in southern Ohio. Seed was carefully harvested and planted. In the rich soil it grew fast and as thick as jungle grass. Its pinkish blue stems bore silvery-white flowering spikes shaped like a turkey foot. In succeeding years, it tended to form clumps and grow even taller. Other native prairie grasses were introduced, along with prairie flowers—splendid tall liatris or purple gayfeather, wild rudbeckia and a variety of yellow daisies. In fall the synthetic Ohio prairie is spectacular. The bluestem could easily screen out a herd of buffalo or hide a column of Indians on horseback, just as early explorers said it did. The clumps are almost like bamboo and stand twelve feet high. If this is the prairie that our pioneers pushed across in their Conestoga wagons, it is no wonder they were impressed.

An Iowa farmer, Rex Gogerty, has preserved five acres of native prairie that have never been plowed as his contribution to posterity, and elsewhere a few nature-appreciators are trying to preserve other small shreds of natural history from the all-pervasive plow and bulldozer.

Another of my farmer-naturalist friends is Ernie Strubbe of Minnesota, a mountain of muscle but with the curiosity of a child and the sensitivity of an artist. His bird paintings are marvels of detail. His ardor for inculcating others with a love of nature never flags.

Years ago an eleven-year-old boy on a farm in New York wrote a school composition, "Birds of the Hudson River Valley," and until he was fourteen kept a detailed diary of the birds he saw and collected. Both works are on display at Hyde Park. The boy was Franklin Delano Roosevelt.

I feel myself in good company.

Another Roosevelt was an ardent student of birds. President Theodore Roosevelt wrote of the thrushes: "In melody, and above all in that finer, higher melody where the chords vibrate with the touch of eternal sorrow, the nightingale cannot rank with such singers as the wood thrush and the hermit thrush. The serene, ethereal beauty of the hermit's song, rising and falling through the still evening under the archway of hoary mountain forests that have endured from time everlasting; the golden leisurely chiming of the wood thrush sounding on a June afternoon, stanza by stanza, through sun-flecked groves—there is nothing in the nightingale's song to compare."

The former chairman of the board of Du Pont, Crawford Greenawalt, a meticulous observer and photographer of hummingbirds, has produced a book that is a classic.

But wait. I'd better stop right there. The last thing I'd want to do is encourage an interest in nature just because it's fashionable.

A naturalist is at home with others of his kind, but

quite content by himself, too. No matter where in my travels I find an hour to kill, I am never bored. On the Kansas prairie I find the Bell's vireo, a furtive creature. The nearby bluff is golden with prickly poppy. At the railway station in Zurich, a bullfinch sitting on a power line is singing his heart out. No matter that my train is still an hour off. In such company I am never lonely.

# 15 🌿 *What does it all mean?*

AND SO THE SEASONS roll around, faster and faster as the years pass by. Life germinates once again, flourishes, reproduces, and dies. The hunted make food for the hunters. Nestling birds feed nestling hawks and owls and squirrels, and we see meaning and purpose in it. Moths emerge and mate and die and their offspring survive. And here too we see plan and purpose.

But for ourselves—and especially for me—does it make any sense? Because for me, I am the whole universe, and after I am gone, does anything really matter?

🌿

A half-grown raccoon came and squeezed open the door of the screened-in porch of a cabin at Itasca State Park, where I was entertaining friends. We fed him cookies and a candy bar, hoping to entice him from the porch into the living room, but he declined. He was quite obviously no one's pet, but a wild animal that had discovered the easy life of panhandling. How would he react, someone asked, if we hooked the screen door? We tried rushing past him to hook it, but he exited too fast. When he returned, I went out the back door and round the cabin in front, moved quickly inside and hooked it. Immediately, the animal dashed for the screen door, gave it a push, promptly stood up and tried unlatching it with his front feet and failing that, flashed upside down and unhooked it with his strong hind feet. It all happened so fast we could hardly follow his movements.

How could he know that the door was locked? Had he been locked in all night sometime and slowly learned about door latches? Normally he would use his dexterous hands for fine work like this, but the catch fitted snugly. He needed the power of his rear feet. What almost instantaneous recognition of his predicament! We tried to lure him again to the cabin but he never returned from the woods. Was this too a learned reaction? Was he angry or just fearful? Perhaps an animal behaviorist may someday give an answer. The riddles in nature are beginning to draw the attention of scientists and amateur observers alike.

On a lake trout-fishing trip in Canada my brothers and I came upon a small stream that had suddenly gone dry, leaving suckers gasping in the empty pools. A few yards upstream where we pitched our tent we found the cause. Beavers had just completed a dam about six feet across that both shut off the water and blocked the passage for the spawning fish. It seemed a shame to let the big egg-filled fish die, so we pulled loose the logs and let the water rush past, then went out for a late afternoon walk. Returning a couple of hours later, the stream was again dry and dozens of suckers were dying. This time we pulled out the logs and sticks and threw them into the brush, then set to broiling filets of lake trout at our camp no more than twenty-five feet from the damsite. While we were eating we detected a change in the gurgle of water nearby. When I went to investigate I found the dam almost completely rebuilt, in almost less time than we had taken to scatter it—all without our seeing or hearing the beavers at work. This time we rooted out brush like bulldozers run amok, shouting all the while. But within minutes after we returned to the campfire they were back at the dam. As darkness fell they sensed they were safe and continued work just out of range of the firelight. Several trees crashed during the night; we wondered sleepily if one might hit our tent, but we didn't stir. In the morning the dam was higher than ever, and scores of suckers lay dead. In the sand of the creek bottom we saw the tracks of mink and of two bear that had been feeding on fish. Where the creek joined the lake we surprised a bald eagle that had been feeding. How shortsighted we had been in believing that because the fish couldn't serve us, they were wasted!

Beavers and their dams will always remain a mystery to me. I have already mentioned the principles of dam building—a pile of trees and rubble with other trees and branches leaning against it facing the stream and anchored in the stream bottom—but how can the water be so evenly dispersed as it trickles across the top of the dam? In my own dam-building, a small seep quickly erodes away all my efforts. Yet even after beavers leave and their dams lie untended they persist, becoming in some instances the early roadbeds across a marsh. One dam has become part of the fine sandy beach at one end of my lake.

Long ago when that dam was still in use by beavers, an Indian watched a brush wolf chase a beaver across the dam and into the water, where the beaver instead of diving swam in circles, luring the wolf farther and farther from shore. Suddenly the wolf disappeared below the surface, accompanied by a great splashing, after which blood stained the water. And though the Indian watched for some time, the wolf's body never reappeared. My father heard the story from the Indian himself, a man with a reputation for integrity. Perhaps the beaver has wisdom or "learned response" beyond dam-building.

Another riddle: next time you see a killdeer on a marsh, watch him closely with your binoculars. Have you ever observed how he stamps the ground ever so fast with one foot? Stamping is not the right word for such a dainty tapping but I know of no other way to describe it. Those small vibrations of the ground cause worms to surface—why, no one knows. Nor can anyone explain to my satisfaction how the birds first discovered the response to stamping. To call it evolution seems simplistic, a cover-up for lack of hypothesis, just as the word "instinct" has served so long and respectably as a substitute for "I don't know."

Another riddle in the bird world is anting, in which a great many kinds of birds, notably the flicker, grasp an ant and rub it over their feathers. The movement is so swift you can barely follow it. Sometimes the bird later eats the ant, more often discards it. Does the formic acid in the ants serve some function in discouraging lice or in grooming the feathers? Or is the smell simply something pleasant, as functional as after-shave lotion? I have seen an oriole begin anting when presented with pieces of cloth soaked in vinegar, which has something of the same smell.

How does a wood thrush sing three notes simultaneously? One tone even vibrates while the other two are sustained. You can listen to a recording, slowed down to a quarter speed, which makes the three notes easy to distinguish. And how can the starling reproduce the sounds of a flock of chickens? The mockingbird, too, can almost duplicate the sound of a flock of laying hens. You can hear a New England mockingbird, inspired by a nearby flock, give his interpretation on a recording, *The Mockingbird Sings,* available from the Laboratory of Ornithology at Cornell University. Southern mockingbirds, being more numerous, have less extensive repertoires than northern birds, since they listen to one another more often than they do other birds.

How does a bird learn to sing? A Cornell scientist reared bluebirds in soundproof enclosures. They grew up making bluebird calls, but never did develop the bluebird song. Other experiments suggest that the common alarm calls of many species are built-in, unlearned, or whatever you might choose to call it, but that what we know as the song is learned from adult birds. Konrad Lorenz has shown that a jackdaw can learn an entire sentence after hearing it just once, given sufficient stimulation. Why cannot the nestlings, just hatched, learn a song equally quickly? On the day that young wrens or bluebirds hatch I have noticed a sudden surge of singing by the male, perhaps more energetic than during courtship days, and sung atop the nesting box with seeming disregard for revealing the whereabouts of the nest. Does this serve to imprint the song firmly, just as the size and form and color of the parents are imprinted on the young birds during the first few moments or hours of life? It seems altogether possible.

One September I was strolling through the Philadelphia zoo when I heard a robin singing from what seemed a long way off, a beautiful song of particular clarity. It seemed remarkable that the song so far away could overcome the noise of passing traffic. Only by accident did I look up to see the bird on a low branch not ten feet from me, singing with his bill nearly closed, a dreamy reverie of spring. So soft was the song that it seemed the bird was singing just for me.

Many birds sing their spring songs in the fall, softly muted in what is called a "whisper song," but that first robin song is the one I can never forget. Did it serve to teach young males to sing? There is an upsurge in the male hormones of birds for a short period every fall that swells the testicles, and this may prompt the fall singing. But scientists cannot say why this happens. Is it only an accident? Probably not. As ignorance drops from man's eyes, increasingly he sees that everything that happens has a plan, marvelously intricate and precise. Perhaps the whisper song is vestigial, dating back to a warmer era when birds had both spring and fall nests. Whatever the origin, do listen for them. You will ever after remember the time and the place and the beauty of the moment.

Perhaps it was a matter of hormones that caused a male Blackburnian warbler to linger far after the rest of his tribe had deserted the chill of Minnesota to appear on my windowsill on October 12, resplendent in his flaming orange breast feathers, to pick at gnats three feet from my chair. Had it not been for his brilliant spring plumage I would have chalked him down as a bird with cataracts, able to survive in familiar surroundings, but unable to see the landmarks that aid in migration.

What causes the feeding habits of orioles to change so abruptly? During migration they come to the feeder en masse to feast on orange halves. As many as four males have shared my three-by-three-foot feeder, feeding ravenously, while half a dozen more waited in the trees to take their turn. Is it the color—so like their own feathers—that first attracts them? Are they in effect doing battle with the orange? If so, why should they largely desert the fruit about the time the females arrive and the urge to do battle with other males is strongest in them? An occasional oriole, male or female, keeps feeding on oranges all summer, but generally the feeders go idle.

There are puzzles in the plant world that intrigue me no less. After a plant graft, how do the two ends join up and particles of food and building materials leap the gap into the strange new plant stem? The process must be somewhat akin to the process of human grafts. Some apple trees reject the new tissue, and it starves. In others the junction thickens with tissue. I would like to look in via microscope on the supply lines. There must be some confusion. A purple plum that I placed atop a wild plum is growing far faster than the wild, and its lush stem is bulging above the lean gray parent stalk.

Two of my brothers and I, out looking for mushrooms one fall, spotted a Norway (red) pine with what we first took to be an enormous hawk's nest in it about twenty feet high. Coming closer we saw it was a witch's broom—a limb that has gone berserk. The limb completely circled the trunk and from it had grown a dense brush of needles that gave the tree the appearance of having a beautiful fur collar. I climbed up to inspect it more closely. Somehow the genetic template had been altered so that the limb instead of reaching out in normal pine fashion had, in addition to being dwarfed, curled around the trunk, its needles pointing outward like blades of grass to catch the sun. Was it an obstruction in the food supply line that dwarfed and deformed the limb? Had a wasp stung the limb years ago? Or had solar radiation caused a rupture in the genes? In most witch's brooms in pine the change is irreversible. And the seeds from them produce trees about half of which are true dwarfs. This is why I searched the limb and found three cones. Though they were largely infertile, my friend Paul Tangjerd has succeeded in starting a single tree to grow. So far we cannot tell if it will be a dwarf or full-size.

Last fall on a trip to the north of Manitoba I saw stretches of otherwise normal jack pine in which it seemed that half the trees had well-developed witch's brooms. Was this an outbreak of insects or maybe even a hot spot of solar radiation? Nobody knows.

Black spruce, the tall slim pyramids that grow in northern swamps, have numerous witch's brooms that in the dusk perch like bears on the trunk, startling me more than I care to admit. Whether or not these have the same origin as those on the pine I don't know, but they seem to sap the tree's strength, making it attractive to carpenter ants that honeycomb the trunk and eventually kill it.

Black spruce have always intrigued me. Below their dense branches is shelter from rain, snow, or sun. Cool, spongy sphagnum grows there, and animals from star-nosed moles to deer like to travel through the rich carpet of moss and needles. At dusk the tall tops become cathedral spires, purely. Or should I say that the architects who designed the first cathedrals modeled them after the spruce? Very often the slender tip of the tree is injured—whether by spruce budworm or by a bird alighting on it as Aldo Leopold suggests, I don't know. At any rate, two tips develop. And this is what surprises me about those two tips: neither one progresses an inch ahead of the other. Years after the accident, the two trunks are precisely equal in height and shape. If a limb emerges at one point on one tree, a limb will develop at the same point on the other. Like identical twins among humans, they never vary, and perhaps this isn't too strange, since they are one organism. But my wonder is by what intricate set of signals the tree keeps each half growing at precisely the same speed. In an average tree, each limb takes advantage of extra light and grows boldly into the open space, but the twins neither forge ahead nor lag behind. When I see what appear to be exceptions to the rule, I find that the trunks are separate trees. I cannot help but marvel at such a precise mechanism that can regulate growth over a vascular roadway fifty to a hundred feet long.

Others have marveled at the precision with which trees arrange their leaves to take maximum advantage of sunlight. In John Kieran's *Treasury of Great Nature Writing* is an essay on the subject that captures the same awe that I am trying to express.

Occasionally a tree that has been tampered with will get its signals crossed. Paul Tangjerd rooted the limb of a white spruce—no mean feat without a greenhouse—and the branch continues to grow like a branch without sending out an upright trunk. It is now ten feet long and still wandering. My brother's little nursery of grafted blue spruce—all descendants of a single spectacular tree in Moerheim, Germany—are still growing like the branches that they are, despite our tying them to bamboo stakes to keep them upright. It will be eight to ten years before they forget their horizontal nature and elect one branch as leader and become a conventional tree.

Aldo Leopold, the Wisconsin naturalist, was struck with wonder, too, at the way a pine tree keeps its leader always growing above the rest of the tree. Only in old age, he said, does the tree seem to forget which sprout is boss, and let its upper limbs spread out into a softly rounded head.

A friend of mine, Kermit Beougher, lived in Quito, Ecuador, only sixteen miles from the equator. The sun shines down almost exactly astride a concrete wall running east and west between his house and garden. Homesick for the blackberries he knew as a child back in Oregon, he brought two plants with him from the United States and planted one on each side of the wall, where they grew luxuriously. But while one is dormant, the other flowers and fruits. Exactly six months later, the second one flowers and fruits. Both are equally healthy, but for some reason one fruits in December, the other in June. Here is a problem for botanists, professional and amateur, and for curious people in general. How could such a minute difference in environment cause summer south of the wall and winter on the other side?

Kermit says that there are visitors who are uninterested in his blackberry riddle. How sad for them! To me, curiosity is a gift of God that enlivens every hour of existence. I find it hard to believe that any human can be devoid of curiosity, except that I have a friend who fits that description. I asked Clive McKay, the Cornell nutritionist who over the years has counseled several hundred graduate students, if it were possible for an intelligent person to be lacking in curiosity. He thought for a long while, and then remembered one or two students who would qualify. But in addition, he said, they were lazy, and that is probably the answer. Curiosity is a needle, a goad that compels you to study further, to consult encyclopedias, and again to observe and study.

My Ecuadorian friend, Kermit, a missionary who was building radios for the former head-hunters of the Andes and upper Amazon, has a profound curiosity. The first time I met him he had just returned from a trip up a tributary of the Amazon in a dugout log where he had cracked three ribs when the boat overturned, been shocked by an electric eel and covered with stinging insects—but would have returned the next day if his vacation time had not expired. Kermit had stored up enough wonders to propel him through a year of reference books at the mission library.

The insect world has wonders for all who have the ability to focus on little things. Someday I am going to enclose a swarm of bees within two panes of glass so I can study them day by day. Some day I mean to have an ant colony. But for now I am more than content to study the same parasitic wasps that I discovered in my sandpile as a six-year-old. My sympathies go to bees and ants, who must give up their whole lives to performing a single task, like laborers on a production line. But my admiration goes to the wasp, which must battle alone the whole process of digging a nesting hole and remembering its location, finding exactly the right grub, stinging it into passivity, transporting it back to the hole and stuffing it in, laying an egg alongside, then plugging the hole and tamping it shut. How did that whole long chain of behavior evolve? Was it trial and error? Probably not, since the adults cannot pass on any learning to their offspring, which they never see, and since learning, according to prevailing theory, cannot be passed on through germ plasm. What about the glowworm—how

did its strange light come into being, and for what purpose?

One of the most feared creatures in all nature is the
owl. Its huge hypnotic eyes cause panic, sometimes para-
lyzing immobility among birds. It is understandable
that birds might well be shocked and fly off or at least
be deterred from eating a moth whose under-wings have
big orbs like owl's eyes. Butterflies, which fly during
daylight hours, have protective coloration on the bottom side of both wings, so that at rest with wings folded
above their backs, they are well camouflaged. Few of
them bear the owl's-eye coloration. Among moths,
though, which fly during the hours that owls are most
active, there are several with beautifully formed eyes,
that probably ward off many flying squirrels, also active
at night, as well as day-flying birds that would otherwise
gobble them up at rest. I can understand how the coloration of such moths might have evolved over untold
ages. But there is one little friend of mine (excuse me if
I wax anthropomorphic for a minute) that I cannot
believe evolved from anything else, no matter how I
strive to be understanding and scientific.

The spicebush swallowtail is a handsome black-and-
white butterfly whose larva feeds on the spicebush or
benzoin, a shrub of the Eastern United States with
leaves that smell strongly of camphor and with bright
red berries that are beloved to the wood thrush. About
the time the wood thrush is nesting in the benzoin
bushes, the tiny brown and white larva emerges. A juicy
morsel for a bird, he escapes—because he looks for all
the world like a bird dropping! As he grows, his color
turns to green and yellow. Now he hides inside the curl
of a leaf. But if uncovered, he is a terrifying creature.
On his front are big, ferocious eyes that are amazingly
like those of a green snake. All summer he grows bigger
and more frightening. But inside that tough exterior is
somebody as timid as a tadpole. His frightening eyes are

pure disguise, not eyes at all, but simply pigmented skin. At the approach of danger, his front end coils beneath his body and his head with its true eyes is sucked in under his body. Only the big threatening orbs with black pupils are visible, so real that I find it hard to believe they are not glaring at me. How and by what strange accidents of evolution did the spicebush larva wind up with two eyes on its back? There is even a stripe through each "pupil" that simulates light striking across it!

As if this weren't enough, below his big fake eyes is a wide fake mouth and out of it—or nearly so—snaps a wicked-looking orange tongue whenever he is disturbed. The tongue, like a snake's, is deeply forked. Like all else with this little bluffer, the tongue is fake. It's actually a scent organ which on demand turns inside out like a glove and exudes a pungent odor that may repel some predator who isn't already terrified by the sight of him. Viewed from behind, the tongue looks like horns, and two extra spots below the fake eyes look like flaring nostrils.

Could random accident have evolved such a creature? Apparently so, but to me it is purposeful evolution, with a God in charge, a God with a warm sense of humor. The feeling grows stronger every time I encounter the little spicebush larva, with his mark of the whimsy of God on him. I am again aware of God's sense of humor when I visit the zoo, and even more so when I visit an aquarium. The garishly decorated parrot fish are as overdecorated as a dance-hall hostess of the 1890's. Such a view, scientific purists will say, is a hopeless conceit. Nature was not put on earth to please and amuse mankind. But perhaps to a thoughtful parrot fish or a sensate spicebush swallowtail, man offers a few light moments in return.

Scientists often discuss at length the meaning of life. One of them is a friend who has spent his life delving into the secrets of plants; his discoveries in the field of 2,4-D, gibberellin, and other hormones have been monumental. One of the brilliant scientists of our day, he is also one of the gentlest.

To him and to some of his associates there are universal laws of life. Disobedience to them means oblivion. One such law is change. To live is to change. Anything that fails to change cannot survive, because the rest of the universe is forever changing. The organisms that flourish are therefore the adaptable ones, and that means they are highly variable—like bacteria, for instance, which often quickly produce new generations which tolerate antibiotics.

The successful moths and butterflies, this scientist would say, are those with such variability that in the past ages some appeared with eye spots which gave them a decided advantage in the battle for survival. Variations that conferred no advantage didn't continue. Such changes were purposeless and met a dead end.

Over millions of years other laws held force: laws of goodness and integrity and honor, so that communities —whether of ants or bees or wolves or humans—which honored the common cause were those that prospered.

To my colleague in science and others, the universal laws of life are no less mysterious, no less powerful, no less awe-inspiring, no less divine, than what the rest of us choose to call God. When this good friend sits in his pew on Sunday, he substitutes "universal law" whenever his pastor uses the word "God," and he says it fits the context perfectly. He believes just as strongly as I in a force all-pervasive and all-powerful, but one whose rules go beyond our Ten Commandments to include the laws that govern all things—trees and mosses and microbes and all the stars in the universe. By the law of nature, perhaps the parrot fish might not seem ridiculous at all, each strange adornment serving a real purpose.

There are some who say that nature proves the existence of God, and hold forth on its infinite beauty and plan, forgetting that tornadoes and hail and disease—of plants and animals and mankind—are also part of nature and the grand design. There is much that is evil and ugly in nature; good and evil are in perpetual conflict. But out of ugliness and conflict, beauty continues to arise. Chestnut trees struck down by blight keep arising from the stump. Superbum lilies chewed up by pine mice leave seeds from which new plants arise. To me the triumph of good over evil is a powerful witness to the existence of God. Out of chaos and ugliness come beauty and strength. The cecropia bursting out of its dead silken shroud becomes the symbol for me of the divine promise.

Aldo Leopold has said that whoever invented the word "grace" must have watched the upland plover as it alights on a fence post, wings above its head, then slowly lowers them with a movement that is pure poetry, finally folding softly against its sides. Why don't other birds alight with wings aloft and follow that same fluid pattern of descending wings? Gulls sometimes do, but few other birds that I know of. And, more puzzling still, what purpose is there in the movement? None that I can imagine, nor can naturalists offer an answer. Is it naive to suggest that perhaps God, too, loves beauty for beauty's sake alone?

Twice in my life I have watched white-tailed deer do a kind of slow trot that naturalists call single-footing. While the rear feet take two steps the front feet take only one, so that alternately each front foot is raised high and arched for a longer interval, with the result that the deer seems to float in midair like the Lippizaner horses of Austria. It is an eerie movement of almost unearthly beauty. I saw a single deer in Minnesota float through the air just as it was about to plunge into the forest. It seemed to want to prolong its look around without diminishing its sense of speed. In Dutchess

County, New York, I watched four deer float slowly across the far end of a meadow and back again, frightened but unwilling to leave without further reconnoitering. Why did they single-foot? Couldn't they simply have trotted more slowly? Until someone provides a better answer, I have one that satisfies me: God loves beauty sometimes without regard to function, simply for beauty's sake.

There is a plan and purpose behind the solitary wasp as it digs its sandy tunnel, behind the cecropia as it spins itself into oblivion, behind the other riddles of the world of nature. For me it is a God who loves humor and beauty as well as life.

RICHARD C. DAVIDS was born and reared below the Canadian border in Minnesota, near the place where the Mississippi River is a creek just beginning its two-thousand-mile journey. His grandparents were immigrants from Norway, one grandfather a farmer, the other a sailor. He was the youngest in a household of six brothers, two sisters, a cousin, and the latter's mother—the beloved "Auntie" of this book—along with assorted lumberjacks en route to and from his father's lumber mill. At eighteen, he taught a rural school of 35 children, ages five to eighteen, keeping fire in the Waterbury wood stove and urging skunks out of the outhouse. After graduating from the University of Minnesota *magna cum laude* and Phi Beta Kappa, he wrote a textbook on conservation, the first in the United States. He has served as an editor of *Better Homes & Gardens* and *Farm Journal* and as an adviser to *The Lutheran,* and is a contributor to *Reader's Digest.* Currently, he lives on a farm in Minnesota which produces no other crop than wildlife. His most recent book, *The Man Who Moved a Mountain,* is the widely acclaimed biography of Bob Childress, the mountaineer who tamed a violent part of the Blue Ridge.

A NOTE ON THE TYPE

This book was set on the Linotype in a type face called Baskerville. The face is a facsimile reproduction of type cast from molds made for John Baskerville (1706-75) from his designs. The punches for the revised Linotype Baskerville were cut under the supervision of the English printer George W. Jones.

John Baskerville's original face was one of the forerunners of the type style known as "modern face" to printers—a "modern" of the period A.D. 1800.

*Typography and binding design by* CLINT ANGLIN.